BERGSON AND THE EVOLUTION OF PHYSICS

BERGSON

BERGSON
AND THE EVOLUTION
OF PHYSICS

Edited and translated by P. A. Y. Gunter

KNOXVILLE ᴜᴘ THE UNIVERSITY OF TENNESSEE PRESS

LIBRARY OF CONGRESS CATALOG CARD NUMBER 77–77844
STANDARD BOOK NUMBER 87049–092–3

PREFACE

THE TWENTIETH CENTURY has witnessed a striking and as yet unfinished series of revolutions in every branch of physics. It is clear in retrospect that Henri Bergson considered such conceptual revolutions in physics inevitable and, further, that he was able schematically to foresee certain of their most important theoretical consequences. This is a remarkable achievement, particularly considering Bergson's reputation as an "anti-scientific" or "literary" intellect; yet, at the present time Bergson's interpretation of the physical sciences remains one of the least understood, least discussed, and least appreciated aspects of his thought. The present collection is an attempt to remedy this unfortunate situation by making clear both the extent of Bergson's insight into the basic concepts of physics and the relevance of his insights to living issues in the philosophy of science.

In the introduction to this volume, I have taken a first step toward suggesting the contemporaneity of Bergson's philosophy of physics by analyzing, at length, his philosophical method and explaining how this method, in spite of appearances, could have been expected to lead to scientifically prophetic insights. The charge of anti-scientific intentions with which Bergson has been saddled is seen to be not merely misleading, but radically false: Bergson's philosophy of intuition is the affirmation, not the negation, of science. Hopefully this realization will serve to unify, in a general way, the readings which follow.

Most of the readings presented below appeared originally in European scholarly journals and have been translated for the first time from French and German.[1] They represent a stimulat-

[1] De Broglie's essay "The Concepts of Contemporary Physics and Bergson's

ing and highly informative philosophical-scientific literature, but one which, apart from studies like the present, would not only be inaccessible to the average reader interested in contemporary scientific thought, but also would remain little, if at all, known among English-speaking philosophers. The physicists and philosophers whose views are expressed in this book are by no means in complete agreement, either among themselves or with Bergson's ideas. Nonetheless, their essays gain in depth and impact when viewed as an interrelated body of opinion. Besides suggesting Bergson's contemporaneity, then, this collection makes available a coherent literature relating to his work.

Though the essays presented here were written at different times and from diverse viewpoints, it has been possible to divide them roughly into four categories. The first, introduced by Louis de Broglie, the originator of the wave theory of matter, concerns the relevance of Bergson's thought to quantum physics, particularly to the problems raised by quantum indeterminacy, the wave-particle duality, and the problem of "time-reversal invariance" (i.e., the problem of whether temporal series can be reversed). The second, which begins with a discussion between Bergson and Albert Einstein, concerns the basic conclusions of relativity physics, particularly those relating to the question of the status of the multiple time series and the "dislocations of simultaneity" required in the special theory of relativity. The third involves the consideration of Bergson's concept of time from the viewpoint of Zeno's famous paradoxes. The fourth and last section consists in Professor Milič Čapek's masterful survey of Bergson's contributions to our understanding of modern physics as a whole.

One final word: the scientists and philosophers in this collection are concerned with Bergson's reflections for other than mere "academic" reasons. These writers seek, by analyzing Bergson's criticisms and claims, to clarify their understanding of basic concepts involved in the evolution of physics. It can be argued that

Ideas on Time and Motion" appears (in translation) as a chapter of his *Physics and Microphysics;* the translation, however, is fragmentary, and omits some of de Broglie's most significant conclusions. My own translation is complete.

Bergson's insights might prove useful not only in giving a coherent and intellectually satisfying interpretation of the basic concepts of contemporary physics, but also, as one of the authors translated here has stated elsewhere,[2] in suggesting further theoretical advances in that science.

I would like to thank Dr. David A. Sipfle and Mary-Alice Sipfle for their very helpful suggestions concerning difficulties encountered in translating several articles and for collaborating with me in the translation of both Professor O. Costa de Beauregard's essay, "Certain Aspects of the Irreversibility of Time in Classical and Quantum Physics," and the dispute between Henri Bergson and André Metz over the interpretation of the special theory of relativity. Dr. John C. Osborne of the Department of Germanic and Slavic Languages of The University of Tennessee is to be thanked for helping me to render a more accurate "complete paraphrase" of Günther Pflug's passages on inner time and the relativity of motion than would otherwise have been the case. I would also like to thank William K. Sipfle, formerly of the physics department of Ripon College, Richard J. Noer, assistant professor of physics, Carleton College, and Dr. John Mowat of the physics department of Auburn University for technical advice and information concerning Professor Costa de Beauregard's "Certain Aspects of the Irreversibility of Time in Classical and Quantum Physics." Finally, I would like to express my gratitude to Professor Milič Čapek and Professor Robert Blanché for carefully correcting my translations of their essays, and to Professor Čapek for suggesting important corrections to the text of certain other translations. *The Journal of the History of Philosophy* is to be thanked for releasing Dr. David A. Sipfle's article, "Henri Bergson and the Epochal Theory of Time," thus making it possible for it to appear here for the first time.

[2] Milič Čapek, *The Philosophical Impact of Contemporary Physics* (New York: D. Van Nostrand, 1961). Čapek's thesis, that modern science has relied too uncritically on visual and spatial concepts for its models and conceptual schemes, in many respects parallels Bergson's attitude toward scientific thought.

CONTENTS

ABBREVIATIONS

BELOW ARE LISTED those of Henri Bergson's works which will be referred to most often in this volume. Abbreviations of these works will be used throughout the book in both text and notes. The English edition will be cited first, with appropriate page numbers, followed by the French edition and its page numbers. Each of these editions is fully described in the Bibliography.

CE	Creative Evolution
EC	L'Évolution créatrice
CM	The Creative Mind
PM	La pensée et le mouvant
DS	Duration and Simultaneity
DSf	Durée et simultanéité
MM	Matter and Memory
MMf	Matière et mémoire
TFW	Time and Free Will
Essai	Essai sur les données immédiates de la conscience

INTRODUCTION

BERGSONIAN METHOD
and the Evolution of Science

HENRI LOUIS BERGSON was born in Paris October 18, 1859, the second son of Varsovie Michael and Katharine Bergson. Michael Bergson (originally Berek-son[1]) was Polish; a composer in his own right as well as a proponent and popularizer of Chopin, he had traveled widely across Europe as a teacher, performer, and conductor. Katharine Bergson, a native of Yorkshire, spoke English to her children and wrote to them in her native tongue. In the words of one French biographer, she remained *"de cœur anglaise."* [2] Katharine and Michael Bergson were both Jewish and shared a common background in the Hassidic tradition. Hassidism, stemming from reform movements in eastern European Judaism, made a direct appeal to religious experience and insisted that personal obedience to God is more important than formal obedience to rabbinic legalisms. Henri Bergson was not subjected to a rigorously sectarian religious training and never considered himself to be Jewish in any orthodox sense. Nonetheless, as he later conceded, the awareness of belonging to an unfairly treated minority was to exercise a lasting influence on his mind.

Bergson's life exhibits few spectacular episodes. His academic record at the Lycée Condorcet in Paris was uniformly brilliant, culminating in prizes in English, Latin, Greek, philosophy, and mathematics. For a time he seriously considered a degree in mathematics. His mathematics professor, Adolphe Desboves, admired Bergson's solution to the problem of the three circles, first posed by Pascal in a letter to Fermat, and published it in his *Étude sur*

---

[1] Ben-Ami Scharfstein, *The Roots of Bergson's Philosophy* (New York: Columbia University Press, 1943), 100.

[2] Rose-Marie Mossé-Bastide, *Bergson éducateur* (Paris: Presses Universitaires de France, 1955), 15.

Pascal et les géomètres contemporaines (1878). The same year Bergson won a national prize in mathematics and saw his work published in the *Annales de mathématiques*.[3] Elated by the facility with which his young scholar solved demanding problems, Desboves predicted for him an outstanding career in the sciences. Bergson, however, remained dissatisfied; he found mathematics "too absorbing"[4] and chose a career in philosophy instead. "You might have been a mathematician," said the disgruntled Desboves, "but you will only be a philosopher."[5] The following description, read by René Doumic on Bergson's reception into the French Academy, reveals Bergson as he appeared to his schoolmates at the Lycée Condorcet:

> I recall quite clearly our first encounter. . . . You were already famous then. You were always famous. . . . I recall the fragile-looking youth you were in those days, with your tall, slender, slightly swaying figure, your charm so delicately fair, for your abundant hair, inclining slightly to red, was then carefully parted on your forehead. . . . The eyes below the arch of that lofty forehead looked out with a slightly astonished gaze, an expression noticeable in reflective persons, unmistakably honest, but veiled and solitary, withdrawn from the outer world and turned inward. . . . You said little, but that little was uttered in a clear, sedate voice, full of deference to your companion's opinion, especially when you were proving to him in your quiet little way, and with that unconcerned air of yours, that his opinion was absurd. We had never seen a school boy so polite, and that made us regard you as somewhat different from ourselves, though not distant—you were never *that*, and you never have been—but rather, somewhat detached and distinguished. From your whole personality emanated a singular charm; it was something subtle, and even mysterious. . . .[6]

In 1870 the French suffered a humiliating defeat at the hands of Prussia, and the next decade was therefore to be a time of con-

[3] *Les nouvelles annales mathématiques*, 1878, pp. 268–76.
[4] Jacques Chevalier, *Bergson* (London: Rider and Co., 1928), 45.
[5] *Ibid.*
[6] René Doumic, *Discours de reception de Bergson à l'Académie française*, 24 mars, 1918.

fusion and internal instability for France. Bergson and his class-mates were to find the name of their school repeatedly changed, from Lycée Condorcet to Lycée Fontaine, then back to Lycée Condorcet, and finally to Lycée Bonaparte, as political parties rose, fell, and rose again. Bergson concluded pessimistically that the compromises required by politics could not be undertaken by an honest man and resolved never to enter political life—a resolution which he was not always able to keep.

Except for a brief stay in Switzerland, where Michael Bergson was director of the Berne Conservatory, the Bergsons remained in France. In 1878, however, the family moved to England, leaving Henri alone in Paris; and his three brothers and three sisters decided to live in Britain. One brother became an actor and novelist, writing in English under a pseudonym; two of his sisters married in England. Katharine Bergson corresponded regularly with her son, keeping him abreast of the family's activities and contemporary British literary life.

Soon after his family's departure Bergson enrolled at the École Normale, where he devoted his energies entirely to philosophy. At the time, French philosophy was sharply divided between antagonistic schools: "A nostalgic spiritualism, a professional rationalism, struggling at its post like the captain of a sinking ship, [and] a stubborn but hesitant positivism—this is what Bergson discovered." [7] Philosophy at the École Normale was split between Kantianism, taught by Émile Boutroux, and mechanistic evolutionism, as represented by Herbert Spencer. Bergson sided with the second, less numerous, group. Spencer's scientific erudition, his attempt "always to bring philosophy back to the ground of fact," [8] seemed to the young philosopher far more promising than Kant's obscure abstractions. Bergson's contemporaries, however, regarded Spencer as the proponent of a "soulless" mechanistic universe. With his taste for British empiricism and his refusal to see in the tenets of traditional psychology anything other than mere

[7] François Heidsieck, *Henri Bergson et la notion d'espace* (Paris: Le Circle du Livre, 1957), 20.
[8] Charles DuBose, *Journal 1921–1923* (Paris: Correa, 1946), 63.

5

words, Bergson was considered by his classmates to be a positivist, or even a materialist. Hence the following vignette. A professor, seeing some books on the library floor, turned to Bergson (who was student librarian) and barked, "Monsieur Bergson, you see those books sweeping up the dirt; your librarian's soul ought to be unable to endure it!" The class cried out, "But he has no soul!" [9]

Although Spencer is little discussed today, the influence which he enjoyed in the heyday of triumphant mechanism was immense. Envisioning the extension of mechanistic explanations to the entire universe, Bergson carefully reread Spencer's *First Principles* and studied the works of contemporary physicists. It seemed to Bergson that Spencer's assumptions, though sound, required to be reformulated and made more precise. Pierre d'Aurec pictures Bergson's intentions quite clearly: "What did the young student in search of a dissertation subject think of the third chapter [of Spencer's *First Principles*] dedicated to the latest ideas of science? Space, time, matter, motion, force, consciousness: Spencer was most imprecise in treating these notions. Bergson realized this, but hoped to remedy it. Was he not better trained in mathematics and more exacting in matters of method?" [10] Bergson's first original work was to have been a model of narrowly scientistic analysis, dedicated, in clarifying the concepts of classical Newtonian physics, to the reduction of cosmic and human phenomena to the purely mechanical "concentration" and "diffusion" of mass particles.

In 1883 Bergson published a translation of Lucretius' *On the Nature of Things*[11] and in 1884 took a provincial teaching post at Lycée Blaise Pascal at Clermont-Ferrand. He spoke little of his preoccupations, even to his closest friends, the librarian Gilbert Maire and the mathematician Constantin, whose study of the differential calculus he read and discussed.[12] Bergson's characteris-

[9] Doumic, *Discours de reception de Bergson*, 51.

[10] Pierre d'Aurec, "De Bergson Spencerien au Bergson de l'*Essai*," special edition, *Archives de philosophie*, XVII (1957), 112.

[11] Henri Bergson, *Extraits de Lucrèce* (Paris: Delagrave, 1883). The notes to this work appear in English as *The Philosophy of Poetry* (New York: Wisdom Library, 1959), edited and in part recast by Wade Baskin.

[12] Mossé-Bastide, *Bergson éducateur*, 27.

tic reserve, however, concealed a profound intellectual ferment. For in comparing Spencer's principles with the facts of experience, he had discovered a concept which caused the overthrow of his mechanistic assumptions and formed the basis for a bold new philosophy: the concept of "lived time" or "duration."

According to Spencer, time is to be treated as if it were very little different from space. Like space, time is measurable and contains juxtaposed parts. Like space, time is a homogeneous medium whose properties are conceived as everywhere alike. Moreover, time, like space, must be capable of being accurately described by mathematical concepts. Thus, Spencer says, it is both accurate and meaningful to state that one time is equal to or twice as long as another, that a given instant precisely divides two periods of time, or that events begin or end at some specifiable instant. It is even meaningful to state that time is composed of instants and to speak of the movement of time as the succession of one instant upon another, much as one speaks of a body moving from one point to another in space.

That Spencer should have reasoned about the nature of time in this way was quite understandable. Not only had previous philosophers made closely similar assumptions, but both science and common sense seemed to agree in treating time as if it could be cut up into neat units, measured, and described with mathematical precision. Our clocks, our calendars, our physics—not to speak of our daily lives—depend upon the space-like character of time. What error, then, could be committed by treating time as if it were little different from space?

Such arguments appeared perfectly valid. Yet, to his surprise, Bergson found that the more carefully he analyzed Spencer's commonsense, spatial concept of time, the less satisfactory it appeared. The briefest examination, for example, revealed that moments of time are not alike; rather, each had its own quality and tone, which varied from that of other moments. Time—or, to use Bergson's terminology, duration—was not a homogeneous medium like space, but instead a heterogeneous stream, ever-flowing, never repetitive. Moreover, to attempt to describe the flow

7

of duration as the succession of one sheer instant upon another was to disfigure experience, which shows us one moment merging imperceptibly into the next, without discontinuous transitions. But to admit that moments of time were qualitatively different, and that they shaded into each other by continuous transitions, was to have dealt a death-blow to the idea of a measurable duration. Measurement implied the juxtaposition of equal (and in this sense identical) units; but this was only possible if what one measured had mutually identical, juxtaposed parts. Objects in space no doubt had these properties. The flux of duration, however, had neither mathematically precise demarcations nor "parts" which were identical with (and in this sense equal to) each other. The concept of a homogeneous, measurable time was therefore a pseudo-concept. Real time was what experience—particularly inner experience—revealed: "Below homogeneous time, which is the [spatial] symbol of true duration, a close psychological analysis distinguishes a duration whose heterogeneous moments permeate one another; below the numerical multiplicity of conscious states, a qualitative multiplicity; below the self with well-defined states, a self in which *succeeding each other* means *melting into one another* and forming an organic whole." [13] The analysis of commonsense "clock" time thus led to the discovery of real duration, and real duration led to a new exploration of the enduring, active, changing self. Bergson's entire philosophy, though to be concerned with issues and concepts far removed from those of his first study, *Time and Free Will*, was nevertheless to consist of a continual widening and deepening of the insights derived from his initial discovery of "real duration."

Bergson's strikingly original analysis of the nature of duration[14] not only made possible a new philosophy, but it also en-

[13] Henri Bergson, *Time and Free Will*, 128; *Essai sur les données immédiates de la conscience*, 95. Hereinafter, these works will be cited in the text as TFW and *Essai*, respectively. In addition, the English and French editions of *Creative Evolution*, *The Creative Mind*, *Duration and Simultaneity*, and *Matter and Memory* will be cited within the text by use of appropriate abbreviations. A complete list of these abbreviations appears on p. *xi*.

[14] The psychologists William James and James Ward published analyses of experienced time (in James's phrase, the "stream of consciousness") almost simul-

tailed the rejection of an old one. If scientific mechanism were correct, all change would be reducible to the predictable motions of material particles, and "freedom of the will," in the sense in which the ordinary man understands it, would therefore be an illusion, rooted in an ignorance of physical causes. But the experience of duration revealed change to be a far more dynamic, organic, and highly interrelated process than could ever be suggested through the motions of mass particles. Bergson saw that each moment of duration was a fresh existence and involved the emergence of new qualities. Thus the present did not repeat the past, but added to it; and what was added, being truly novel, had to be unpredictable as well. Mechanism was doubly false then: false because of its impoverished conception of change and false because of its assumption that the future is uniformly predictable. And human acts, where they are creative, must therefore be free acts.

In 1888 Bergson returned to Paris to teach and in 1889 defended and subsequently published two theses: *Quid Aristoteles de loco senserit* and *Essai sur les données immédiates de la conscience (Time and Free Will)*.[15] The former, an exposition and criticism of Aristotle's doctrine of "place," was a purely academic exercise and has been little studied. The latter, destined ultimately to go through countless editions, introduced the concept of experienced duration and sharply criticized theories based on the "spatialization" of time: for example, psychophysics, associationist psychology, psychic determinism. To Bergson's great surprise, he was not called on in his thesis defense to discuss the concept of duration. His thesis supervisor, the psychologist Paul Janet, thought only the first chapter, dedicated to the analysis of sensation, was significant, while the philosopher Émile Boutroux limited discussion

---

taneously with Bergson's similar analysis. It is clear that each arrived at his conclusions independently, however. (Cf. Bergson's letter to the director of the *Revue Philosophique* on his relation to Ward and to James, *Revue Philosophique,* LX [August, 1905], 229–31.)

15 Henri Bergson, *Quid Aristoteles de loco senserit* (Paris: Félix Alcan, 1889). A French translation of this study may be found in *Les Études Bergsoniennes* (Paris: Éditions Albin Michel, 1962), II, 9–104. For a brief summary of Bergson's conclusions, see Heidsieck, *Henri Bergson et la notion d'espace,* 29–40.

to special aspects of Bergson's concept of liberty. Though the young philosopher was furious,[16] his anger failed to unsettle his good manners. Bergson was declared doctor of letters à l'unanimité.

The Essai received polite reviews and then passed into temporary obscurity. Bergson taught, married (Mlle. Maurine Neuberger, who bore him one daughter), and continued his researches. The Essai had explored the subjective experience of duration, contrasting it with the static homogeneity of space. Bergson now approached the experience of duration in terms of the mind-body problem, attempting to relate consciousness to the material world and to answer those who conceived consciousness as entirely dependent on, or identical with, brain states. Matter and Memory, published in 1896, is therefore both a reply to materialist theories of mind and the statement of a new theory of mind-body interaction.

Those who conceived the mind to be either dependent on or identical with the brain rested their case, in the main, on what was then known of the maladies of verbal memory—the aphasias. Scientific investigation of the aphasias was interpreted as showing that the brain was literally a "storehouse" for memories and other mental contents and as proving, therefore, that "mind," "soul," or "will" were merely functions of the cerebral mechanism. It took Bergson six years to master the immense literature on aphasiology. His study convinced him that the then classical "braintrace" theory of memory was not supported by the facts. Memories, he concluded, are not stored in the brain, which is an organ of adaptation and not of thought. Rather, memories are retained in the unconscious, from which they are recalled by the brain to aid us in the sphere of action:

> The role of the brain is to choose at any moment, among memories, those which can illuminate the action begun, and to exclude the others. Those memories capable of being inserted into the motor framework forever changing, but always prepared, emerge once more to consciousness; the rest remain in the unconscious.

16 DuBose, Journal 1921–1923, 67.

The role of the body is thus to reproduce in action the life of the mind, to emphasize its motor articulations as the orchestra conductor does for a musical score; the brain does not have thinking for its function but that of hindering the thought from becoming lost in dream; it is the organ of *attention to life* (CM 86–87; PM 79–80).

This being the case, it is not difficult to understand why a complex brain structure and nervous system are necessary to the existence of a highly developed mentality. Only a fully developed brain and nervous system can transmit the complex intentions of a reflective and creative consciousness into appropriate acts. The complexity of man's neurological system is thus an indication of the diversity of the acts which he may choose to perform; it is a symbol of man's potential freedom, and not an evidence that the mind is a product of the brain.

By denying, like Descartes, that the brain can be said to "think," Bergson by no means hoped to reinstate the sharp Cartesian distinction between the extended material body and the unextended mind or soul. On the contrary, he hoped to show that mind and body are intimately interrelated and that the spontaneous, creative self described in *Time and Free Will* is firmly rooted in the material world. The close interrelations between mind and body are explained by Bergson as a mutual accommodation of two contrasting schemas. In response to a stimulus, he holds, the body calls up the various responses at its disposal, and these organize themselves into a "corporeal schema." Except in the case of involuntary or thoroughly conditioned reflexes, however, the stimulus does not elicit an immediate and overt response. Where intelligent action is concerned, this response awaits the action of the mind, which draws memory-images from its past experience and organizes them into a "dynamic schema." The ensuing act, constituted by the process of adjustment of these two schemas, is thus a union of mind and body. In describing this union, Bergson both escapes the criticism, leveled at Cartesians, of having introduced a "ghost" into a "machine," and anticipates later phenomenological accounts of the "lived body" and the "body-subject."

11

Matter and Memory, though destined, in Ian Alexander's words, to be "the bed-rock of Bergsonism," [17] received little attention. Like *Time and Free Will*, it received its share of reviews and was forgotten. In 1898 Bergson was named to a teaching post at the École Normale and in 1900 to a professorship at the Collège de France, where his lectures began to attract a following. In 1903 he published *An Introduction to Metaphysics* and in 1907, after eleven years of thorough preparation, *Creative Evolution*, the book that was to make him famous.

In *Creative Evolution* the psychological and physiological insights of Bergson's earlier work are broadened to include a metaphysical vision on a grand scale. Though a thoroughgoing evolutionist, Bergson remained skeptical of Darwin's and Spencer's mechanistic accounts of evolution, both of which seemed to him clearly based on an illicit spatialization of time. Viewed as an ongoing process, evolution appears to be a continual springing-up of new forms, similar to the history of a human consciousness. The fact that these forms are truly novel additions to the universe suggests—mechanistic theories notwithstanding—that their emergence is unpredictable, although their ever increasing complexity suggests that the process which engenders them is not random but directed. To the force which drives the evolutionary process Bergson gave a name: the *élan vital*.

The *élan vital* or "vital impetus" is described by Bergson as being engaged in a continual struggle with physical matter. The results of this struggle are twofold: while life is forced to take on many of the characteristics of its material environment, matter is nonetheless shaped into ever more complex and active organisms. Evolutionary advances are therefore products of both vital and material tendencies, much as effective actions (as portrayed in *Matter and Memory*) are products of the interaction of dynamic and corporeal schemas. Besides being opposed by inert matter, the vital impetus is constrained by its own characteristics. Not only are its energies limited, but also its various potentials are un-

[17] Ian Alexander, *Bergson, Philosopher of Reflection* (London: Bowes & Bowes, 1957), 30.

able to develop jointly and as a whole. Thus life diverges from a common source to create sharply contrasting biological forms, each of which is only a partial expression of the original impulse. In plants the tendency toward torpor and immobility, in animals the tendency toward irritability and motion are dominant, while other evolutionary developments express still sharper contrasts.[18] Although this divergent evolution is accompanied by increasing conflict between species, there is, Bergson demonstrates, a degree of complementarity between living things. Plant life depends on the microbes of the soil for the nitrogen necessary to photosynthesis; animals are dependent on plants for the energy which the photosynthetic process stores; man, in turn, is dependent on the balance achieved by plant and animal life. In spite of its contrary tendencies, life achieves a measure of internal coherence, therefore, and is able to triumph over both its own weaknesses and the obstacle of matter: "All the living hold together, and all yield to the same tremendous push. The animal takes its stand on the plant, man bestrides animality, and the whole of humanity, in space and in time, is one immense army galloping beside and before and behind each of us in an overwhelming charge able to beat down every resistance and clear the most formidable obstacles, perhaps even death" (CE 271; EC 271). There are, to be sure, no fixed goals and no pre-established ends. Yet each of us, it is implied, can have a part in the creation of goals and the envisaging of ends and thus share in the creative evolution of humanity.

One of the paradoxes of human existence, Bergson insists, is that although man shares in the universal flux of things, his intellect is unable to understand evolution. This congenital nearsightedness may be explained by the place that man occupies in the evolutionary scheme. A survey of the main directions of evolution discloses in animal life a dissociation between two opposed tendencies: instinct, the possession of arthropods, and intellect, the determining

---

[18] Species are to be defined, Bergson insists, not through the possession of specific properties but through the *tendency* to emphasize these properties. Thus there are plants capable of movement and animal species which have fallen into torpor; yet the general tendency to emphasize mobility nonetheless is sufficient to distinguish animals from plants (CE 108; EC 109).

feature of vertebrates, including man. Intellect is an ability to manufacture tools out of nonliving matter, instinct a capacity to shape biological instruments, that is, tools that are a part of the structure of the organism. In the most highly developed instinctive societies, those of ants and bees, the tools through which the society survives consist either in special organs (the bee's pollen sacs and sting, for example) or in a "polymorphism" through which specific types of organisms (for example, drones, workers, and queens) are fitted by their structure to perform only specific tasks. The contrast with human societies is obvious. From the very moment *homo faber* emerged as a distinct species, his technology has been an attempt to shape inert matter rather than an effort to restructure the human form. Man has thus avoided the stereotyping and the extreme limitation of function inherent in instinctive societies; but he has at the same time acquired mental habits, Bergson says, that deform his view of reality. Instinct, which has taken up the task of shaping life, is by its nature capable of understanding living things; intellect, on the other hand, has as its task the profitable manipulation of inert matter and, understandably, tends to view the living as it views the nonliving.

Bergson's analysis of instinct and intellect therefore arrives at a dual result. Man, he indicates, is the product of evolutionary processes that have emphasized intellect at the expense of instinct. But intellect tends toward static and mechanical conceptual schemes and thus fails to understand the creative advance of life. Either man must give up the hope of understanding life, or he must draw near to a new kind of knowledge, one which is capable of grasping the inner dynamics of evolution. Such a mode of knowledge would necessarily be instinctive, but an instinct that has become "disinterested, self-conscious, capable of reflecting upon its object and of enlarging it indefinitely" (CE 176; EC 178). Bergson terms this highly concrete and creative reflection "intuition."

The philosophy of *Creative Evolution*, with its celebration of vital spontaneity and its rejection of "intellect," quickly attracted adverse criticism. Irked by Bergson's seemingly glib and dangerous anti-intellectualism, Bertrand Russell retorted, "Intellect is the misfortune of man, while intuition is seen at its best in ants, bees, and Bergson." [19] Scientists, similarly, tended to view Bergson's biological theories as naïve, if fascinating, poetry and, like most poetry, invalid from a scientific point of view. Thus Julian Huxley complained, "But to say that biological progress is explained by the *élan vital* is to say that the movement of a train is 'explained' by an *élan locomotif* of the engine. . . ." [20] Nonetheless, Bergson's message struck a responsive note in a wide variety of minds. To intellectuals chafing under the restraints of dogmatic mechanism, to religious thinkers struggling with persistent doubts, and to free spirits at odds with the rigid inflexibility of turn of the century morals and institutions, *Creative Evolution* came as both a release and an inspiration. Bergson's works were translated into every European language, newspaper and magazine articles breathlessly discussed his "wonder-working" philosophy, and philosophical journals bristled with discussions of "duration," "novelty," and *"élan vital."* His lectures at the Collège de France, already popular, became so crowded that the philosopher was forced to reserve several rows in order that students might be able to attend. Journalists, priests, tourists, students, and fashionable matrons vied for seats in the cramped lecture hall to hear the philosopher discuss Spinoza's conception of time, Aristotle's physics, or Berkeley's concept of sensation. The *grande dames* of Parisian society made themselves conspicuous by stating that they would understand philosophy partly through the intellect and partly "through the heart"—and by sending servants hours ahead to reserve seats. On Bergson's reception into the French Academy the hall was so choked with flowers and admirers that he was forced to push his way bodily to the platform, his protests *("Mais . . . je ne suis pas une danseuse!"* [21]) unheard among the clamor. To his still great-

[19] Bertrand Russell, *A History of Modern Philosophy* (New York: Simon and Schuster, 1945), 793.
[20] Julian Huxley, *Essays of a Biologist* (London: Chatto and Windus, 1926), 34.
[21] Mossé-Bastide, *Bergson éducateur*, 34.

15

er embarrassment, the newspapers began to debate whether Bergson's lectures ought to be moved to a larger building. Perhaps, it was suggested, the Paris Opera would be large enough.

The popular vogue of Bergsonism was also parallelled by its profound influence among serious intellectuals. Not only did professional philosophers—William James, Alfred North Whitehead, Martin Heidegger, Gabriel Marcel among them—learn from his critical analyses and his evocation of the freshness and fluidity of experience, but also writers, musicians, educators, artists, political thinkers, and even military strategists appropriated elements of Bergson's thought and transformed his philosophy into a multitude of "Bergsonisms." The philosopher of the vital impetus was hailed as the initiator of a new era in Western thought, and enthusiastic followers ranked his works alongside—or slightly above —those of Plato, Aristotle, Kant, and Hegel.

Yet the twentieth century, though indeed a new era in Western thought, was to be dominated by philosophies very different from Bergson's; and interest in his ideas was to decline almost as rapidly as it had arisen. The reasons for this decline were many and deserve careful consideration. The contemporary philosopher who sets out to chronicle them is fated to ask whether they constitute a final verdict on Bergson's philosophy, or whether they constitute a development that invites reassessment.

In 1914 Bergson, anxious both to avoid further embarrassments and to cut short the vogue that by now had indissolubly associated his name with fashionable matrons and unreflective enthusiasm, resigned his teaching post. His gesture, however, went unheeded. Already the press professed to find his philosophy "flattering to an idle and worldly public; to an audience composed for the most part of women who belong to the lower and upper middle class; to a public to whom study or effort is instinctively repugnant." [22] One wag had even gone so far as to publish an imaginary lecture on the tango by "the celebrated metaphysician of the Collège de France, M. Blagson." [23]

[22] Gabriel Reuillard, in *Les Hommes du Jour* (quoted at length in *Current Opinion*, LVI [May, 1914], 372).
[23] *Ibid.*, 371.

Although Bergson's intellectual following was able to survive the taint of popularity, it was unable to survive its own inner divisions. Perhaps these are best illustrated by the disputes between French revolutionary syndicalism and French militarism, both of which appealed to the Philosophy of Intuition for support. "France," Barbara Tuchman observes, ". . . needed some weapon that Germany lacked to give herself confidence in her survival. The 'idea with a sword' fulfilled the need. Expressed by Bergson it was called *élan vital*, the all-conquering will." [24] The doctrine of creative evolution suggested that a heroic "spiritual" force might overcome a massive "material" obstacle; translated into military terms this was taken to mean that France might overwhelm the German war machine through sheer *élan*. As a result of the teachings of the extravagant Colonel Loyzeau de Grandmaison, the French military establishment became convinced—quite to the detriment of France, whose strength lay in her defensive position—that the "impetus" of the footsoldier must never be lost and that mere intelligent prudence was out of the question when it was a matter of "keeping the offensive."

To Georges Sorel, however, Bergson's philosophy seemed to lead not to militant nationalism but to a politics of pacifism and internal social revolution. In *Reflections on Violence* and *The Myth of the General Strike*, Sorel transformed the *élan vital* into the *élan révolutionnaire*, proclaiming that the effete intellectualism of modern parliamentary government must be overcome by the spontaneous—and, if necessary, violent—action of the working classes. In spite of Bergson's denials,[25] including personal communications to Sorel,[26] Bergson's philosophy came to be closely associated with Sorel's revolutionary syndicalism, a fact which thus cost Bergson the support not only of conservatives and "liberals," but also of many disinterested scholars who felt justified

---

[24] Barbara Tuchman, *The Guns of August* (New York: The Macmillan Co., 1962), 31. (Cf. also Alistaire Horne, *The Price of Glory* [New York: St. Martin's Press, 1963], 11–12).

[25] Isaac Benrubi, *Souvenirs sur Henri Bergson* (Paris: Delachaux et Niestlé, 1942), 20.

[26] Pierre Andreu, "Bergson et Sorel," *Séances des Amis de Bergson*, March 19, 1949.

17

in concluding that Bergsonism was of necessity a philosophy of violence.[27] It is ironic, therefore, that Bergson's syndicalist followers were also to defect from his camp. Although he was ill-disposed toward bloodshed in any form, when Germany attacked France, Bergson was willing to turn violence against violence. His patriotic speeches[28] during the war years 1914–18 wholly alienated the syndicalist movement, including its spokesman Sorel, who lamented to the Italian philosopher Croce, "Bergson . . . prattles like a child about the war." [29] Thus, while radicals reproached him for his conservatism and while conservatives reproached him for his radicalism, the racist *Action Française* attacked him for his Jewishness, the scientifically oriented Sorbonne disparaged him for his "mysticism," and the Catholic Church, so little opposed to mysticism, concluded by placing his works on the Index. For all his efforts at consensus, Bergson had in the end not only his own enemies but also the enemies of his enemies.

In retrospect, it is clear that the radical transformation of Europe's intellectual climate played a greater part in the eclipse of Bergson's philosophy than either the vogue associated with his name or the disintegration of his following. The First World War deeply disillusioned a world that had known fifty years of peace and had believed itself secure and stable. To the generation living in its aftermath, the comfortable optimism and the facile assumptions that had prevailed before the great conflict appeared ironically empty. Materialism, mechanism, vitalism, idealism, even positivism: almost all the major philosophies endemic to the nineteenth and early twentieth centuries possessed an implicit faith in evolutionary progress. But it was precisely this faith that the slaughter in the trenches brought into question. In the new era, as D. H. Lawrence remarked, there were no Big Words. What was true of the era generally was also, though for somewhat more complex reasons, true for philosophy. The imposing philosophical

[27] For example, George Santayana, *Winds of Doctrine* (New York: Charles Scribner's Sons, 1926).
[28] For an English translation of Bergson's patriotic diatribes, cf. Henri Bergson, *The Meaning of the War* (London: T. Fisher Unwin, Ltd., 1916).
[29] Pierre Andreu, "Bergson et Sorel," *Les Études Bergsoniennes*, III, 62.

18

schemes and the sweeping slogans of the past were soon superseded by existentialism's painstaking explorations of human forlornness and despair and the logically precise but piecemeal studies of analytically minded philosophers. It is only a slight exaggeration to state, therefore, that Bergson's philosophy—like many another full-blown evolutionary ideology—became a casualty of war.

Granted these historical factors, it remains true that the fate of a philosophy is also in large measure determined by its own merits and defects, or at least by those that its contemporaries conceive it to possess. It is highly significant, therefore, that many of Bergson's most astute contemporaries, including Bertrand Russell, George Santayana, and A. O. Lovejoy, should have attacked his philosophy as incoherent and illogical. Not only did the negative conclusions of these critics have a profound impact on the fortunes of Bergsonism, but also their evaluations continue today to influence the prevailing interpretation of Bergson's philosophy, at least among English-speaking philosophers. For the purposes of discussion, the objections of these critics may be reduced to three: (1) Bergson's critique of the intellect, besides calling into question our most reliable and well-established knowledge, is ultimately destructive. In attempting to remove an obstacle to his world view, Bergson undermines and frustrates precisely those intellectual capacities without which man could not survive, much less progress. (2) Having discredited the scientific intellect, Bergson then introduces his touted "intuition"; but intuition, far from being able to resolve philosophical problems, is nebulous, vague, and irrational. Therefore, to found a philosophy on unreasoned "intuition" is to invite justified denunciation, for one thereby sanctions both puerile enthusiasms and dangerous thoughtlessness and, in addition, places his insights beyond the reach of all responsible analysis and grounded criticism. (3) Finally, it is objected, one may search Bergson's writings in vain to find any coherent connections between intuition and its arch-foe, the intellect. On the one hand, intellect deforms reality for practical ends; on the other, intuition is resolutely turned away from pragmatic considerations. Bergson so thoroughly fails to interrelate

19

these two modes of thought that he appears in the end to defend two philosophies simultaneously, while remaining almost oblivious to their contradictions.

Such criticisms, especially when developed by able and perceptive critics, appeared quite valid to many thinkers who might otherwise have felt a certain sympathy for Bergson's thought. There can be no question that even today each judgment remains relevant to the interpretation of Bergsonism. Nonetheless, it is my conviction, and the manifest conviction of most of the authors translated in this study, that such criticisms spring from a misunderstanding of both the essential spirit and the basic structure of Bergson's philosophy and that a more accurate analysis would shed an entirely new light on his treatment of intuition, science, and their interrelations. Before suggesting such an analysis, however, it is necessary to complete the chronicle of Bergson's life.

Apart from prolonged sieges of insomnia, Bergson had always enjoyed good health. But in 1924 he was suddenly stricken with paralyzing arthritis and, as his condition rapidly worsened, was forced to retire from public life. His last years, spent in virtual seclusion, were a continual struggle against the illness which sapped his strength, deformed his hands, and rendered every movement painful. His enforced isolation, moreover, coincided with the general decline of interest in his philosophy; the news of his death, in 1941, was shocking precisely because the world had already fallen into the habit of thinking of him as dead.[30]

The contrast between Bergson's years of illness and his earlier years of international prestige is made all the more striking by the political and diplomatic services which consumed his energies prior to his retirement. In 1916 Bergson, along with other French intellectuals, was sent on a diplomatic mission to Spain with the hope of bringing that nation into the war on the side of the allies.[31]

[30] Irwin Edman, Introduction, Creative Evolution (New York: Modern Library, 1944), ix.
[31] Henri Bergson, "Discours prononcé à la Résidence des Étudiants, Madrid, Le 1er mai 1916," Écrits et paroles (Paris: Presses Universitaires de France, 1959), III, 445–48.

The mission, while it failed in its ultimate objective, probably succeeding in assuring Spanish neutrality.[32] The next year he was sent to the United States to try to convince President Woodrow Wilson of the magnitude of German designs and the danger of German authoritarianism, and thereby dislodge the American government from its policy of neutralism.[33] Although he was unable to exert a direct influence on Wilson, who purposely isolated himself from all but a few intimates, Bergson did influence the President indirectly through Colonel Edward M. House, Wilson's advisor, and through Secretary of the Interior Franklin Lane. In the end Lane assured Bergson that the philosopher had done "more than he knew" to shape the President's decision to enter the war.

Wilson's fateful decision was made, Bergson held, not in terms of calculated national self-interest but on the basis of sincere moral idealism.[34] America entered the war to sustain threatened Western liberal traditions, to prevent the ruin of Britain and France, and to make possible an organization for preventing future world conflicts. It is not certain whether, in Bergson's conversations with House, the phrase "League of Nations" was mentioned. But the two did agree that such an organization was needed, and Wilson's inability to bring the United States into the League of Nations was for the philosopher a bitter disappointment. In spite of his disappointment, Bergson devoted several years to the League of Nations, as president of the International Commission for Intellectual Cooperation (the forerunner of UNESCO). From our present vantage-point the efforts of the League of Nations appear sadly ineffectual. Considering the circumstances under which the International Commission for Intellectual Cooperation was forced to operate, its efforts could scarcely have been expected to result in unqualified success. Nonetheless, Bergson—who assessed quite realistically the obstacles confronting the commission—managed on a vanishingly small budget to see it organized and housed. Through a combination of tact and sheer persistence, he was also

---

[32] Mossé-Bastide, *Bergson éducateur*, 109–110.
[33] Henri Bergson, "Mes missions (1917–1918)," *Écrits et paroles*, III, 627–41.
[34] *Ibid.*, 637.

able to see several programs put into action. It is difficult to know what more he might have accomplished. In 1924 illness forced his resignation, and he retired from public life.[35]

Creative Evolution had transmuted the essentially psychological insights of his earlier writings into a bold, far-reaching philosophical system. In spite of its speculative scope, however, this system was conspicuously silent on two key points. First, although Bergson had made many remarks on the evolution of human societies, he had neglected to fashion a social philosophy. And, second, although he had made suggestions concerning the nature of God (CE 248; EC 249),[36] he had not yet committed himself to a specific philosophy of religion. *The Two Sources of Morality and Religion* (1932) contains both Bergson's theology and his reflections on man's social evolution. Human societies, he suggests, exhibit a perpetual struggle between two contrasting moralities: that of the closed society, turned inward on itself and structured toward self-preservation, and that of the open society, which overflows national boundaries and static social structures, seeking the ultimate unity of mankind. The tension between these two moralities, present at every point in human evolution, is clearly visible in the disputes between pharisees and essenes, sectarians and liberals, literalists and mystics—that is, between what might be called the clerks and the heroes of the moral life. *The Two Sources of Morality and Religion,* like *Creative Evolution,* argues for the dominance of dynamic and creative tendencies over static and conservative ones. Ultimately it is dynamic religion or mysticism that makes possible man's emergence from the closed society into the open society, the brotherhood of man.

In *The Two Sources of Morality and Religion* Bergson describes Christianity as the religion that has most adequately expressed an open, creative morality. Through the Christian saints and mystics an impetus has been imparted to humanity that transcends both rigid creeds and mechanical formalisms and thereby

[35] Mossé-Bastide, *Bergson éducateur,* Chapitre V, "L'Activité de Bergson à la Société des Nations," 119–50.
[36] See also *An Introduction to Metaphysics* (New York: Bobbs-Merrill, 1949), 49.

22

translates into history the creative love of God. Although the last years of his life found the philosopher increasingly sympathetic toward Roman Catholicism, he saw quite clearly the direction in which Europe was moving and refused to renounce his Jewish heritage. A storm of anti-Semitism was about to vent itself upon the world, and he preferred, under the circumstances, to remain among the persecuted.[37] He was to live to see the fall of France, amid the triumph of Nazi armies and Nazi brutality. Rather than accept special treatment from the German government, which insisted that all French Jews register their names and wear yellow arm bands, Bergson renounced all honors and privileges and waited his turn to register on the street in line with other Jews, in the December weather. He died January 3, 1941, and was buried three days later at the cemetery of Garches, in Paris.

Paul Valéry, shortly after Bergson's death, concluded his brief address before the French Academy with the following tribute:

Very high, very pure, very superior figure of the thinking man, and perhaps the last of those men who have exclusively, profoundly, and superiorly thought, in an age of the world in which the world thinks and meditates less and less, in which civilization seems, from day to day, to be reduced to the memory and the vestiges which we guard of its free and superabundant intellectual creativity, while miseries, anguishes, constraints of every kind frustrate or discourage the enterprises of the spirit, Bergson already seems to belong to a bygone age, and his name, the last great name in the history of the European intellect.[38]

M. Valéry's rhetoric is deeply moving. But would it not, we might ask, be more realistic to reverse his evaluation? Far from seeming the last, or one of the last, of great European intellects, does not Bergson begin to appear, more and more, as simply the final expression of a now outworn intellectual milieu? His thoroughgoing

---

[37] Jacques Chevalier, *Entretiens avec Bergson* (Paris: Librarie Plon, 1959), 282.
[38] Paul Valéry, "Henri Bergson, Allocution prononcée à la séance de l'Académi du jeudi 9 janvier 1941" (Paris: Domat-Montchrestien, 1945), x–xi.

evolutionism and his mechanistic concept of science, it can be argued, belong to the nineteenth rather than to the twentieth century, as do his romanticism and his optimistic assessment of man's future, while the scientific knowledge employed in the development of his philosophy is now out of date. In short, have not the passage of time and the emergence of a new sophistication rendered Bergson's philosophy of duration obsolete?

There are compelling reasons for thinking that this evaluation is invalid. Because of the restricted scope of this book, it is not possible here to enter into all the considerations relevant to a more just assessment of Bergson's contemporaneity. Instead, this study is limited to an examination of his philosophy of science or, still more narrowly, his philosophy of physics. Perhaps this will be found surprising. Bergson's name has always been so closely associated with the biological and social sciences that any attempt to link his name with the science of physics must be quite unexpected. Some, like Professor Thomas Hanna, might go further and insist that such an attempt is basically ill-conceived: "The best explanation for Bergson's impressive failure as a scientific theoretician is the same as that for his failure to succeed as a metaphysician: he was not sufficiently conversant with the outlook and problems of mathematics and physics." [39]

This opinion, however, is not justified. From the beginning Bergson was not only thoroughly conversant with the outlook and the problems of physics—whose basic concepts he once studied with a view toward constituting a new philosophy—but also well aware, at a time when few possessed equal foresight, of impending crises in the "foundations" of physical theory. Bergson, therefore, did possess a knowledge of physics, and his thought remains increasingly relevant to recent physical discoveries as well as to puzzling issues in the contemporary philosophy of physics—relevant, and also strangely prophetic.

It is not the purpose of this introductory essay to review in de-

[39] Thomas Hanna (ed.), *The Bergsonian Heritage* (New York: Columbia University Press, 1962), 23.

tail the development or the significance of Bergson's physical theories. The philosophers and scientists translated here succeed quite admirably, both in analyzing Bergson's essential insights and in discussing (and, at times, disputing) the implications of these insights for the science of physics. Instead, the remaining pages of this introduction will consist in an effort to resolve a very general puzzle, which must confront anyone trying to interpret not only the Bergsonian physics but also any other aspect of his philosophy: that is, the problem of Bergson's seemingly anti-intellectual and anti-scientific standpoint. If the French intuitionist does indeed defend the anti-scientific philosophy his critics have interpreted him as possessing, how could he possibly utter scientifically useful or prophetic remarks? And if he does achieve significant insights into matter, energy, space, causality, or time, how could these insights issue consistently from his philosophy?

In answering these questions, one should recall the three major objections pressed by Bergson's critics against his philosophy. These were that his intuition is vague and irrational, that his critique of the scientific intellect is destructive, and that the relations which he establishes between intuition and intellect remain thoroughly obscure. If these criticisms are examined, it will become apparent that each rests, in the main, on a thorough misunderstanding of Bergson's philosophical goals and the methods by which he hoped to attain them.

One of the best known interpretations of Bergson's theory of intuition is that of Bertrand Russell, who insists that "Intuition . . . is an aspect and development of instinct, and like all instinct, is admirable in those customary surroundings which have molded the habits of the animal in question, but totally incompetent as soon as the surroundings are changed in a way which demands some non-habitual mode of action." [40] Like instinct, therefore, intuition lacks, "largeness of contemplation, impersonal disin-

[40] Bertrand Russell, *Mysticism and Logic* (Garden City, N.Y.: Doubleday and Co., Inc., 1957), 16.

terestedness, freedom from practical preoccupations." [41] And what, Russell concludes, can be the value of an unreflective impulse which is shared only by "ants, bees and Bergson"?

It would seem, however, that Russell's instinctive dislike for Bergson precluded largeness of contemplation, disinterestedness, or careful reading on Russell's part.[42] In Bergson's philosophy the concept of development or evolution is fundamental: new organic forms and modes of awareness come into existence through evolutionary processes. But Bergson is, of all philosophers, the first to insist that what has developed from antecedent conditions need no longer share the attributes it possessed under those conditions. Hence, in *Creative Evolution*, when he describes intuition as the development of instinct into a mode of awareness which is "disinterested, self-conscious, capable of reflecting" (CE 176; EC 178), these qualifications must be taken quite seriously and not merely brushed aside as Russell does. No one would conclude that a man is in no essential way different from an amoeba merely because both arise from similar conditions and are the outcome of similar tendencies; but it is equally absurd to assume, simply because intuition is in a special sense an evolved form of instinct, that it is not to be distinguished from instinct per se. Intuition is lucid, far-ranging, creative, and in these respects the direct negation of sheer instinct, which Bergson describes as unchanged, riveted to its special function, and "turned outward by it into acts of locomotion" (CE 177; EC 179). It is no wonder then that Bergson should protest so emphatically against the interpretation of his intuition as sheer instinct: "in every line that I have written there is assurance to the contrary: my intuition is reflection" (CM 103; PM 95).

The discovery that Bergson's intuition is a form of reflection is vitally important to any understanding of his philosophy of science. Yet it is equally important to understand that this form of

[41] *Ibid.*, 17.
[42] Bergson believed that Russell's attack on his philosophy was motivated, at least in part, by Russell's inability to forgive him for a critique which he once gave, in Russell's presence, of Russell's theory of Platonic ideas. (Cf. Chevalier, *Entretiens avec Bergson*, 197.)

reflection is carefully controlled and involves an intense effort of concentration. On this point, too, Bergson has been thoroughly misunderstood. A. O. Lovejoy, for example, insists: "The type of ordinary experience which approximates his much-extolled intuition is none other than sleep—or at least, dream. For in this state the mind is relatively, though even yet not absolutely withdrawn into itself; it is freed from the exigencies of action, and its points of contact with the material world in which action takes place are obstructed." [43] It should follow from this, Lovejoy concludes, that "a method, if not the method of philosophizing is to dream." [44]

A more careful reading on Lovejoy's part would have clearly shown the injustice of this interpretation. In his earliest writings Bergson does cite the dream state as a state in which it is possible, to a high degree, to experience the continuity of real duration. In his later work, however, it becomes apparent that though in dreams we may experience the continuity of consciousness, we experience it there at the passive level of sensation:

> The more we succeed in making ourselves conscious of our progress in pure duration, the more we feel the different parts of our being enter into each other, and our whole personality concentrate itself in a point . . . pressed against the future. . . . It is in this that life and action are free. But suppose we let ourselves go, and instead of acting, dream. At once the self is scattered; our past . . . is broken up into a thousand recollections made external to one another. . . . Our personality thus descends in the direction of space (CE 201; EC 202).

For Bergson, to live by sheer habit is to live as an automaton, while to live wholly in a dream is to lose one's ability to choose (MM 198; MMf 166–67).

If we are to have an intuition, therefore, we must be fully active and highly conscious. Without this active effort it is impossible to rise above habits of representation developed by purely rational judgment. It is impossible to bring our vague intuitions into the

[43] A. O. Lovejoy, *The Reason, the Understanding, and Time* (Baltimore: Johns Hopkins Press, 1961), 68.
[44] *Ibid.*, 71.

focus of thought and develop them there. Hence Bergson says of intuition: "In spite of appearance, it is nothing more than concentrated attention, and therefore is a form of voluntary effort. The greater this effort, the more profound, the more complete, is the resulting intelligence. . . . It is an effort that may become painful—indeed so acutely painful that most men put it off indefinitely." [45] Even those who put off the effort of intuition for good, however, must concede that Bergson intends it as a form of painstaking, discriminating awareness.

The realization that Bergson's intuition is a concentrated and discriminating effort of attention entails, once and for all, the rejection of any interpretation of it as simply a surrender to nebulous impulse.[46] Instead, intuitive awareness resembles the phenomenologist's *epoché*, a disciplined attempt to cast off the prejudices of everyday thought and allow phenomena once again to speak for themselves.[47] Intuition is, as Maurice Merleau-Ponty sees, "a sort of Bergsonian 'reduction' which considers all things *sub specie durationis*—what we call subject, what we call object, and what we call space." [48] What is puzzling, then, about Bergson's unique phenomenology is that it can satisfy the interests and claims of both science and philosophy. The key to this puzzle lies in an understanding of Bergson's empiricism.

A young saint, it has often been said, makes an old sinner. Those who place great faith in such aphorisms might be inclined to believe that Bergson's youthful immersion in the traditions, methods, and assumptions of British empiricism was merely a prelude to his rejection of all such straight and narrow paths in philosophy. It is true that Bergson reacted against Mill, Spencer, Taine, and the other empiricists of his day. But it must be kept clearly in mind that this reaction involved not a rejection, but a reformulation, of

[45] Algot Ruhe and Nancy Margaret Paul, *Henri Bergson* (London: Macmillan and Co., Ltd., 1914), 27.

[46] For a recent example of such an interpretation, see Mario Bunge, *Intuition and Science* (Englewood Cliffs, N.J.: Prentice-Hall, Inc., 1962), 12–17.

[47] Cf. on this point Gaston Berger, "Le progrès de la réflexion chez Bergson et chez Husserl," in Albert Béguin and Pierre Thévenaz, *Henri Bergson, essais et témoignages recueillis* (Neuchatel: Editions de la Baconnière, 1943), 257–63.

[48] Maurice Merleau-Ponty, in Hanna (ed.), *The Bergsonian Heritage*, 137.

empiricism. Bergson, in fact, was never anything other than an empiricist. The philosophical method that he was to perfect gradually from the period of *Time and Free Will* involved joining the empiricism of Mill and Spencer to a new empiricism, which he conceived to be equally well founded on perceived fact. The result is that Bergson practices two empiricisms: an analytical empiricism, close to the methods and assumptions of science, and a dynamic empiricism, the complement of the first.

Bergson's philosophy begins with analysis, typically the analysis of one or more of the sciences. This has generally been thought a paradoxical strategy in an anti-intellectual philosopher, and particularly in Bergson. The intellect, especially the scientific intellect, is for Bergson a pragmatic faculty that, rather than comprehending things, utilizes them, and in utilizing them spatializes, fragments, and materializes them beyond recognition. Why then should the analyses of intellect be necessarily important to intuition? Why, above all, should a seemingly anti-scientific method involve an intense initial concern with science?

The answers to these questions are twofold. First, if intellectual analyses distort reality, then a philosophy critical of the intellect must make us aware of the presence, nature, and degree of this distortion. Merely to say in an abstract way that intellectual analysis distorts is not to have said much; but to have shown the nature and degree of this distortion *concretely*, with regard to a particular subject-matter, is to have said something illuminating. Second, the view that the intellect in most respects fragments, spatializes, and distorts reality is not inconsistent with the view that the intellect can in some sense arrive at truth. The complexity of Bergson's interpretation of the intellect is ignored by those who fail to see that Bergson believes the intellect, at its most general, can and does bear abstractly on the "sinuosities" of reality (CE 102; EC 103). That this is and must be so can be proved either by a careful study of the text or by a general analysis of Bergson's entire position. We will reserve proof of these points for later and remark now that for Bergson, if intellectual analysis spatializes and fragments reality, it should be possible to return, though ab-

29

stractly, to reality by picking up these spatial pieces and putting them back together again. In both cases, whether we view the intellect's negative or positive relations to reality, we will have been forced to view, concretely and afresh, whatever the intellect studies. Indeed, had the intellect never begun by viewing its object abstractly and then distorting it, we would never have had the opportunity to end with a fresh, concrete reflection on real things.

Bergson's initial treatment of the knowledge and limitations of the intellect is many-sided and, insofar as possible, thorough. In some ways intellect bears upon reality, and in other ways the intellect distorts it; consequently, we must take account of both effects. The intellect also has a characteristic way of both perceiving and conceiving things. An intellectualized perception is one that isolates, spatializes, and makes static whatever is encountered. Turned outward, intellect will perceive independent physical objects in an empty space; turned inward, it will perceive isolated "states" of consciousness, "intellectual atoms" separated from their context. The theorizing intellect simply carries on the same operation at a more general level. Turned outward toward the world, it will hypothesize the atoms of Lucretius, the mass-particles of Newton. Turned inward toward the self, it will posit the isolated mental states of Hume, the intellectual atoms of associationist psychology.

Philosophy begins by retracing the work of intellect in both thought and perception—but, it must be insisted, of intellect understood in no simple-minded way. Bergson therefore attempts as regards any given subject matter to learn whatever the intellect has (to date) to teach about it; this attempt is sincere and determined, moreover, because only through it can the philosopher discern the extent to which the intellect has distorted our view of a particular phenomenon, and in the process re-reflect on that phenomenon directly. The scientific studies to which Bergson devoted many years, and which preceded each of his major works, were not treated by him as merely incidental to his aims as a philosopher, for apart from "the sum of observations and experience gathered together by positive science," he asserts, significant philosophical insights are not possible: "And it is not merely a question of assimilating the most conspicuous facts; so immense a mass of facts must be accumulated and fused together, that in this fusion all the preconceived and premature ideas which observers may unwittingly have put into observations will be certain to neutralize each other. Only thus can the bare materiality of the fact be exposed to view" (CM 236; PM 226). Philosophy, then, must begin as an analytical and scientific empiricism. On this point Bergsonism and Spencerian empiricism are agreed. But at this point, for the moment, they part company. Philosophy, unlike scientific empiricism, aims not at practical effectiveness but at a more and more encompassing reflection, that is, an intuition. It takes the inverse direction from intellect and instead of fragmenting what the intellect has to teach, tries to weld together the intellect's observational and theoretical "atoms" and, without losing sight of particulars, to bind them together into a synthetic intellectual picture of the world.

That this has not generally been seen to be Bergson's real intention is in part a result of his refusal to artificially separate the intellect's pulverizing, generalizing views of a thing from concrete reflection's (intuition's) immediate encounter with it. In all segments of his work Bergson blends intellectual analysis with intuitive insight: this is natural because he wishes at all points to contrast the two. To those who have misunderstood his intent, however, his writings have seemed to be an intolerable mishmash of undigested science and indigestible poetry. But this is, surely, to miss the point.

There is still another reason why Bergson's attempt to assimilate the perceptions, theories, and methods of the intellect definitively has gone virtually unrecognized. Kant, writing in the eighteenth century, could hold that only one logic, one physics, one geometry existed; he could assume on the basis of this that there must be some one definitive intellectual picture of the world. His first critique, therefore, simply posits this assumption and asks: what must be the structure of the mind if it has constructed and understood this definitive account of things? And his reply is: the

31

mind already possesses certain forms and categories a priori, and these make our definitive intellectual picture of the world inevitable—and final.

But Bergson realized from the beginning that alternative logics, geometries, and physics were possible and that no absolutely final scientific conclusions or purely intellectual world view could ever be reached. Hence, Bergson's accounts of intellectual knowledge and intellectual conclusions are stated hypothetically and conjecturally and thus lack the force and prima facie clarity of a more definitive presentation.

Very well, intuitive philosophy must come to grips with whatever the intellect has to say about a thing in order to see (1) the extent to which the intellect has distorted our view of the thing and (2) the extent to which some of its representations picture the thing with a certain abstract adequacy. By coming to grips with the intellect and its knowledge, intuitive philosophy will have been enabled to reflect with precision on the phenomena that intellect has already investigated. But, in the beginning, intuition's phenomenology of the immediately given will touch only on the more material aspects of things because it is precisely on these aspects alone that the intellect is capable of effecting an analysis.

There is no need here to open a long parenthesis on Bergson's precise definition of "matter": perhaps it will suffice to point out that for Bergson matter is a species of "slackened" movement or creativity. The motion of a shooting star across the sky is movement itself, in its vitality; the path traced by this motion, which we are liable to mistake for the motion itself, is the motion's "materiality." An organism as a whole, with its vitality and direction, transcends or is "more than" its mechanisms; the mechanisms of an organism are only the organism's "materiality." Mental mechanisms set up by habit, by persistent conditioning (e.g., "rote memory"), are the materiality of the conscious mind; they are, according to Bergson, the residuum or resultant of a vital process that made their initial construction possible, and as material they are transcended by the vital and creative activity of the mind as a whole (e.g., especially, "active memory," which binds our mental life together). More pertinent to our present purposes, physical matter is also portrayed as the slackening or "interruption" of an initial creation, a slackening that science interprets as entropy and that marks matter's basic tendency. Now in all cases, as Bergson explains in his analysis of the natural history of the human mind, it is the material component of movement that the intellect seizes on, and that it analyzes with greater or lesser accuracy.

Hence, intuitive philosophy, commencing with analysis by the intellect, soon shifts its attention to the material structure that the intellect has analyzed; however, unlike the intellect, which perpetually abstracts, intuition attempts to reflect on these structures concretely. In so doing, philosophy transcends its intellectual labors and begins a new kind of analysis—a reflective analysis of the qualitative "given" of immediate awareness. This painstaking phenomenology of the perceptually "given" focuses first, and more analytically, on the material components of perception and then climbs by degrees to the more vital pole of events, which can be confronted in itself only by a highly conscious and fully synthetic reflection.

Bergson thus begins with an intuition of "matter" and ends with an intuition of vitality. He begins with a relatively plain experience and ends with its more obscure condition.

But once again it must be stressed, even at the cost of tedious repetition, that an intuition which grasps the dynamics of experience is for Bergson just as thoroughly grounded in perception as the modes of sense awareness appealed to by "scientific" and analytical empiricisms. In fact, he would insist, his intuitive awareness is far truer to experience than the so-called empiricism of his predecessors, precisely because intuition involves no implicit subtraction of change from experience. Where Locke or Spencer sought, as a rule, discrete and unchanging sense elements (for example, isolated sense-data, mental states) through which experience could be reconstituted, Bergson seeks simply to confront experience without presupposing for it any static substratum. His intuition is thus the culmination and expression of a thoroughgoing empiricism—*sub specie durationis*.[49] At this point, however, it finally becomes possible to appreciate the full ingeniousness of Bergson's philosophy. It is true—as his critics never tire of pointing out—that for Bergson intuition definitely transcends the analyses of the scientific intellect. In this respect intuition is the negation of science, which, it is held, never fully comprehends vitality, spontaneity, duration. But in another respect Bergson's intuition must be a most powerful affirmation of science because intuition fully comprehends the fundamental natural processes that the scientific intellect endeavors more and more adequately to analyze. Thus, at every point where Bergson's intuitive phenomenology appears most obviously and irrefutably to be "anti-scientific" and "anti-intellectual," it should have achieved insights that can be useful to science's "spatial" analyses.

If this suggestion appears strange, perhaps it will become clearer by being put in still another way. Intuition, once attained at the heights of reflective tension, returns to symbols, to language, to abstract representations in order to express itself. Having transcended science, intuition does not simply regard it with Byronic contempt. For intuition has gained insights into concrete reality. Further, by dealing with concrete reality, intuition has gained increased vitality, awareness, and flexibility. Because this is the same concrete reality with which the intellect, in science or philosophy, seeks to deal, the insights of intuition should be of value to the intellect.

If Bergson's philosophy of science is approached with this thought clearly in mind, then many of his remarks concerning the evolution of science appear in an entirely new light. Modern mathematics, Bergson suggests, is an effort to substitute the "ready-made" for the "being-made" (CM 225; PM 214). Thus, analytical geometry was discovered through the introduction of motion into the genesis of figures (CE 334–35; EC 334), while the calculus was made possible through reflection on the con-

[49] From this point of view Bergson's intuitionism and James's radical empiricism are very similar.

34

cept of acceleration, *i.e.*, through consideration of the "tendency to change" (CM 225; PM 214). Similarly, modern physics—and indeed, modern science generally—is held to date from the day when Galileo began to consider motion in and for itself instead of attempting to conceive it through static Aristotelian concepts (CM 228; PM 217). What is true of mathematics and physics is still more true of modern biology, whose evolutionary theories are rooted in an increased awareness of the dynamic nature of living things (CE x; EC vi). The moral of this account of the history and foundations of the sciences, however, is not that scientists must henceforth desist from the metaphysically immoral "spatialization of time," but rather that the evolution of science is potentially unlimited and that we should expect the various sciences from time to time to be transformed by the emergence of new insights and new, more supple spatializations. The intuitive method in philosophy thus points to the future, and not the futility, of science.

Once this is realized, Bergson's critiques of scientific concepts are seen to be not destructive but creative in intent. To criticize present theories and opinions in the sciences may be to open the way toward new scientific insights, particularly when these criticisms are made in the light of concrete fact. That is what Bergson attempted to accomplish. It is easy to see why, in spite of this, many of his critics, like Santayana, remained both puzzled and indignant: "M. Bergson never reviews his facts in order to understand them, but only if possible to discredit others who may have fancied they understood. He raises difficulties, he marks the problems that confront the naturalist, and the inadequacy of explanations that may have been suggested. Such criticism would be a valuable beginning if it were followed by the suggestion of some new solution; but the suggestion only is that no solution is possible. . . ." [50] If this essay has succeeded in proving a single thesis, it is that for Bergson not only are new solutions always possible, but also that a fully empirical philosophy might conceivably be of use in their attainment.

[50] Santayana, *Winds of Doctrine*, 67.

A careful analysis of Bergson's philosophical method, although it reveals that Bergson was aware of the philosophical aims that he wished to achieve and of the means necessary to realize them, still does not wholly remove the paradoxical appearance of his thought. At least, however, it is now clear that the air of paradox that hovers about Bergson's philosophy results from his unique aims and not from deep-rooted confusions on his part. Bergsonism is an "anti-intellectualism" intended to stimulate the intellect; it is an anti-scientific mode of thought based on the serious study of science; it is a negation of science that is intended to affirm and strengthen scientific thought. Above all, this last point must be insisted on and clarified. The fundamental goal that Bergson sought, as he states in his last philosophical essay,[51] was "a philosophy which would submit to the control of science and which in turn could enable science to progress" (CM 77; PM 70). As long as this aim is not fully understood, that is, as long as Bergson's protest against the spatialization of time is taken to be simply a reaction against science and clear thought, the obstacles that confront any accurate interpretation of his philosophy will remain insurmountable.

Laudable intentions, however, even when joined to a coherent and clearly envisioned program, do not guarantee the validity of a philosopher's ideas. In Bergson's case in particular, a further question must be posed. Did the philosopher, in fact, accomplish what he set out to accomplish? Answering this question conclusively is far more difficult than deciding, for example, whether Bergson's philosophy is destructively anti-intellectual. In the first place, it is no easy matter to specify what amount of influence on, or degree of prophetic anticipation of, the course of scientific thought would constitute a "verification" of his philosophical methods. Were such a standard proposed, the objection could still be made that Bergson was not sufficiently well understood by his contemporaries for his methods to be adequately tested. A satisfactory evaluation of Bergson's philosophy of

[51] The first two "introductions" to *La pensée et le mouvant,* 1934 (*The Creative Mind* [1946]).

science, therefore, cannot be achieved easily but must involve both a careful study of the philosopher's critical insights and a thorough knowledge of the recent history and basic concepts of the sciences to which he devoted his attention. The following remarks concerning Bergson's approach to biology, the behavioral sciences, and physics are intended only as suggestions.

Bergson's biological speculations have in general been construed as a series of flagrant violations of Peirce's maxim—never block research.[52] The majority of contemporary biologists have consistently viewed Bergson's vitalistic biology as an attempt to introduce a "transparently primitive god"[53] (the *élan vital*) into scientific thought in place of a valid scientific hypothesis. But a more thorough analysis of the philosophy of *Creative Evolution* will put us on our guard against such an imputation of total naïveté and will suggest that Bergson had a more profound purpose in studying biology than that of making the study of biology appear impossible. The most characteristic feature of biological evolution, viewed as a process, is, precisely as Bergson held, the ceaseless emergence of increasingly complex forms. Nothing prevents us from studying this basic *fact* simply as a process, *sub specie durationis*, without presupposing for it some static substratum or, for that matter, any "explanation" at all. It will be retorted that such a phenomenological study can do little more than entertain a handful of philosophers and is scarcely relevant to the serious investigations of science. The history of science, however, suggests to Bergson that the effort to reflect on process per se has in the past been of critical importance: "Modern science dates from the day when mobility was set up as an independent reality. It dates from the day when Galileo, setting a ball rolling down an inclined plane, firmly resolved to study this movement from top to bottom for itself, in itself, instead of seeking its principle in the concepts of *high* and *low*, two immobilities by which Aristotle believed he

[52] C. S. Peirce, "Fallibilism, Continuity, and Evolution," in Walter G. Muelder, Laurence Sears, and Anne V. Schlabach, *The Development of American Philosophy* (Cambridge: Houghton, Mifflin Co., 1960), 364–71.
[53] Garrett Hardin, *Nature and Man's Fate* (New York: New American Library, 1961), 225.

could adequately explain mobility" (CM 228; PM 217). The discovery of the phenomenon of acceleration—a discovery that eluded Greek science—was possible only for a scientist capable of reflecting concretely and disinterestedly on motion without allowing his more conventional presuppositions to overcome his fresh insights. Galileo, of course, was able to give his "intuitions" a precise mathematical expression; but Bergson from the beginning insists that a valid intuition is one that can be given a "symbolic" formulation. From a more adequate qualitative insight, he proclaims, a more subtle quantitative analysis must follow. Thus several of the discoveries that have transformed the positive sciences or created new ones have been "so many soundings in the depths of pure duration" (CM 228; PM 217). Such "soundings" may transcend mathematical conceptualization, but (paradoxically?) they have not inhibited mathematical creativity. "The more living the reality touched" (CM 228; PM 217) by these soundings, the more powerful have been the resulting modes of analysis.

The resemblance between Bergson's account of Galileo's discovery and his description of the aims of *Creative Evolution* is too striking to be accidental: "We believe that if biology could ever get as close to its object as mathematics does to its own, it would become, to the physics and chemistry of organized bodies, what the mathematics of the moderns has proved to be in relation to ancient geometry" (CE 32; EC 32). Biological evolution accelerates as it advances (CE 249; EC 250); it is a "continuous" motion (CE 19; EC 19); it embodies a ceaseless "tendency" toward change (CE 85; EC 86). Philosophy is precisely the attempt to follow the dynamics of life's development in order to suggest new modes of "spatialization" to the mathematician and biologist.[54]

Bergson therefore must not be interpreted as refusing to apply

[54] An example of such a "spatialization"—one in part suggested by Bergson's researches—may be found in the studies by Alexis Carrel and Lecomte du Noüy. The conclusion that these investigators draw from, respectively, the study of the growth of tissue cultures and the study of the "cicatrization" of wounds is that there is a measurable "physiological time," which must be distinguished from physical time. Cf. André George, "Le Temps, la Vie et la Mort," *La Vie Intellectuelle*, XLII (1936), 121–46.

his philosophical method to the life sciences. A careful reading of *Creative Evolution* reveals instead the constant effort to suggest, through a phenomenology of evolutionary processes, new directions in scientific research. Considering Bergson's stress on the metaphysical limitations of biology, it is no wonder that his faith in its future *as a science* should have been denied and his intuitive grasp of the development of life taken to be the negation of science. Again, however, we must heed Bergson's explicit statement. Scientists, he wrote in 1913, six years after the publication of *Creative Evolution*, have been quite correct in the past to reproach vitalism for its scientific sterility; but in the future this reproach will no longer be necessary.[55]

Whether the reproaches that Bergson's biological speculations have drawn in the past will in the future be transformed into critical acclaim on the part of thoughtful biologists is a matter for conjecture.[56] The possibility that his approach to biological problems might yet prove heuristically sound ought to be raised, however, if only to make the hopes that inspired *Creative Evolution* undeniably evident. It is interesting to note that the status of certain others of Bergson's insights do not remain problematic. His philosophical conceptions have had a definite creative effect on the young sciences of social psychology[57] and psychophysics;[58] and he can be credited with having founded a unique school of psy-

[55] Henri Bergson, *Mind-Energy* (London: Macmillan and Company, Ltd., 1920), 80.

[56] It is, of course, not true that Bergson has received no support from biologists or that his biological speculations have had no salutary impact whatever on the science of biology. Cf. Eugenio Rignano, "Ce que la biologie doit à Bergson," *Les Nouvelles Littéraires*, No. 322, December 15, 1928; Édouard Morot-Sir, "What Bergson Means to Us Today," in Hanna (ed.), *The Bergsonian Heritage*, 46–48; James Johnstone, *The Philosophy of Biology* (Cambridge: at the University Press, 1914).

[57] Barbara Tuchman, *The Proud Tower* (New York: Macmillan Co., 1962), 383–84.

[58] Bergson's brilliant critique of the methods and assumptions of psychophysics is contained in *Time and Free Will*, 52–72. For a brief account of this critique, see my article, "Bergson's Reflective Anti-Intellectualism," *The Personalist*, XLVII (Winter, 1966), 49–53. I am indebted to Dr. J. E. Smith of Yale University for information concerning Bergson's influence on psychophysics, of which Bergson has been termed a founder.

chology,[59] with having been one of the precursors of Gestalt psychology,[60] and with having anticipated important conceptions in contemporary anthropology.[61] Nor should a survey of Bergson's contributions omit to mention the extent to which his findings have influenced and found corroboration in pathology[62] and neurology.[63] Finally, it may be suggested that his anticipations of major features of twentieth-century physics are as remarkable as they are unexpected.

With the exception of Duration and Simultaneity (Bergson's criticism of the special theory of relativity, published in 1922), the philosopher's reflective analyses of physical concepts are nowhere presented in a unified fashion but are scattered throughout his writings. A persistent concern with the problems and the concepts of physics is, as Louis de Broglie demonstrates,[64] evident even in so psychologically oriented a study as Time and Free Will. In the works which follow, this concern is developed with great effectiveness. The wide variety of Bergson's insights and the difficulty of discovering their precise interrelations should not be allowed to obscure the fact that his reflections on the science of physics were dominated by a single preoccupation: the problem of the relationship between the properties of experienced duration and the properties of physical matter.

It must not be forgotten that the starting point of Bergson's philosophy lay in a dual criticism not only of Spencer's mechanistic philosophy but also of the physics from which it was drawn. In analyzing Spencer's basic principles and at the same time con-

[59] Richard Müller-Freienfels, The Evolution of Modern Psychology (New Haven: Yale University Press, 1936), 90–92, 263–66.

[60] Heidsieck, Henri Bergson et la notion d'espace, 53.

[61] Claude Lévi-Strauss, Totemism (Boston: Beacon Press, 1963), 92–99, 102–103.

[62] Cf. Raoul Mourgue, "Le point de vue neuro-biologique dans l'oeuvre de Bergson," Revue de métaphysique et de morale, XXVII (1920), 27–70. Also Vladimir Jankélévitch, Henri Bergson (Paris: Presses Universitaires de France, 1959), Ch. III, "L'âme et le corps," 80–131.

[63] Cf. Eugene Minkowski, La schizophrénie (Paris: Payot, 1927); Henri Piéron, Traité de Psychologie (Paris: Presses Universitaires de France, 1949), I, La psychologie différentielle.

[64] See "The Concepts of Contemporary Physics and Bergson's Ideas on Time and Motion," translated on pp. 46–62 of this book.

sidering the philosophical implications of certain new ideas in physics, Bergson was led to see the fundamentally a-temporal conceptual framework upon which all mechanistic systems of thought must rest. The fundamental characteristics of time-as-experienced are, or appeared to Bergson to be, the "interpenetration" of present states, the total transformation of states with the passage of time, and the felt or experienced flux of continuous activity. But for Newtonian physics as well as for mechanistic philosophy, all of these characteristics are specifically denied. For mechanism, the ultimate constituents of physical nature are discrete mass particles, externally related to each other; the only sort of change that matter can exhibit is the simple translation of such particles from one part of space to another. And rather than speak of activity or energy in physical nature, the mechanist appeals instead to the basic property of inertia—literally, *resistance* to change of motion. It was not simply that the mechanist in philosophy or physics utilized a mathematical and therefore "spatialized" time. What appeared really striking to Bergson was the extent to which mechanistic physics had driven *all* the essential characteristics of experienced time out of physical nature.

Bergson was unable to believe that any existence could be utterly devoid of the characteristics that are basic to temporal experience. Moreover, arguments drawn from psychology, from "immediate intuition" (MM 262; MMf 221), and from the researches of those physicists (Faraday, Kelvin, and Clerk Maxwell) who had most thoroughly criticized classical Newtonian physics (MM 263, 265; MMf 222, 223) seemed to suggest the possibility of a very different kind of physics and a very different concept of physical matter. Sooner or later, Bergson speculated, science would accept a more dynamic view of matter: ". . . a theory of matter is an attempt to find the reality hidden beneath . . . customary images which are entirely relative to our needs. . . . And, indeed, we see force and matter drawing nearer together the more deeply the physicist has penetrated into their effects. We see force more and more materialized, the atom more and more idealized, the two terms converging towards a common limit

41

and the universe thus recovering its continuity" (MM 264–65; MMf 222–23). Physical nature is thus seen to consist not in discrete, inert mass-particles, but in *"modifications, perturbations,* changes of *tension* or of *energy,* and nothing else" (MM 266; MMf 224). Motionless on its surface, in its depths physical nature "lives and vibrates" (MM 270; MMf 228). In such a world the parts of matter, like the parts of duration, interpenetrate; change, rather than consisting in a simple translation of particles through empty space, involves the transformation of both moving object and its surrounding force-field—in short, a global transformation —and vibratory energy, not inertia, is a primary fact.

It is scarcely necessary to draw the parallels between the aspects of Bergson's theory of matter that are revealed in these passages and certain of the main features of twentieth-century physics; they are drawn with great skill in the essays that follow. These remarks concerning Bergson's philosophy of physics are intended only to make clear at the beginning his belief that the understanding of experienced time is a key to the interpretation, and the evolution, of physics. Insofar as twentieth-century physics bears out this belief, Bergson may be said to have succeeded in his philosophical quest, and to be fully contemporary.[65]

[65] Portions of this essay appeared in *The Personalist,* XLVII (Winter, 1966), No. 1. I would like to thank the editors of *The Personalist* for allowing me to use those passages here.

QUANTUM PHYSICS

LOUIS DE BROGLIE

The Concepts of Contemporary Physics and Bergson's Ideas
on Time and Motion

Remarks by the Editor. Assessing the philosophy of duration
from the vantage point of quantum physics, Louis de Broglie
finds that Bergson anticipated certain essential features of contemporary physical theories. Interestingly, many of these anticipations are found in *Time and Free Will,* the philosopher's first
work. While it is well known that Bergson protested against the
spatialization of time, it is not as widely recognized that he protested against the "spatialization of matter" as well. Just as duration cannot be represented by discrete, static points, so matter,
Bergson held, cannot be represented as an aggregate of discrete,
static particles having absolutely precise locations. In both cases,
spatialization deforms reality, substituting immobility for change,
externality for interrelationship.

By criticizing the spatialization of matter and thus drawing a
distinction between its static and its dynamic characteristics, Bergson arrived at insights closely resembling those of quantum physics. Werner Heisenberg's uncertainty relations, which assert the
incompatibility of location and momentum, find their parallel in
Bergson's denial that the dynamics of motion are compatible with
geometrically precise location, just as Niels Bohr's principle of
complementarity, which states the irreducible duality of wave
and particle, strongly suggests certain other of Bergson's "intuitions" of the nature of matter. Nor do these prophetic observations exhaust the philosopher's insights. Bergson was old and in
ill health when the new physics began to emerge and become
established. It would have been most interesting, de Broglie concludes, had he been able, with his penetrating intellect, to review
the new conceptions of quantum physics. *Professor de Broglie's*

W E HAVE NO INTENTION of analyzing or of discussing here
the entire philosophical doctrine associated with the name
of Henri Bergson. We have neither the time nor the desire to submit to a critique the many and various theses which, from *Time
and Free Will* to *The Creative Mind*, Bergson progressively develops around certain central ideas. These theses have been pas-
sionately discussed, a fact which proves their originality; they have
been made the object of numerous critiques, many of which were
certainly justified—at least in part. In Bergson's books there are frequently brilliant suggestions which, on reflection, appear frail or
exaggeratedly paradoxical; too many opinions which call for
solid demonstration are supported by certain beautiful but imprecise images evoked in an admirable style which, at times, conceals feebleness of argument under the beauty of form. Nonetheless, these reservations made, it should be recognized that, taken
as a whole, the work is powerful: it is impossible to examine it
without experiencing, almost on each page, the impression that it
makes us perceive a number of questions in a different light, that
it places constantly before us windows through which we perceive, in a flash, unsuspected horizons.

Personally, from our early youth, we have been struck by
Bergson's very original ideas concerning time, duration, and
movement. More recently, turning again these celebrated pages
and reflecting on the progress achieved by science since the already distant time when we first read them, we have been struck
by the analogy between certain new concepts of contemporary
physics and certain brilliant intuitions of the philosophy of duration. And we have been still more surprised by the fact that most
of these intuitions are found already expressed in *Time and Free*

Will, Bergson's first work and also perhaps the most remarkable, at least from our point of view: this essay, its author's doctor's thesis, dates from 1889 and consequently antedates by forty years the ideas of Niels Bohr and Werner Heisenberg on the physical interpretation of wave mechanics.

Without doubt it would be taking things too far to state that one found in Bergson, formally stated, certain principles of quantum physics: one cannot identify the precise statements of quantum physics with the profound, but often vague and fleeting, intuitions of the celebrated thinker. The analogies exist nonetheless, and it is these which we wish to isolate as precisely as possible in the present essay, without allowing ourselves, however, to read into the texts of the philosopher the meanings which interest us, for this is the principal danger of a study of this kind.

Throughout his life Bergson was obsessed by the idea that our intelligence falsely represents the real nature of time. Preoccupied above all with noting coincidences rather than observing the time which flows, our intelligence unconsciously substitutes for real duration a geometrical schema, that of a homogeneous time conceived as a sort of one-dimensional continuum. In doing so, if Bergson may be believed, our intelligence refuses to face the true nature of concrete duration, which is a veritable progress, a creation of new forms and a continuous invention. We do not wish to discuss the Bergsonian conception of concrete duration; but one can agree with its author that science has in fact always allowed, almost without discussion, the possibility of representing time as a simple variable, which can be plotted along a line like a spatial dimension, and that, by that very fact, science condemns itself to not being able to comprehend why time and space present themselves in our experience under different aspects, why, in particular, time always flows in the same direction, though any dimension of space can be pursued indifferently in two directions. Our intelligence projects in some manner the succession of events on a homogeneous axis and desires henceforth to see nothing more in the flow of time than a displacement along that axis. It is quite

47

possible, in fact, that in thus excessively schematizing, it allows certain essential properties of real time to escape.

If our representation of time is perhaps excessively schematized, will it not be the same for our representation of space? In order to represent to ourselves the localization of objects in space, we project them, in the same way, on a homogeneous three-dimensional framework which is an abstractly conceived geometrical space. In proceeding thus, do we not again risk misunderstanding certain essential characteristics of concrete space? In his writings Bergson has approached this question much less often than the analogous question related to time. While in none of his works does one fail to find, many times, the idea of a profound opposition between concrete duration as he imagines it and the abstract and homogeneous time employed by science, it is only in certain passages, notably in Chapter IV of *Matter and Memory*, that he has opposed abstract space and concrete duration. "We spread," he tells us, "beneath the continuity of sensible qualities, which is concrete extensity, a net whose meshes are indefinitely deformable and indefinitely decreasing: this simply conceived substratum, this entirely ideal scheme of abstract and indefinite divisibility, is homogeneous space. . . . Homogeneous space and time are therefore neither properties of things nor essential conditions of our faculty of knowledge: they express in an abstract form the double work of solidification and division to which we submit the moving continuity of the real in order to obtain there a fulcrum for our action, in order to establish bases of operation" (MM 278, 280; MMf 234, 235). Insisting on this point he says again that one can find the origin of all the difficulties relative to time and space "no longer in that duration and that extension which actually pertain to things and are immediately manifest to consciousness, but in the homogeneous space and time which we spread out beneath them in order to divide the continuous, fix becoming, and furnish points of impact for our activity." Farther on, resuming his thought he concludes: "What is given, what is real is something intermediary between divisible extension and pure inextension: it is what may be termed the *extensive*. Extensity is the most salient quality of

48

perception. It is by solidifying and subdividing extensity by means of an abstract space, stretched by us beneath it for the needs of action, that we constitute a multiple and indefinitely divisible extension" (MM 326; MMf 274). We have cited texts, perhaps less known than those relative to duration, in order to show that Bergson's philosophy was to lead him, and has in fact led him, to the conclusion that the representation of extensity by homogeneous geometrical space has, at least in part, the fallacious character which in his eyes is possessed by the representation of duration through the homogeneous time of mathematicians and physicists.

It is possible therefore that our representation of extensity by homogeneous geometrical space is too schematic and that it errs in pulverizing the extension of the material world into a simple juxtaposition of localizations in an abstract framework. Nonetheless, and this is probably the reason why Bergson insisted more on the case of duration than that of extension, the representation of the flow of time by displacement along a homogeneous axis implies a more complete abandonment of many more incontestable properties of felt reality. Nothing prevents us in this abstract representation from supposing that we may reverse the course of time, contrary to the most certain property of real duration. Nothing prevents us either, as Bergson has well noted (CE 338; EC 337), from supposing that the flux of time operates with an infinite speed, so that the entire past, present, and future history of the world might be found instantaneously spread out before us. It is really such a representation, basically at variance with all the immediate data of our experience, which appears in relativity theory when it invites us to represent the totality of events past, present, and future in the framework of an abstract four-dimensional continuum, space-time. From this point of view, each observer successively discovers the events contained in space-time: at each instant of his proper time, he will be able to regard as simultaneous all events localized in a particular three-dimensional section of space-time and, as his proper time flows, this section will traverse progressively the entirety of space-time. Thus, ac-

49

cording to this audacious schemza, events in their entirety will in some manner be given a priori: it will only be through a sort of infirmity of our means of perception that we will discover them successively in the course of our own duration. Such a purely static vision of the universe, which excludes all novelty and spontaneity, Bergson always rejected with the greatest energy. "If time," he says, "is thus spread out in space and succession turned into juxtaposition, science has nothing to modify in what it tells us, and in what it tells us it takes account neither of what is essential to *succession* nor of *duration,* insofar as it flows. It has no other sign for expressing the succession and the duration which strike our consciousness. Such a representation no longer applies to what is moving in becoming, as the bridges extended from place to place across the river do not follow the water which flows under their arches" (CE 338; EC 337).

Let us lay aside these pretty images whose charm may be misleading; let us lay aside what may be contested of Bergson's conception of duration. It nonetheless remains true that the schematic representation of time employed by classical science and pushed to its extreme consequences by relativity theory may be a useful but fallacious schema, which masks for us a part of the real character of the flow of things. And, we have seen, even for extensity, it is not certain that extensity can be entirely described through localizations in the homogeneous framework of geometrical space.

Bergson attempted to draw to him, if one may say so, the theory of relativity and to show that it does not contradict ideas which he holds dear. He was thus led to write the least estimable of his books, *Duration and Simultaneity,* a work which has justly been criticized because it seems that its author has misunderstood the real meaning of the conceptions of Albert Einstein and his continuators. In truth, relativity physics seemed to be in flagrant opposition to Bergson's views, precisely because it pushed the spatialization of time and the geometrization of space to their extreme limits, because it is from this point of view the final development of classical physics. But relativity physics is not the last word in science, for there is no last word in matters of scientific progress.

In spite of the undeniable and admirable light which it brings to bear for us on many questions, relativity theory has not succeeded in interpreting phenomena in which quanta intervene; and in order to do so it was necessary to develop theories stranger than that of relativity. Today, it is certain that quantum theories penetrate into more profound strata of reality than all previous theories. The theory of relativity itself now appears to us as simply a macroscopic and statistical view of phenomena: it describes things approximately and in bulk and does not descend profoundly enough into the detailed description of elementary processes to allow us to perceive quantum discontinuities there. It is quantum physics, whose most advanced form is wave mechanics, which has enabled us to penetrate into the mysteries of elementary processes and to take account of the discontinuities bound up with the existence of the quantum of action. The question is thus posed whether this new physics will not better accord with certain of Bergson's ideas than did the relativistic doctrine. This is a question which we will examine later.

Before approaching this question it is necessary for us to recall how Bergson criticized the habitual notion of movement. He dedicated a considerable number of pages throughout his diverse writings to this critique. His idea seems to have been essentially that in describing the motion of a point as a continuous series of positions attained successively in the course of time, science commits a profound error because it allows what is essential to motion to escape: mobility, dynamism. The variable t of classical mechanics, which serves to mark the instants of the passage of the moving object at the diverse points of its trajectory, may be conceived as unrolling infinitely fast without anything being changed in the previsioned coincidences: the entire trajectory is then found to be spatialized, and it is actually thus that relativists imagine things in their space-time when they evoke the "world-line" of a moving object. But Bergson never admitted this point of view which, according to him, deprives duration of its concrete and, in some manner, its creative character. More than once, in his critique of the classical image of motion, he appealed to the arguments of Zeno of Elea for support, arguments by which the ancient philosopher so curiously attempted to clarify the mystery which attaches to the apparently simple notion of movement. The most striking of these arguments, in our eyes, is that of the Arrow, which, according to Zeno, can occupy a really determinate position at no instant of its flight, since if it occupied such a position, *it would be immobile*. Commenting on the Eleatic's subtle remark, Bergson writes, "Passage is a movement and stoppage an immobility. . . . When I see the moving object pass through a point, I . . . conceive that it *might* stop there, and even when it does not stop, I tend to consider its passage as an arrest, though infinitely short. . . . All points of space necessarily being fixed, I must be careful not to attribute to the moving object itself the immobility of the point with which it coincides. . . . How can a *progress* coincide with a *thing*, a movement with an immobility?" (MM 247–48; MMf 207–208). Thus the philosopher of duration retains an invincible distrust regarding the representation of motion through the displacement of a point on a trajectory. He sees there an illusory description. "At bottom," he states, "the illusion rises from the fact that the motion, *once completed*, has deposited along its course an immobile trajectory on which one may count as many immobilities as one wishes. From this, one concludes that motion deposits at each instant a position with which it concides."

Without insisting any further on the exposition of Bergson's ideas on duration and motion, ideas which have often been effectively analyzed, we approach now the question which constitutes the principal goal of this article: Is there any analogy between Bergson's critique of the idea of motion and the conceptions of contemporary quantum theories? It seems that the reply ought to be in the affirmative.

One of the important results of the development of the new quantum and wave mechanics has been to demonstrate the impossibility of simultaneously attributing to an elementary particle a well-defined state of motion and an entirely determinate position. The existence of the quantum of action, whose size is measured by

Planck's constant, opposes all simultaneous and perfectly precise determination of the coordinates which fix the particle's position and the magnitudes, such as energy and quantity of motion, which specify its dynamic state. In other words, it is impossible to know at the same time with precision the dynamic aspect of elementary processes and their spatial localization; and this impossibility is expressed quantitatively by Heisenberg's famous uncertainty relations. To be sure, it is always possible through an appropriate measurement to determine the spatial position of an elementary physical entity; but this measurement, which projects in some way the elementary entity as a point in the fixed framework of our geometrical space, deprives it, so to speak, of all mobility and leaves us in complete ignorance of its motion. Inversely, another sort of measurement permits us to fix the dynamic aspect of the physical entity in attributing to it a determined quantity of motion or energy, but then, having determined its mobility, we remain totally ignorant of its spatial location. Intermediate cases can be presented in which we come to know partially at the same time both the geometric and the dynamic aspects of the physical entity; but this partial knowledge of each of these two aspects is always limited and remains subject to Heisenberg's uncertainties. All this is true on the microscopic scale of elementary particles and atoms. By contrast, if one makes only macroscopic observations, experimental uncertainties and the imperfections of our senses can give us the *illusion* of simultaneously knowing the position and momentum of a particle; then we can attribute to it a trajectory on which, at each instant, it will possess a certain speed. But this will be only an approximative image and, if we can analyze things more precisely by measuring positions with more precision, we can now grasp only a succession of localizations between which the motion will escape us.

The analogy between these ideas and those of Bergson seems real, and one can even say that if Bergson's critique of motion here failed in certain respects, it failed above all through an excess of prudence. It retains in fact, as the statements made at the end of the last paragraph show, the idea of a trajectory described by a moving object, and it then has difficulty in explaining that movement in its dynamism does not coincide with geometric displacement along a trajectory. But with the ideas of quantum physics, when one regards things on a small enough scale there is no trajectory assignable to the moving object, for one can determine through a series of necessarily discontinuous measurements only certain instantaneous positions of the physical entity in motion, and each of these determinations implies a total renunciation of the possibility of grasping at the same time its state of motion. Always guided by Zeno of Elea, Bergson seems to have foreseen this when he wrote: "In space there are only parts of space and at whatever point one considers the moving object, *one will obtain only a position*" (TFW 111; *Essai* 84). He could have said, using the language of quantum theories, "If one attempts to localize the moving object, through a measurement or an observation, at a point of space, one will obtain only a position and the state of motion will entirely escape." But he wrote these lines in 1899, more than forty years before Heisenberg's uncertainty relations became part of science!

A page later Bergson states again: "In short, two things must be distinguished in motion, the space traversed and the act through which it is traversed, the successive positions and the synthesis of these positions. . . . But here a phenomenon of endosmosis is produced, a mixture of the purely intensive sensation of mobility and the extensive representation of the space traversed." From the point of view of wave mechanics, this way of speaking does not seem to us entirely satisfactory. What must be said is that an elementary physical entity may in turn be represented through the concept of a *particle*, that is, as a point precisely located in geometrical space, and by the concept of a *wave*, which in wave mechanics represents motion in a pure state with no spatial location. Thus wave mechanics, in dealing with two opposed images, comes to distinguish mobility and localization and considers that these two images cannot be simultaneously employed with full precision, for this is the content of Heisenberg's uncertainty relations. At the same time, we remark in passing, in the microscopic domain the classical notion of velocity bound up with the continuous description of a trajectory disappears. It is only within the limits of macroscopic experience, where precision is limited, that one can employ two images simultaneously, approximate knowledge of localizations and motions justifying by virtue of approximation the use of the notion of trajectory. It is in the macroscopic, hence in the domain of man's usual perception, that the mixture of the idea of mobility and of space traversed which Bergson speaks of in the text cited above can operate.

In another passage of *Time and Free Will* we discover the following: "Now, in the analysis of variable motion as in that of uniform motion, it is a question only of spaces already traversed and of simultaneous positions already attained. We are thus justified in saying that, if mechanics retains of time only simultaneity, it retains of movement only immobility" (TFW 119; *Essai* 90). This affirmation may be true of classical mechanics, which knows how to represent motion only through successive positions on a continuous curve; but it seems much less exact to us for wave mechanics, which knows how to represent mobility, without being preoccupied with localization, by means of the analytical image of the plane monochromatic wave. In wave mechanics, precise location and pure mobility can meet in turn, being, according to this new doctrine and according to Bohr, complementary aspects of reality.

The examples we have just cited show that certain of Bergson's phrases must be modified if one wishes to render more precise the analogy between the philosopher's conceptions and the new theories of the physicists; but in the text of his books, the analogy appears clearly enough at times. Thus, when at the present time a professor of wave mechanics wishes to explain to his students how the plane monochromatic wave represents the rectilinear and uniform motion of a corpuscle, he begins his explanation by saying, "Let us consider a corpuscle animated with a perfectly definite state of motion, that is, corresponding to an exactly known energy and quantity of motion and *let us abstract entirely from the position of the particle in space:* this non-localized state of motion is described in wave mechanics through the propagation of a plane monochromatic wave. . . ." And now let us listen to Bergson: ". . . fix your attention on these movements by abstracting from the divisible space that underlies them and considering only their mobility!" (MM 276; MMf 232). Isn't there an undeniable analogy between the teaching of the scientist and the exclamation of the philosopher?

And *Creative Evolution* contains a passage that inevitably suggests a corpuscle of wave mechanics, which is represented by a wave extended throughout an entire spatial region and which, not being localized, may manifest its presence in all points of this region: "As the shrapnel, bursting before it falls to the ground, covers the explosive zone with an invisible danger, so the arrow that goes from A to B displays with a single stroke, although over a certain extent of duration, its indivisible mobility" (CE 309; EC 308).

Let us continue our parallel. According to the new concepts of physics, when an experiment or an observation makes it possible to define the state of a particle at an instant t_1 with all the precision that Heisenberg's uncertainty relations permit, wave mechanics is in a position to announce what will be the particle's possible locations at a succeeding instant t_2 and their respective probabilities; but it can not generally make definite predictions, and it is in thus substituting for the definite predictions of the older mechanics simple probabilities referring to diverse possibilities, that quantum mechanics finds itself renouncing the rigorous determinism of classical physics. If now, at the instant t_2 which follows t_1, an experiment or observation permits us to precisely locate the particle, the situation changes completely for us, since it is one of the possibilities and no other which is realized. Thus in quantum theory far more than in classical theories, time seems to produce, in flowing, new and unforeseeable elements. Now these are the words which appear beneath Bergson's pen when he writes: "The more I examine this point, the more it appears to me that, if the future is condemned to *succeed* the present instead of being given alongside it, this is because the future is not entirely de-

56

termined at the present time and if the time occupied by this succession is something other than a number, it is . . . because there is unceasingly being created in it . . . something unforeseeable and new" (CE 339–40; EC 339).

If Bergson could have studied quantum theory in detail, he would doubtless have observed with joy that in the image of the evolution of the physical world which it offers us, at each instant nature is described as if hesitating between a multiplicity of possibilities, and he would doubtless have repeated, as in *The Creative Mind*, that "time is this very hesitation or it is nothing" (CM 93; PM 101).

The following objection to Heisenberg's assertions concerning quantum physics has sometimes been made: "Let us consider a particle in motion outside of any field; we determine first through two successive measurements its exact position A at an instant t_1, then its exact position B at a succeeding instant t_2, which is possible even when Heisenberg's uncertainties are taken into account. We will then be able to admit quite naturally that the corpuscle has described a uniform rectilinear motion AB during the interval t_2-t_1, with the velocity $\frac{AB}{t_2-t_1}$. One therefore knows the trajectory of the corpuscle during that interval of time and also its velocity, which is contrary to the impossibility postulated by Heisenberg of knowing location and motion simultaneously." To this it has been justly replied that the rectilinear trajectory AB is only attributable to the moving object "as an afterthought" when it manifests itself at point B, and that consequently this trajectory can in no way be predicted at t_1 when nothing more is known than its position A. Furthermore it is arbitrary to maintain that the particle, since one has successively seized its presence at A and then at B, really described the straight line AB in coinciding progressively with all its points. It is curious to compare this argument with that which Bergson developed, with a perhaps exaggeratedly subtle artfulness, in pages 175 and following of *Time and Free Will* concerning the very controversial question of free will. On pages 181–82 one may read: "Time is not a line on which

57

one can pass again. Certainly, once it has elapsed, we have the right to represent the successive moments to ourselves as external to each other and to think thus of a line which traverses space; but it remains understood that the line symbolizes not the time that is passing, but the time that has passed. This is what critics and partisans of free will both forget—the first when they affirm and the others when they deny the possibility of acting differently than we have acted. The first reason thus: 'The path has not yet been traced; hence it can take any direction whatever.' To which one may reply: 'You forget that you cannot speak of the path until the action has been accomplished, but then it will have been traced out.' The others say: 'The path has been traced thus: hence its possible direction was not just any direction whatever, but actually this particular direction.' To which one may answer, 'Before the path was traced out, there were no possible or impossible directions for the very simple reason that there could not yet be any question of a path. . . .' "

The problem examined by Bergson in this passage is evidently not identical with the problem in wave mechanics which we cited above, but in transforming certain parts of Bergson's text one can adapt it to this problem, and the rapprochement of these two arguments will then become very suggestive.

To effect these comparisons, we will cite the following text, which appeared recently in a work presented to the Faculty of Sciences in Paris: "In quantum physics, if one places oneself at state t_1, the events of the interval $t_1 t_2$ will be described by *uncertainties of prediction;* if one places oneself at instant t_2, the events of interval $t_1 t_2$ will be described by measurements already made and by their results. Because of indetermination, the *future of now* will appear as distinct from *the past which will be.* . . . The future of the present moment is far richer in possibilities than the past which will be." [1] Does not this quite exact summation of the present position of quantum physics suggest a certain aura of Bergsonism?

[1] Diplôme d'études supérieures of Mlle. Pasturaud.

Still other passages of Bergson's works are interesting to compare with the new concepts of quantum theory.

In wave mechanics[2] it is impossible in general, when one deals with a group of particles of the same physical nature, to attribute to each an individuality making it possible, for example, to number it permanently. The basic reason for this is that, for particles of the same physical species having identical properties, it is possible to distinguish between them only through their different spatial positions: now, in wave mechanics, one cannot in general attribute to particles well-defined positions in space, and these particles *can* be found in an entire extended region of space. If their regions of possible presence merge or overlap—which will most often happen—how can one follow their individuality? Thus wave mechanics has given up individualizing particles and following the evolution of each separately with the course of time: it can only consider the total number of particles of the same kind and the variations of these numbers. And again these total numbers are not effectively ascertainable save through new observations which isolate and locate the diverse particles, permitting them to be counted.

Thus it is clearly apparent in quantum physics how the possibility of numbering is tied to location in space and why, each time the spatial location blurs or disappears, it becomes impossible to attribute to these apparent units a permanent numbering. Now Bergson, from the already distant time when he wrote *Time and Free Will*, seems to have grasped certain of these fundamental ideas. This may be verified by re-reading the curious pages which he has devoted in his book to numerical multiplicity and space (TFW 75–90; *Essai* 57–67). He writes: "We say therefore that the idea of number implies the simple intuition of a multiplicity of parts or units, which are absolutely alike. . . . And yet they must be somehow distinct from one another, since otherwise they would merge into a single unit. Let us suppose all the sheep in a

---

[2] See the author's article "Individualité et interaction dans le monde physique," *Revue de métaphysique et de morale*, XLIX (1937), 353 (or the volume *Continu et discontinu*, 117).

flock to be mutually identical: they will be distinguished at least by the place in space which they occupy: if not they would not form a flock" (TFW 76-77; *Essai* 58). From this it must follow that if locating each sheep were impossible, the animals could not be distinguished, and one arrives at the idea of the indiscernibility of identical particles introduced by wave mechanics.

In wave mechanics, the possibility of two particles being found at the same point of space leads to the attenuation of the old notion of the impenetrability of matter. In fact, the notion ceases to have value the moment the permanent numbering of particles is recognized as being impossible. This fact may be reconciled with a profound thought of Bergson: "To admit the impenetrability of matter is therefore simply to recognize the solidarity of the notions of number and space: it is to state a property of number rather than of matter" (TFW 89; *Essai* 67).

One of the essential ideas introduced into quantum physics since its inception is that of *stationary states*. According to Bohr, the structures of the atomic scale are capable of being changed to stationary or quantified states which have no temporal evolution and are as if placed outside of duration. But these quantified systems are also susceptible of a swift *transition* from one stationary state to another; and it is the succession of these sudden transitions, whose probabilities quantum physics today is able to calculate, that is brought about by the evolution of the material world envisaged at the atomic scale. These conclusions of modern theories may perhaps be found closely similar to the following sentence from *Creative Evolution*: "Let us say only that intelligence represents becoming as a series of *states* each of which is homogeneous with itself and seems not to change" (CE 179; EC 177), as well as the passages in the same work where the kaleidoscopic character of our knowledge of things is described, though to be sure the analogy is here vague enough.

We wish to follow these comparisons no further, the subtle and often fleeting thought of the philosopher being very difficult to compare with the precise assertions of scientific theories. The rapprochements which we have believed we have perceived between the former and the latter concern only certain new ideas, so varied and perhaps so paradoxical, which Bergson took pleasure in maintaining in the course of his works. But these ideas, ideas relative to time, duration, and motion, are at the heart of the doctrine; it is these which have served as points of departure for the philosopher's thought; it is to them that he always returned under different forms.

It would have been very curious to learn Bergson's opinion concerning the philosophical aspects of contemporary physics, to see how he would have reacted in the face of a scientific evolution which seems, we have tried to show, to lead to conclusions which present a few analogies with certain affirmations dear to him. Unhappily, when quantum theories began to take on their present form Bergson was already old and in poor health: he doubtless could not explore them sufficiently to attempt to utilize their results in his philosophical investigations. Nonetheless, in his last work, *The Creative Mind,* he made allusion to these theories in a footnote whose text appears as follows: "One can therefore, and one even should, speak of physical determinism even though one postulates with the most recent physics the indeterminism of the elementary phenomena which make up the physical fact. For this physical fact[3] is perceived by us as subjected to an inflexible determinism and by that fact is radically distinguished from acts which we perform when we feel ourselves free. As I suggest above, one might ask himself if it is not precisely in order to pour matter in this determinism, in order to obtain in the phenomena that surround us a regularity of succession permitting us to act on them, that our perception stops at a certain particular degree of condensation of elementary events. . ." (CM 303; PM 61–62). A curious suggestion according to which livings beings inevitably would have a "macroscopic" perception, since the apparent determinism which renders possible their actions on things reigns only in the macroscopic realm. In reading this isolated text, one deeply re-

[3] We would add "macroscopic."

grets that the great philosopher was not able to scan the unforeseen horizons of the new physics with his piercing gaze.[4]

SATOSI WATANABÉ

The Concept of Time in Modern Physics and Bergson's Pure Duration

Introduction by Louis de Broglie.[*] M. Satosi Watanabé is a young Japanese physicist who visited France some fifteen years ago and who, during this visit, prepared and defended a very interesting doctoral thesis on the manner in which the interpretation of the second law of thermodynamics is presented in quantum theories: in this thesis he utilized the ideas of M. Johan von Neumann, which he deepened and made more precise from contrasting points of view. But M. Watanabé is not content to be an excellent theoretical physicist; he is also a philosophical spirit. In the article which follows, he has developed very interesting and original concepts concerning the profound meaning of Nicholas Carnot's principle while agreeing in his conclusions with certain of Bergson's ideas.

[4] Other resemblances between Bergson's ideas and those of modern physics can also be shown. André George has kindly called my attention to certain analogies between Bergson's conception of causality and the distinction between strong and weak causality which we ourselves introduced, some years ago, in the light of quantum ideas (see especially *Continu et discontinu*, 64). Thus, speaking of weak causality, Bergson writes on page 209 of *Time and Free Will* (*Essai*, p. 161), "If therefore one decides to conceive the causal relation under this second form, one can assert a priori that there is no longer between the cause and the effect a relation of necessary determination, for the effect will no longer be given in the cause. It resides there only as a possibility and as a confused representation which will perhaps not be followed by the corresponding action."
The analogy with the probabilistic conception of the causal relation as conceived by contemporary quantum physics is evident.
On this question, one might also examine other remarks in *Continu et discontinu*, p. 294 and following.
[*] M. de Broglie's introduction appeared along with Watanabé's original article in the *Revue de métaphysique et de morale*, LVI (1951). Both are reprinted here in translation with the permission of the authors and the *Revue de métaphysique et de morale*.

62

The opinions which he sustains will doubtless provoke discussion, but it is certainly the case that the fundamental idea of closely relating the increase of entropy to the development of our "cognition" is entirely consistent with the actual quantum interpretation of entropy. M. Watanabé's ideas are of particular interest, since he is at present one of the theoretical physicists who have reflected most penetratingly, from the scientific point of view, on the place of the second law of thermodynamics in quantum physics.

SAINT AUGUSTINE has written in his *Confessions*, "I know what time is, if no one asks me, but if I try to explain it to one who asks me, I no longer know."

After fifteen centuries of scientific progress this opinion ought still to be that of contemporary philosophers. It can be said that the efforts of physicists, biologists, psychologists, sociologists, and finally of all philosophers have the common goal of grasping the essence of something which we know through the experience of life and which we designate by the name "time." Nonetheless, the notions which scholars form of time seem to diverge farther and farther from each other in the course of their researches.

Henri Bergson, the great French genius of our century, made a decisive advance in the investigation of time. Most notably, he forced us to recognize the essential difference between physical time and real inner duration, the first being everywhere homogeneous, measurable, and reversible and the second always heterogeneous, unmeasurable, and irreversible. We understand by "physical time" that variable which enters into the equations of physics under the name of "time."

As is well known, Bergson attributes no reality to this notion; at least, he does not put it on the same level as extended space and inner duration (TFW 100, 113, 234; *Essai* 75, 84, 176). According to him, physical time is only the projection of pure duration into space, and is only measurable by means of spatial extension.

However this may be, it is a fact that physical time is as indispensable as spatial coordinates to the precise predictions of physical theory. Hence there is every reason to examine the relations between pure inner duration and physical time and to attempt, if possible, to erect a bridge between them. For those who adopt Bergson's thesis, this essay consists in the discovery of how this projection of pure duration into the external world is accomplished.

It is universally known that Einstein's theory of relativity caused a revolution in the concept of time. It is recognized also that quantum theory has forced us to modify our conception of the principle of causality. But few realize that this quantum theory implies a completely new point of view for the philosophy of time: this constitutes a revolution with far more significant implications for philosophy than that provoked by relativity theory.

We have stated since 1935 that this new point of view, introduced by quantum theory, leads us to re-establish an intimate relationship between physical time and psychological duration.[1] We would like today to sum up what, in our opinion, quantum theory signifies with respect to the evolution of the concept of time.

Quantum physics is able to reveal the basic character of time precisely through the new interpretation which it affords us of the second law of thermodynamics or, more briefly, of the principle of entropy. Before proceeding to the exposition of this new interpretation it is necessary to note at the beginning the agreement between Bergson's philosophy and the principle of entropy. As Albert Thibaudet has clearly demonstrated in his work on Bergson's philosophy, the central problem of his philosophy can be revealed in the light of the principle of entropy.[2] But it is a curious fact that Bergson seems not to have known of the existence, or at least to have felt the importance, of the principle of entropy at the time, in 1888, at which he wrote the first essays of *Time and Free Will*, essays which are the basis of his philosophy of pure duration. And it will not be until *Creative Evolution*, in 1907, that he will

---

[1] See Pierre Lecomte du Noüy, *L'homme devant la science* (Paris: Flammarion, 1939), in which my unpublished article is cited.
[2] Albert Thibaudet, *Bergsonisme*, livre I, pp. 201–27.

term the principle of entropy "the most metaphysical of the laws of physics" (CE 243; EC 244), and employ this principle to characterize physical time in opposition to real duration. It can be believed that Bergson would have formulated his philosophy of duration in a more precise form if he had known how to utilize the principle of entropy to his advantage from the beginning.

The new interpretation of this principle by quantum physics appears to permit us to penetrate still further into the path which Bergson's philosophy has opened for us.

We would like to begin by briefly explaining the meaning of the principle of entropy. To do this it is necessary to distinguish two categories among natural phenomena: those which are *reversible* and those which are *irreversible*. Imagine that a natural phenomenon is photographed, and that the film is then shown backward in the movie projector. For example, you have perhaps seen a movie in which a diver breaks through the surface of the water, his feet above his head, and rebounds through the air to land on the diving board. Such a movement is the reversed movement of the natural phenomenon. A phenomenon is said to be reversible if its inverse movement is admissible according to the laws of nature. Otherwise the phenomenon is said to be irreversible.

Consider a pendulum whose movement is subjected to no resistance, that is, whose oscillation does not diminish in amplitude. The inverse movement is exactly the same as the original movement. Hence this is a reversible phenomenon. Similarly, the movement of billiard balls is reversible, if one abstracts from the dissipation of energy which results from shock and from resistances of all kinds.

Imagine on the other hand that you allow a drop of ink to fall into the water. After a time the ink will be mixed almost uniformly in the water. Such a diffusion phenomenon is evidently irreversible. We suppose now that we have two bodies, A and B, which touch each other in such a way that heat can pass from the first to the second. We further suppose that at a given instant body A is warmer than body B. Even a ten-year-old knows that in time

65

the difference between the two temperatures will diminish. From the point of view of the conservation of energy the inverse phenomenon would be possible, that is, one in which a warm body becomes warmer while a cold body becomes colder, in such a way that the total heat remains the same. But this cannot happen, for the phenomenon of heat conduction is irreversible.

What law, then, decides the direction in which an irreversible phenomenon unfolds? This is decided by the second law of thermodynamics, or the principle of entropy, which is stated as follows: "In a thermally isolated system, entropy increases with time." This means that in a system externally isolated in such a way that heat cannot traverse the wall of isolation, the irreversible phenomenon flows in the direction which increases entropy. The entropy of a system is a physically calculable quantity, but we do not have to define it rigorously here. We say that the entropy is greater in the state in which the ink is uniformly mixed with the water than in the state in which it is concentrated in a small region of the water. Similarly, entropy becomes greater as the difference in temperature between the two bodies becomes less.

This principle of increasing entropy is sometimes termed "the principle of the degradation of energy," since the utilizable energy in general diminishes with the increase of entropy, though the total energy is conserved.

This principle of entropy defines the "unique direction" within the flow of physical time. But let us note how the principle is stated. All physical treatises, even those which are worthy of the greatest confidence, state the principle quite simply: "Entropy increases with time." Such a statement must be construed as the definition of the actual direction of time.

But if it states only this, the principle will become a tautology. To avoid this result, the statement can be modified to read, "If two systems are supposed, each of which is thermally isolated, the increase in entropy of one coincides with the increase in entropy of the other." Unfortunately, it is evident that this statement is much too narrow to express the entire content of the principle of entropy. Actually, when the increase of entropy is spoken of, it is understood that the actual direction of time, which according to the principle coincides with the increase of entropy, is known a priori. The following formula ought therefore to be chosen: "The entropy of a thermally isolated system increases in the direction of the flow of psychological time."

To this it can be objected that such a proposition goes beyond the limits of physics. But we have seen that, in the form usually adopted, the principle is a mere tautology. We believe therefore that the formulation we have given, unsettling as it may appear at first glance, states the essence of the principle. Above all it has the advantage of making us realize that we are dealing, not merely with an external phenomenon left to itself, but with the relationship between the external phenomenon and the consciousness which observes it.

Until the end of the nineteenth century, scientists had succeeded in producing an entire system of physical laws which seemed to exhaust all the possible regularities among physical phenomena. This system, which we today term classical physics, was a closed system, free from all intrinsic contradictions. It consisted in two distinct theories: that of mechanics and that of electromagnetism. All physical phenomena seemed to be explained by one or the other of these theories, or by a combination of both. It is not surprising, therefore, that the physicists of the time should have attempted also to explain the second law of thermodynamics with the aid of the fundamental laws of the classical system. The motion of the molecules constituting a system ought, it was thought, to obey these fundamental laws; and all global laws of the system, like that of the increase of entropy, ought to be deducible.

Now this conclusion was destined to encounter a very grave difficulty. All the equations of physics are symmetrical with respect to time reversal, just as they are symmetrical with respect to the change from left to right. Consequently, all physical phenomena permitted by the fundamental laws are reversible, and it is clear that any combination whatever of reversible phenomena is also reversible.

It was thus necessary to add a further principle to this system, in order to draw an irreversible conclusion from reversible premises. This further principle involved considerations of statistics or chance. The conclusion drawn from this was that "if the state of a system is fully known at a given instant, it is more probable that at a succeeding instant the system will be found to have an increased rather than a decreased entropy." The vague term "fully known" signifies that the state of the system is determined by thermodynamic measures such as temperature, density, pressure, etc., but that the state of motion of each molecule is not known.

Clearly what is at stake here is the probability of a succeeding state based on the knowledge of a preceding state. When the reasoning which led physicists to this conclusion is examined, it is discovered that the preceding instant could be exchanged with the succeeding instant, so that the following formulation could be substituted for the formulation stated above: "If the thermodynamic state is given at a certain instant and the attempt is made to predict—or better, retrodict—the state of a prior instant, it is probable (far more probable than the contrary case) that the system possessed a greater entropy at the prior instant than at the originally given instant." [3] This proposition is a prediction which reverses the direction of time, a prediction which is the inverse of the conventional form of scientific prediction [prévision].

The two statements which we have formulated seem to contradict each other since one proclaims the increase and the other the decrease of entropy with physical time. Nonetheless, they do not stand in contradiction, for both affirm this: that entropy is found to be increased in the state known after the other is known —after in the flow of thought! This shows that there is no privileged direction to physical time and that, if a unique direction is found in the development of physical phenomena, this direction is simply the projection of the flux of our psychological time. All this is quite in accord with the content of the second law of thermodynamics. In this way we have attempted to reconcile the

[3] This conclusion can be deduced from the argument developed in the celebrated article by Paul and Tatiana Ehrenfest, *Encycl. Sci. Math.*, *Mec*, IV, 2, ii.

reversibility of classical physics with the irreversibility of thermodynamics. We are led by this consideration to think that the increase of entropy is not a characteristic of the external world left to itself, but that it is the result of the liaison between the subject and the object.

This last point has been established in a decisive fashion by quantum theory, which in the first years of this century undermined the foundations of classical physics and ended by revolutionizing the philosophy of scientific knowledge. We would like now to glance, without entering into details, at quantum physics' conclusions concerning entropy.

In classical physics the state of a system is entirely determined independently of the knowledge of its observer. This is no longer the case in quantum physics, for which knowledge of the state and the state itself are synonymous. If probability is invoked in classical physics, it is because the observer does not know in detail the precise state of the atoms which constitute the system. Classical physics is, at bottom, deterministic, and presupposes a rigorous causality. In quantum physics, on the contrary, the most precisely defined state in principle does not allow a deterministic prediction as a result of a prior observation. Everything is subordinated to statistical laws.

In quantum mechanics, a physical state changes according to two completely different kinds of processes. First, the state changes gradually with the course of time, following a certain differential equation termed a wave equation. This process is causal and reversible. Second, the state changes abruptly the moment the observer makes a new observation of the system. This process is statistical and irreversible. Quite naturally, the renewal of the investigation changes the knowledge of the state, and hence the state itself.

It can be demonstrated that entropy is not in the least changed by the first process. (This is intimately bound up with the fact that the process of change is reversible.) On the other hand, entropy changes rapidly in the second process, and always so as to increase.[4] This means that the act of observation itself increases the entropy: a shocking situation in the eyes of classical physicists since an objective physical measure is now closely dependent on the intervention of the observing subject. The principle of entropy is no longer a simple physical law, but must be considered as the law of the development of knowledge. In the new mechanics, entropy measures, so to speak, the degree of precision of our knowledge.

For the rest it must be noted that entropy does not increase gradually with time but that it increases suddenly at the moment of observation. Entropy becomes always greater after the observation than it had ever been before. Now these terms "before" and "after" do not refer to the flow of time, but simply to the order of the development of our cognition. We are dealing here with the direction of psychological time.

Physical time, taken in itself, that is, taken as a variable intervening in the equations of physics, is comparable to a straight line in space, in the sense that its two directions cannot be distinguished from each other. If man discovers a privileged direction in natural phenomena or, what amounts to the same thing, if physical time seems to him to flow in a unique direction, it is because he projects, through observation procedures, the stream of his own consciousness into nature. Thus modern physics recovers the lost tie between psychic and physical time, the tie established by the act of observation, which is in the last analysis a mutual interaction between the observer and the observed.

Moreover, the fact that the stream of consciousness in all men, or still more, in all living beings, flows in the same direction, demands an explanation since this fact is too remarkable to be contingent. We have not seen this problem posed in any scientific or philosophical work. Nonetheless, it will merit being posed and attentively studied. The solution will be found only in the assumption that all living beings on earth share in a single, unique life, a

4 See Johan von Neumann, *Mathematische Grundlagen der Quantenmechanik* (Berlin, 1932); see also Satosi Watanabé, *Le Deuxième Théorème de la Thermodynamique et la Mécanique Ondulatoire* (Paris, 1935).

thesis which is in harmony with Bergson's concept of creative evolution. It is conceivable, further, that on a distant star, with which we have no means of communicating, a group of living beings having a common life evolves in the opposite direction.[5] All these results, which follow from the new interpretation of the principle of entropy, can have immensely important philosophical consequences, although no physicist or philosopher seems to have appreciated their importance up to the present time.

We must now consider the real duration proper to consciousness, whose essence Bergson has so gloriously succeeded in grasping. He states in his *Introduction to Metaphysics*, "... there are no psychological states, however simple, which do not change at every instant, since there is no consciousness without memory, no continuation of a state without the addition to the present feeling of the memory of past moments. This is what duration consists in. Inner duration is the continuous life of a memory which prolongs the past into the present" (CM 211; PM 200–201). He also writes, "My conscious state, in advancing in time swells continually with the duration it gathers, rolling upon itself like a snowball in the snow" (CE 4; EC 2).

Similar explications of pure duration can be found throughout his works. If pure duration has these characteristics, it will not be difficult to deduce its irreversibility from them. "From this survival of the past," Bergson asserts, "it follows that consciousness cannot go through the same state twice.... In changing, our personality prevents any state, however identical with itself on the surface, from ever repeating itself in its depths. This is why our duration is irreversible" (CE 61; EC 6).

In effect, the complete inversion of duration will signify a continual inward impoverishment of the Self which, in such a case, will possess prediction but no memory and which, further, will be completely deprived of freedom of action. This will be a being which will not even merit the name monster, a being which is foreign to life.

---

[5] This hypothesis is rather difficult to reconcile with Bergson's concepts developed in *Duration and Simultaneity*.

It is clear, as Bergson demonstrated, that pure duration is not measurable. It can be said therefore that the characteristics of pure duration are its nonmeasurability and its irreversibility. Interpolate, "By contrast, physical time, properly stated, is characterized by its measurability and its reversibility." From this fact alone it will already be possible to infer that the irreversibility of natural phenomena results from the duration characteristic of consciousness. We do not wish to defend Bergson's thesis too rigorously and to claim that physical time is only the projection of pure duration into external space, for physical time is as real for physicists as physical space.[6] Nevertheless, reflection on the recent conclusions of modern physics suggests to us that the apparent irreversibility of physical time is the projection of the irreversibility of pure duration. And this conclusion seems to us to be capable of being put in accord with Bergson's general ideas.

We now propose to note briefly how Bergson himself interpreted the principle of entropy. Here we ought not to lose sight of the fact that in Bergson's era quantum theory had not appeared, and that the interpretation of this principle, even in terms of classical physics, was incomplete.

First we must recollect Bergson's concept of the ideal genesis of matter, the central concept of his *Creative Evolution*. He begins with an ideal experiment: he proposes to us that we concentrate more and more intensively on what we possess within us, that is, our pure duration, to detach ourselves from matter and from intellectuality and, at the same time, to experience the tension of our will. Through an effort in this direction, we approach the limiting state of pure life. Inversely, in relaxing the vital duration we approach [the limit of] materiality, in which memory and will disappear.

Bergson then concludes: "At the base of spirituality on the one hand, and of materiality and intellectuality on the other, there would be therefore two processes of opposite direction, and one passes from the first to the second through an inversion, perhaps even a simple interruption ..." (CE 201; EC 202). The inversion

---

[6] This is necessary to justify the Lorentz transformation.

described here is, by definition, different in nature from the inversion of physical time which we mentioned above. It will become clear, however, that there is a certain correspondence, if not coincidence, between these two inversions.

Let us go further: there is, according to Bergson, an order whenever the object satisfies our thought or, rather, every time our mind rediscovers itself in things. Hence the distinction between order and disorder depends on what we wish to see in things. "Now," Bergson writes, "whether experience seems to us to take the first direction [the direction of life], or whether it takes the second [the direction of matter], in both cases we say that there is an order, for in both processes the mind recognizes itself" (CE 223; EC 224). The first order may be termed, for lack of an appropriate phrase, "the willed order" or order of finality, while the second will be "the automatic order" or the order of causality.[7]

Causality is connected with the point of view according to which the automatic development of natural phenomena are followed from the direction of the past into the present. Finality, by contrast, is connected with the point of view in which the will, having a goal to realize in the future, acts on the present. The passage from one of these viewpoints to the other corresponds, in a sense, to the inversion of time. It is in this sense that we have said that Bergson's inversion corresponds to the inversion of physical time.

Now let us see how Bergson relates this notion of two orders to the principle of entropy, or to the principle of the degradation of energy. In the material world, according to this principle, utilizable energy gradually diminishes, and this, says Bergson, is the material order. The material order ought to be produced where the vital order is suppressed. Bergson therefore wishes to see in life an order opposed to the degradation of energy. Let us hear what he states: "Note that the direction in which this reality proceeds now suggests to us the idea of a thing which unmakes itself; this is,

---

[7] According to Bergson, the first order "oscillates doubtless around finality, yet nonetheless cannot be defined by it" (CE 223; EC 224).

beyond doubt, one of the essential traits of materiality. What is to be concluded from this, if not that the process through which a thing makes itself is directed in the opposite direction of a physical process and that it is consequently, by definition even, immaterial?" (CE 245; EC 246). It is clear from the context that the direction of the march of reality spoken of here signifies the degradation of energy, that is, the increase of entropy which was considered in Bergson's time to be a property of matter independent of mind.

Further on Bergson does not hesitate to declare, "All our analyses in fact show us in life an effort to climb the slope which matter descends. In that, they reveal to us the possibility, the necessity even, of a process the inverse of materiality, creative of matter by its interruption alone" (CE 245; EC 246).

It is clear here how the concept of the ideal genesis of matter is based on the consideration of the principle of entropy.

In observing living beings accumulating energy in their bodies, many hasty thinkers have concluded that such beings act so as to violate the principle of entropy. On this point Bergson is very careful. He says: "[Life] does not have the power to reverse the direction of physical changes, such as the principle of Carnot [i.e., the principle of entropy] determines it. . . . Incapable of stopping the course of material changes downwards, it succeeds in retarding it" (CE 245–46; EC 246–47).

Life signifies, according to Bergson, "primarily a gradual accumulation of energy, secondly an elastic canalization of this energy in variable and indeterminable directions, at the end of which are free acts" (CE 253–54; EC 254). The élan vital is not unlimited; it must struggle against the resistance presented by matter. Hence, "the evolution of the organized world is simply the unfolding of this struggle" (CE 254; EC 254–55). This is the essence of Bergson's thought concerning the principle of entropy.

The goal of our lecture is not to analyze the metaphysical thesis of *Creative Evolution*. We wish to limit ourselves to adding, from the point of view of modern physics, certain remarks which can be reconciled with Bergson's thesis.

74

We ought first, above all, to insist on the fact that the principle of entropy applies only to the object observed by the observer. This involves two important consequences. In the first place, to speak of the entropy of the entire universe is to risk passing beyond the boundaries of science. Not long ago it was common to speak of the death of William Kelvin's universe, that is, the state of the universe in which entropy attains its maximum value or that in which utilizable energy is completely used up.[8] At that moment, it was thought, there would no longer be motion or life in the universe. The horror of this universal death, it will be found, provides one of the motives for Bergson's having represented the tendency of entropy as something opposed to life. This is apparent enough in his *Creative Evolution* (CE 245; EC 264). But to tell the truth this horror seems to have been the result of too hasty a generalization.

Secondly, the increase of entropy applies only to what is observed, and consequently not at all to the observer. As Johan von Neumann has well shown, the distinction between the observer and the observed may be displaced arbitrarily, but it must be drawn somewhere.[9] The observing Self is thus always excluded from the field to which the law of entropy applies. Insofar as men exchange information about an object, they ought to be considered as a single observer. Hence, one is here dealing with the abstract Self. Pure duration is found precisely within this abstract Self. It follows therefore that since the *élan vital* is not a material thing capable of becoming an object of investigation, it can have a nature [*allure*] completely different from that observed in the external world.

Before concluding, we would like to suggest a speculative proposition which can be based on the above considerations, a somewhat daring proposition which concerns a central problem of metaphysics.

[8] It is well known that in classical physics this death cannot be eternal because of Poincaré's theorem of recurrence, or because of the "ergodic" theorem. Cf. Ehrenfest, *Encycl. Sci. Math.*, Mec, IV, 2, ii. For the analogous theorem in quantum physics, cf. J. von Neumann, ZS.f. Phys. 57 (1929), 300.

[9] J. von Neumann, *Mathematische Grundlagen der Quantenmechanik.*

It is, without doubt, one of Bergson's great merits to have related the problem of entropy to that of consciousness. But had he known that the increase of entropy is the direct result of observation by the observing Self, he would, we believe, have given a different account of his theory of Creative Evolution, without, however, altering its essence. Speaking of the original state in which the utilizable energy (of the solar system) was as yet very great, he writes: "In reality, the problem will be insoluble if we remain on the terrain of physics, for the physicist is obliged to attach energy to extended particles . . .; he would renounce his role if he sought for the origin of these energies in an extra-spatial process. It is there, however, in our opinion, that it must be sought. . . . Extension, we said, appears only as a tension which is interrupted" (CE 244; EC 245).

It is quite remarkable that Bergson should have foreseen, so to speak, a certain possible tie between entropy and life; but the effect of life on entropy seems rather to be, in a sense, contrary to that which Bergson believed. It seems to us closer to the truth to say that life, in order to be, must increase the entropy of the external world, and that the increase of entropy is the manifestation in matter of the action of life. This relationship, established by the act of observation between mind and matter, ought to be interpreted as the necessary condition of matter's being matter and, at the same time, of the spirit's being spirit. For no mind can be conscious without observing matter or, consequently, without increasing the entropy of matter; and no matter can become the object of our awareness without being susceptible of being observed and, consequently, without obeying the principle of entropy.

In other words, the existence of matter is made possible by the existence of the spirit, and the existence of the latter by that of the former. To say that the observing act, as a reciprocal intervention between mind and matter, outlines an interrelation between the two does not sufficiently express its role. Rather, it should be said that the act of observation is a productive agent which gives rise to both of these realities. Observation, taken in the most general sense, signifies the action of consciousness; it is life itself. It is something which exists before the subject and the object, before the spirit and the matter. The principle of entropy can henceforth be considered the expression of the reciprocal condition of the existence of the two aspects of the single substance.

These conclusions, drawn from our new interpretation of modern physics, can serve to establish a reconciliation between the opposed theses of the materialists and the idealists. It is really to a superior path, above the viewpoints of materialism and idealism, which Bergson seems always to have tried to lead us by means of his philosophy of life.

OLIVIER COSTA DE BEAUREGARD

Certain Aspects of the Irreversibility of Time in Classical and Quantum Physics

Remarks by the Editor. Scientists have attempted with great success to demonstrate the reversibility of time. Yet the irreversibility of certain physical processes, and the consequent dissymmetry of the future and the past, appears to be a deep-rooted trait of nature. In the following article, Professor Olivier Costa de Beauregard endeavors to reconcile these two contrasting aspects of reality. This reconciliation begins with an analysis of the physical principles (the principle of increasing entropy and the principle of retarded actions) which assert the irreversibility of physical processes. The term "retarded action," along with the correlative term "advanced action," is doubtless unfamiliar to the scientific layman. The diver who plunges from the diving board into the pool provides an example of a retarded action: that is, a causal sequence proceeding from the present into the future. Should the diver burst from the water feet first and land, nicely balanced, on the diving board, his act would constitute an advanced action: that is, a causal sequence proceeding from the present into the past. The processes with which physicists deal are far more exotic than those provided by a diver and a diving board. But in every case, exotic or familiar, physicists have insisted that nature exhibits only retarded and never advanced actions. This "principle of retarded actions," however, like the principle of increasing entropy, has never been fully established. To the contrary, Costa de Beauregard argues, both principles have been assumed to be valid without satisfactory justification in order to secure a desired result. Moreover, in microphysics elementary processes are found to be completely reversible. The true source of the irreversibility of physical time, therefore, must be found neither in the "microcosm" nor in *ad hoc* physical principles, but in the constraining effect which the universe as a whole exercises on its parts. Temporal irreversibility is a "macrocosmic" phenomenon which should be accounted for through "equations of condition," that is, equations stating the extrinsic conditions under which physical processes occur.

These general conclusions are buttressed by Costa de Beauregard through an examination of the treatment of time in quantum and pre-quantum physics. In pre-quantum physics the irreversibility of time was taken to be an indisputable fact and was enshrined in the basic principles of thermodynamics, statistical mechanics, and electromagnetism. Thus Henri Poincaré's "theorem of return" (according to which a swarm of small planets created through the explosion of a large planet could recreate the large planet again, which could once again explode) was rejected even though certain aspects of pre-quantum theory seemed to require it. In quantum physics, however, a complete symmetry is established between the future and the past, and both "prediction" and "postdiction" are allowed. Nonetheless, in dealing with large numbers of elementary particles, the quantum physicist rediscovers temporal irreversibility. What was implicitly true for pre-quantum physics is in quantum physics explicitly proved: irreversibility is a characteristic of macroscopic phenomena. Radioactive disintegrations, which provide an example of a process that can-

78

not be reversed, are therefore to be interpreted as macroscopic in nature.

Professor Costa de Beauregard closes his essay with an analysis of psychological and biological considerations related to the concept of temporal reversibility. It is not possible to reverse the arrow of psychological time. (Imagine, for example, trying to unlearn, in reverse order, a mathematics text whose concepts one has learned in succession.) This fact is to be explained through the macroscopic character of our total brain apparatus. Biological evolution, like psychological time, is irreversible and is opposed to the degradation of energy found in physical entropy. Life is a veritable network of *negative entropy*, amassed through macroscopic physical processes which operate with extreme slowness.

Thus the irreversibility of biological, psychological, and macroscopic physical times establishes a dissymmetry between the future and the past. In other respects, however, a great deal of symmetry may be discovered between the future and the past. Much like the yet unread portions of the mathematics text which one is attempting to learn, Costa de Beauregard suggests tentatively, the future pre-exists, waiting to be encountered, while the past, like the theorems which have already been read and learned, is virtually present. Costa de Beauregard's essay ends, therefore, with a very un-Bergsonian suggestion: past, present, and future are equally real, and in this sense symmetrical. *Professor Costa de Beauregard's essay was originally published in the* REVUE DES QUESTIONS SCIENTIFIQUES, *Ve Série (April 20, 1952). It appears here in translation with the permission of the author and the* REVUE DES QUESTIONS SCIENTIFIQUES. *Professor David A. Sipfle and Mary-Alice Sipfle have collaborated with the editor in the translation of this article.*

INTRODUCTION

1. *Fleeting time which is forever lost, the impossibility of re-making the past or knowing the future:* these are truths of everyday experience even more obvious than the fact that a cycli-

cal isothermal transformation of heat into work is impossible. These facts are, however, particularly difficult for mathematical physics to justify because in its elementary laws of motion [*lois élémentaires d'évolution*], both quantum and classical, this science persistently maintains that there is a total symmetry between the future and the past, making it impossible to doubt that his elementary symmetry represents one of nature's deep-rooted traits. Yet the dissymmetry so often manifested between the future and the past is certainly another such trait. The whole problem is to reconcile these two fundamental facts. A closer examination of the classical explanations of physical irreversibility reveals, not surprisingly, that the irreversibility found in the result of these demonstrations is actually postulated in the premises by a categorical decree. In this respect phenomenological thermodynamics and statistical mechanics do not differ radically from electromagnetism, where it really is a decree, inspired by experience, which causes solutions of the advanced type to be set aside in favor of those of the retarded type. In our opinion there is a close relationship between the basic postulates of statistical mechanics and this other fundamental postulate of irreversibility, the *principle of retarded actions* (§§ 2 and 3). Since, as we have said, the basic interpretation of this universal principle of irreversibility, in its many aspects, cannot be found in the elementary equations of motion, it seems clear that it must be contained in an all-inclusive law of the universe, and that this law is expressed by equations of condition, that is, by equations of the same type as the extrinsic conditions which, for example, theoretical mechanics takes as initial conditions (§ 4).

In discussing a problem such as the nature of time, where the perception of phenomena by consciousness is so important, it is obvious that psychological considerations must be treated explicitly. Thus the physicist is confronted with the whole subjective aspect of time, which he must characterize as exactly as possible without, however, falsifying all that is perfectly objective in the irreversibility of time. This is what we attempt to do, first in the domain of classical physics (§ 5), where we see one of

80

Poincaré's famous arguments in a new light, then in the domain of quantum physics (§ 9), where we will comment on von Neumann's already celebrated theory of irreversibility.[1]

But what appears to be a harsh constraint imposed by the cosmos on our psychological aspirations—a constraint suggested in the very first words of the introduction and so frequently the subject of poetic lament or stoic commentary—is simply the other side of quite a different view of time, which the theoretical physicist finds it even harder to deny. For duration also demands the progressiveness found in creation, whether in action or in thought or in moral effort; it is the same progressiveness found in the creation of biological life, in *ontogenesis* and *phylogenesis*. We have not been able to resist the strong temptation to make a few very modest comments about these vast problems, although their only merit may be to draw attention to some minute details. In the realm of creation itself, the cosmos is indeed quite constraining, but this constraint now appears to be the necessary and precious element of a progress which words cannot express. It is not surprising, then, that the modest remarks of a professional physicist might seem prosaic and disappointing to students of philosophy— and perhaps at the same time appear too audacious to many of his colleagues.

PRE-QUANTUM CONSIDERATIONS

2. *Thermodynamics and theoretical mechanics.* We have already pointed out elsewhere [2, 4] that phenomenological thermodynamics would not conclude that physical phenomena are irreversible if its premises did not already contain this conclusion. In the elementary demonstration of Carnot's theorem, this irreversibility is included in the two premises—the one which excludes

---

[1] We take note, in completing this study, of S. Watanabé's "Le concept de temps en physique moderne et la durée pure de Bergson [The Concept of Time in Modern Physics and Bergson's Pure Duration]," a most interesting study which deals with quite similar preoccupations [*see pp. 63–77 of this book (ed.)*]. The reader will find that though many of the remarks in these two studies appear remarkably similar, in the end our conclusions diverge notably from those of Watanabé [15].

cyclical isothermal transformations producing work, and the one which states that when two conductors are put into contact heat will flow from the one with the higher temperature to the one with the lower temperature.

If the direction of time's arrow were reversed, the formulation of the two premises of Carnot's theorem, and hence the theorem itself and all its consequences, would also be reversed. A little later, in our discussion of Poincaré, we shall consider the paradoxical properties of the hypothetical universe thus obtained. For the moment we simply wish to insist on the fact that classical thermodynamics constitutes, for the first time in the history of science, a systematization of multiple aspects of irreversibility, which it has deduced from a particularly familiar aspect of this irreversibility. Classical thermodynamics does not, and could not, derive irreversibility from premises which did not contain it.

One other point which we must make here is that there is a sort of pre-established harmony between theoretical mechanics and classical thermodynamics. We know that in a conservative system of theoretical mechanics the positions of equilibrium correspond to the extrema of potential energy since the positions of stable equilibrium are associated with the minima of potential energy. This property derives from the essentially non-negative nature of kinetic energy. It follows, indeed, that the total energy of a conservative system represents an upper limit of its potential energy. Therefore, in the vicinity of a *minimum* of potential energy, the different values possible for it, and, consequently, for kinetic energy as well, are bounded, maximally and minimally, by zero and a small positive value. In the vicinity of a *maximum* of potential energy, on the other hand, the symmetrical property of the preceding does not hold, for no lower limit is imposed on the potential energy. Now, the definite positive character of kinetic energy results from the essentially positive character which classical mechanics attributes to mass. If established concepts were extended, requiring us to consider negative masses, the whole theory of stable equilibrium would have to be revised, and with it, as we shall soon see, the whole theory of irreversibility. It is beyond the scope of this study to pursue this discussion as far as R. P. Feynman's theory of electron-positron pairs [5], where negative masses actually are taken into account.

On the other hand, we wish to point out the following characteristic of theoretical mechanics: not only is it true that a system remains eternally in an approximate state of stable equilibrium if it finds itself there at a given instant t_0; it is also true that a real system tends inevitably toward stable equilibrium as soon as the thermodynamic dissipation of its kinetic energy is taken into account. By contrast, in order to bring a system to a state of unstable equilibrium, it would be necessary to 1) increase its total energy by just the right amount and 2) do this in such a way that the ensuing evolution tends (asymptotically) toward the projected position of unstable equilibrium; in other words, it would be necessary to go against the principles of thermodynamics and statistical mechanics.

In sum, there seems to be a pre-established harmony between the notion of stable equilibrium according to theoretical mechanics and the idea of dissipation of energy into heat according to thermodynamics. The positive nature of mass is absolutely essential for this, and perhaps this is where a thorough study of irreversibility in quantum physics would lead.

3. *The connection between the law of increasing entropy and that of retarded actions.* We now take up the reasoning by which Poincaré [9] demonstrates the uniform deployment of minute planets on their common orbit. Let a be the average velocity [*mouvement*] and b the initial position [*longitude*] of one of these tiny planets, $l = at + b$ its position at instant t, and f (a, b) the planet density distribution attached to point a, b. The mean value of the function $e^{il(t)}$ is written:

$$M(t) = \int \int e^{i(at+b)} f(a, b) \, da \, db.$$

If one supposes merely that the function f is continuous, then $M \rightarrow O$ as $t \rightarrow +\infty$; the same being true for the mean values of cos t and sin t, it follows in particular that whatever the law of the initial explosion of a large planet (f [b] $\rightarrow 0$ for values of b not immediately adjoining the position of the large planet b_0) the distribution of residual fragments which describe the initial orbit will tend toward uniformity.

But if $t \to -\infty$, $M \to O$ in the same way. If it were necessary to take this result literally, one would say that the large planet observed at instant O was created through the reassemblage of small planets which were equally spaced on their common orbit in the distant past. Precisely the same paradox is met with again in the fundamental formula of ergodic theory [2, 8, 12] which states that the evolution [of a system] during the instants preceding the initial instant is symmetrical to the evolution during the instants which follow it. This is not a theoretical paradox since, in both cases, the elementary laws of evolution are temporally symmetrical. But the actual fact is that an exceptional configuration of elements can be imposed on a system only as an initial condition, never as a final condition; this principle, implicitly applied by all authors, contains the radical dissymmetry between future and past which appears in the conclusions of the theory. No more than phenomenological thermodynamics, therefore, does statistical mechanics succeed in deducing irreversibility from principles which do not contain it, since, on the contrary, this irreversibility is contained in one of the theory's postulates.

The postulate just considered is plainly nothing but a precise formulation, adapted to statistical problems, of the somewhat vague principle which all men spontaneously apply under the name of the principle of causality; it is by virtue of this same principle that in a problem of theoretical mechanics the extrinsic conditions are imposed on the evolution of the system by virtue of initial conditions and not at all by virtue of final conditions. But the very object of this study is not to accept, as given, the data dictated by our experience of each instant but to attempt to comprehend what these data imply.

We must now show that the fundamental postulate (F.P.) of statistical theory, which has just been brought to light, is closely related to another very general principle of physical irreversibility, the principle of retarded actions. In fact, if, as has just been re-

O. COSTA DE BEAUREGARD

called, the exceptional configuration imposed at instant O by ergodic theory[2] never results from the prior natural evolution of the system, this exceptional configuration must always be the result of the momentary interaction of the system under examination with another system: the explosion of a large planet engenders the swarm of minute planets; a stone falls into a calm pool and creates a train of diverging waves; the experimenter opens the spigot separating two fluids of different temperatures or kinds. The temporally unsymmetrical fact with which we are concerned receives the following new formulation: all action imposed momentarily from without on a system previously and subsequently isolated produces in this system an entirely retarded effect, to the exclusion of any advanced effect; for example, the momentary interaction of the stone with the pond does not erase a train of convergent waves whose existence it has previously determined, to be then thrown back onto the bank by the energy it has acquired. It must be noted that the criterion of statistical equilibrium (as it appears in the present discussion) proves in a strictly objective manner that advanced effects are excluded, leaving only retarded effects. It is by virtue of purely subjective arguments that a tennis player knows that his stroke determines the ball's final trajectory as a function of its original trajectory, and not the contrary; but it is in an objectively controllable manner that one knows that, if between two instants t_1 and t_2 one displaces an element of the partition containing a gas in thermodynamic equilibrium, the Maxwellian distribution of velocities is altered for the reflected molecules, but not for the incident molecules.

In sum, the principle of causality which ergodic theory implicitly applies, and from which the irreversibility it demonstrates is, in the last analysis, wholly derived, is nothing less than the principle by virtue of which an external action has a purely retarded effect. Thus a very close connection can be seen between two of physics' great irreversibility principles: that of increasing entropy, and that of retarded actions.

[2] Our reference to ergodic theory concerns essentially the theory of the unfolding of the element of extension in phase. (Note added in 1967.)

85

4. *The universal significance of the fundamental postulate of statistical theory.* For a system with a finite number of degrees of freedom, Poincaré's well-known theorem of return leads periodically or, speaking more precisely, pseudo-periodically, to the improbable initial situation. This is no longer true if the number of degrees of freedom is infinite, but in this case there remains the total temporal symmetry of the equations of ergodic theory, which, by themselves, would furnish the heterogeneity assumed initially as the accidental offspring of a homogeneous past.

As we have just stated, the demonstration of the law of increasing entropy succeeds only by the suppression, through a categorical decree, of the entire half of the entropy curve preceding the initial instant, an operation which, we have shown, is equivalent to an appeal to the principle of retarded actions. Now, it is easy to see that this important principle is none other than the link which imposes on each partial evolution the same direction as on evolution as a whole; it expresses, as will be seen more clearly in a moment, the existence of a constraining action of the whole on the part, of the total universe on the partial system studied.

Whether the partial evolution studied results from the disruption of a metastable equilibrium, or from the encounter, limited in time, of two "independent" systems which previously were not in thermodynamic equilibrium, in either case it follows from an improbable situation which the past potentially contained, and which is suddenly actualized. It thus appears that all the improbable situations placed by ergodic theory at the inception of various natural evolutions are like fragments, conserved and transported across time, of a highly improbable all-inclusive situation of the universe as a whole, a situation which existed in a still recent past.

Finally, if the world studied by physics lends itself, at least in the first approximation, to being ideally separated into distinct systems or phenomena which interact during finite durations, this isolation is never sufficiently perfect or sufficiently durable to allow Poincaré's theorem of return to come into play. The evolution of the part is irremediably contaminated by that of the whole, and this is shown to us by each of the partial views which we take of it. The diffusion of a drop of ink in a glass of water provides an analogy. Wherever there subsists a particle which rebels at this dissolution, one is on the track of a metastable equilibrium in which a fragment of the initial improbable state of the world remains congealed; when finally this fragment submits in turn and breaks up, one is present at the start of a partial, irreversible evolution of a well-known kind.

Now, in what category must we place the mathematical principles which express this basic irreversibility of the universe? Certainly not in the category of the equations which mechanics, classical or quantum, calls equations of motion [*équations d'évolution*], for these are always rigorously symmetrical between the future and the past. The lesson of statistical mechanics in this regard is clear: the equations or principles which express the evolution of all physical systems in a unique direction, and particularly the evolution of the universe, belong to the same category as the extrinsic conditions initially assumed by theoretical mechanics. Considered as a gigantic statistical system, the entire universe must be given at the beginning in a highly improbable state.

To sum up: the mathematical expression of the irreversibility of the universe is definitely not of the same type as equations of motion, but of the type of equations of condition.

5. The arrow of psychological time cannot be reversed. Let us represent the evolution of the universe, relativistically, as a four-dimensional phenomenon being viewed as a single continuum [*à la fois*] with its temporal thickness. From this viewpoint, the traditional idea according to which universal time impels the universe toward its most probable states vanishes as if it were completely meaningless. The only meaningful question is why, since the temporal dimension possesses the objective dissymmetry between the future and the past previously analyzed, life and consciousness explore this dimension in the direction which makes it appear that entropies increase and actions are retarded, and not in the opposite direction.

Let us first study the direction of change of entropy. If biological and psychological time led us in the reverse of their actual direction, we would live, as Poincaré states [10], in a universe devoid of laws. Two initially indiscernible temperatures would become different without its being possible to predict which would increase and which would diminish. Viscosity would increase instead of decreasing and would cause moving objects to be displaced from their state of rest in unforeseeable directions. All equilibriums would become unstable. No prediction would be possible under these conditions; on the contrary, it is "postdiction" [*postvision*], or the estimation of the probabilities attached to past states, which would be possible as a function of data relative to the present, following the same technique now employed in our predictions. But since, by definition, the course of psychological time impels us toward our future and not toward our past, there would be no relation whatsoever between the temporal domain open to our calculation and that open to the unfolding of our action: reasoned action would be impossible. Moreover, the most prudent of our actions would cause enormous and unforeseeable catastrophes: life would therefore be impossible.

The same conclusion results from the consideration of retarded actions. From this it follows that it is possible to act in the future and to see in the past. To act in the future, because the consequences of our present action will unfold in the demi-cone of the future having as its apex the point-instant in which we initiate the act. To see in the past because our present action does not affect the past demi-cone which ends at the point-instant from which we view things, and so the things we see are really things as they were. Consequently it turns out that the flow of our psychological time transports us to the region of space-time where our action unfolds: we accompany our action. This same flow continually transports all the point-instants which our action has attained into the region of space-time which our vision explores: we can thus see what we have done. If, on the other hand, the arrow of our psychological time were oriented in the opposite direction, our vision would be unrelated to our action; it would be useless for us to be able to shape the past in our own way or to see with absolute exactitude what will happen to us.

In sum, the arrow of biological and psychological time represents an adaptation of life to the conditions with which it finds itself confronted at a point on the slope of the entropy curve neighboring an exceptional fluctuation: on pain of being impossible, and even inconceivable, life is obliged to explore that slope in the direction of increasing entropy. Furthermore, although there is no need to belabor the point, it is certain that life would not be possible in a world in thermodynamic equilibrium. We will return, in section 12, to the modalities of the sort of colonization which life makes on the slopes near an apex of the entropy curve of changing sign.

QUANTUM CONSIDERATIONS

6. *The complete symmetry between the future and the past in the individual quantum phenomenon.* A) Consider an ordinary divergent or retarded wave created by a measurement taken at instant t and making possible the calculations of predictions associated with this measurement. It is possible to make correspond symmetrically to this a converging or advanced wave which figures in the problems of the probability of the causes associated with this same measurement [3, 6]. As a well-known example of the intervention of this wave we cite the problem of Heisenberg's microscope [7], in which the probable distribution of a photon's emission point in the object plane is deduced from its point of arrival in the image plane. The convergent wave in question evidently merits the name wave of postdiction [*postvision*].

B) The quantum probabilities of two reciprocal transitions are equal:

$$P_{if} = P_{fi}.$$

P_{fi} can be interpreted equally well as the probability of predicting the transition $f \rightarrow i$ or as the "probability of postdicting" the transition $i \rightarrow f$, that is, as the probability that, given the state f, this state has resulted from the transition $i \rightarrow f$.

In second quantization theory [*théorie superquantifiée*] P_{if} and P_{fi} contain occupation numbers, and it is naturally essential that these be taken with their true values in those transitions qualified as reciprocal. To illustrate this point let us consider the transition of a single corpuscle, first in Bose statistics, then in Fermi statistics, letting the P's now represent the ordinary quantum mechanical probabilities of this motion.

In Bose statistics, if n_i and n_f indicate the number of corpuscles *initially* present in the initial state i and in the final state f, and consequently $n'_i = n_i - 1$ and $n'_f = n_f + 1$ indicate the numbers *finally* present in these same states after the transition of a corpuscle is supposed complete, then one has, since $P_{if} = P_{fi}$,

$$n_i P_{if} (n_f + 1) = n'_i P_{fi} (n'_i + 1);$$

the second member represents indifferently the probability of predicting the transition $(n'_f, f) \rightarrow (n'_i, i)$ or the probability of "postdicting" the transition $(n_i, i) \rightarrow (n_f, f)$.

In Fermi statistics

$$P'_{12} = n_1 P_{12} (1 - n_2), n_1, n_2 = 0, 1$$

represents equivalently the probability of predicting the transition $1 \rightarrow 2$ or the probability of postdicting the transition $2 \rightarrow 1$; to see this, it is enough to recall Wolfgang Pauli's principle and to remark that P'_{12} is non-zero (and moreover equal to P_{12}) only if $n_1 = 1, n_2 = 0$.

The two results we have just shown, quite unusual because of the total symmetry which they manifest between future and past, do not have a parallel in the classical statistics of Clerk Maxwell and Ludwig Boltzmann; *they are essentially connected with that quite revolutionary characteristic of both of these theories of quantum statistics, the intervention of the number of corpuscles in the final state.*[3]

C) The interpretation of negative energy states, which is at

[3] We reproduce here verbatim an interesting remark, confirming our views, which Allard has been kind enough to communicate to us: "The quantity $n_i P_{if}$ $(n_f + 1)$ can certainly be obtained in classical statistics, but through a seemingly paradoxical kind of reasoning in which an individuality is given to the particles when they are found in a determinate state (i or f), but is taken away from them during the transition. For simplicity of argument we represent states i and f as *compartments;* there are *initially* n_i and n_f particles in each compartment; one of the n_1 particles can undergo the transition, and since it has an individuality, it is possible to choose this individuality in n_i ways. But since P_{if} is the same for all particles, because there is no individuality in the phenomenon of transition, the expression $n_i P_{if}$ $(n_f + 1)$ will actually be found to be the total probability. For

once the most elegant rationally and the simplest mathematically, is set forth by E. C. G. Stueckelberg [13] and Feynman [5]: corpuscles which occupy such states propagate themselves backwards in the time of Minkowski space. This interpretation completely re-establishes a symmetry between the future and the past based on the symmetry between states having positive and negative energies. It must be remarked that it is essentially the substitution of the quantum statistics of Bose or Fermi for classical statistics which makes this new interpretation possible: in Maxwell's and Boltzmann's classical statistics, this would raise the insurmountable paradox of retrograde causality, and would therefore be unacceptable [3].

To see this, let us re-examine a thought experiment we have studied previously [3] in which a corpuscular wave is projected onto a plane screen provided with a variable opening which is initially and finally closed. If the spatial axis $0x_1$ is taken perpendicular to this screen, there exists in Minkowski space a three-dimensional plane screen parallel to the time axis, and the diffraction-splitting experiment is interpreted as a diffraction related to the three directions x_2, x_3 and $x_4 = ict$. The spectral distribution of the diffused wave is easy to calculate, and it is found that, for all particles with a spin greater than zero, the spectral distribution contains plane waves of negative energy. It may thus appear a priori that an inadmissible effect of retrograde or advanced causality is found to be predicted by the equations; in fact this is not the case, for the particles with which one operates are either *bosons* or *fermions*, and the intensity of the plane "emergent" wave under consideration must be multiplied by the number $n'_f = n_f \pm 1$ previously introduced. If this "emergent" wave has negative energy, it is in reality an incident wave, and n'_f is the number of particles projected by it *before* the splitting operation. Thus, as was claimed, the intervention of Bose statistics or of Fermi statistics completely removes the paradox which arises in the classical statistics of Maxwell and Boltzmann.

---

the inverse transition $n'_f P_{fi}$ ($n'_i + 1$) is likewise given, and is equal to the preceding expression."

Finally, quantum formalism as a whole presents an extreme and very remarkable coherence with respect to the symmetry between past and future. This is seen to be as perfect as that previously admitted by theoretical mechanics, and it is certainly one of the more surprising traits of the two new statistics that they should be able to reconcile this perfect symmetry with the essential probabilism attributed to the elementary phenomenon.

But it also follows from this that if macroscopic irreversibility is not found in the elementary quantum phenomenon, it must necessarily be a phenomenon of the statistics of ensembles, just as in classical physics. This is what we now wish to show in certain examples, without returning to our earlier discussions of pre-quantum considerations which could be repeated, *mutatis mutandis,* here.

7. *The macroscopic nonexistence of advanced electromagnetic waves.* In order to deal with the emission and absorption of photons by quantified electronic oscillators, quantum theory and the statistical theory of ensembles both suppose at the outset that the entire system is contained by a perfectly reflecting enclosure of volume V (a hypothesis whose fictitious character is manifest); the phenomenon is thus reduced, on the one hand, to the exchange of photons between electronic oscillators (annihilated photons), and, on the other, to stationary waves (free photons) existing in the enclosure. Distributing the various corpuscles present (free photons, atoms at a given level of excitation, or free electrons) into the different available "compartments" according to the applicable statistical rules (Bose or Fermi), statistical mechanics easily computes the equilibrium distribution of the population under consideration. Taking into account the different probabilities of quantum transition as well, statistical mechanics can write the law according to which the arbitrary initial distribution of the population tends toward the equilibrium distribution.

To simplify the discussion, suppose that all the electronic oscillators enclosed in the container V are capable of only two energy levels, W_1 and W_2; the photons to be considered will then all have the same frequency $\nu = (W_2 - W_1)/h$ at the width $\triangle \nu$ (essentially

92

supposed very small) near the spectral line. Finally, let us ignore the probability of direct encounters between photons, that is, the phenomena of creation-annihilation of electron pairs and the concommitant fluctuations of the vacuum; with this approximation the spectral profile of the line under consideration will remain unaltered, and the spectrum of thermal radiation will never be established. Given these hypotheses it can be said that, in a state of equilibrium the number $\bar{n}$ of annihilated photons of frequency v is determined, with a very small uncertainty, $\triangle n$. Still for the sake of simplification, we shall henceforth speak as if the annihilated photons, whose numbers can differ from $\bar{n}$ in the general case, were distributed in a particular compartment. It goes without saying that this is a *purely fictitious* manner of speaking, since it is actually oscillators of the two types W_1 and W_2 which are distributed in the compartments, according to the appropriate statistics.

Consider at $t_0 = 0$ a configuration of the system in which the number n_0 of annihilated photons of frequency v differs greatly from the mean value $\bar{n}$: according to the fundamental postulate (F.P.) of statistical theory, it is not possible on the macroscopic level for this exceptional configuration to have resulted from the prior natural evolution of the system. However, statistics can derive the law according to which the system tends (asymptotically) toward its equilibrium state in which $\bar{n}$ photons of frequency v are annihilated.

Of course, it is always possible to suppose $n_0 \gg \bar{n}$, which amounts to saying that there is no restriction on retarded emission of the well-known kind. On the other hand, it is possible to have $n_0 \ll \bar{n}$ initially only if $\bar{n}$ is large; this means that retarded absorption, of the familiar kind, is possible only if photons capable of being absorbed exist prior to the process of absorption. Moreover, two other possible microscopic processes are excluded by the postulate F.P.: advanced absorption and advanced emission, in which the values $n_0 \gg \bar{n}$ and $n_0 \ll \bar{n}$ respectively would be realized by the natural evolution of the system during the instants immediately preceding instant 0.

93

We can briefly complete the preceding schema by constructing an image, also schematic, of the processes of continuous retarded emission and absorption. As the fictitious "annihilated enclosure" is emptied of or filled with photons of frequency v at the speed prescribed by the probability of quantum transition, it is possible to artificially maintain the number n at its initial value n_o, different from $\bar{n}$, by introducing from without or by withdrawing annihilated photons at the rate required. In the first case a nonelectromagnetic energy is furnished to the system from outside, and in the second case a nonelectromagnetic energy is given up by the system and recovered. In the first case (nonelectromagnetic energy expended), the postulate F.P. authorizes the maintenance of the value $n > \bar{n}$ but forbids the maintenance of a value $n < \bar{n}$; this agrees with the idea that the emission of the electromagnetic wave is *caused* by the expenditure of nonelectromagnetic energy, and not the contrary. It can be said, in other words, that the postulate F.P. authorizes continuous retarded emission but forbids continuous advanced emission. In the second case (nonelectromagnetic energy recovered), postulate F.P. authorizes the maintenance of a value $n < \bar{n}$ but forbids the maintenance of a value $n > \bar{n}$; this agrees with the idea that the absorption of radiant energy implies the pre-existence of this radiant energy, but that it is not possible, by putting a receptor apparatus into operation, to determine the existence in the preceding instants of a wave which converges onto it, to recall this wave from the past. It can be said, in other words, that postulate F.P. authorizes continuous retarded absorption, but forbids continuous advanced absorption.

There is an obvious relationship between the preceding statements and those of Carnot's principle concerning isothermal transformations, and our thesis is precisely that these diverse statements are of basically the same nature. This relationship does not go as far as identity, however, for the spectrum of the radiation emitted or absorbed in the transformations under consideration is not the spectrum of thermal radiation: although the entropy of the system contained by the reflecting enclosure is augmented at the time of the emission of the photons of frequency ν, it does not thus attain its *maximum maximorum*.

The contrast between the temporal symmetry of the elementary phenomenon and the dissymmetry of the macroscopic phenomenon appear perhaps most vividly when the quantum treatment of *Brehmstrahlung* is compared to the classical treatment of acceleration radiation. Initially, an energetic electron of energy W_2 approaches a nucleus, decelerates, and results in a slowed electron of energy W_1 ($W_1 < W_2$) and a photon of energy $h\nu = W_2 - W_1$: a nonelectromagnetic energy is consumed and an electromagnetic wave is emitted. The reciprocal process $W_1 + h\nu \rightarrow W_2$ exists, of course, with the same quantum probability, but its macroscopic parallel is rigorously excluded. This disparity derives entirely from the fact that the probability of the initial state *nucleus + slow electron* (W_1) + *photon* ($h\nu$) is absolutely negligible compared to the probability of the initial state *nucleus + fast electron* (W_2): the population of the elements in question is definitely not a population in statistical equilibrium, as would be the case if the whole system were enclosed in a perfectly reflecting container of *finite* volume V; however, the fact that the system is thrust into boundless Euclidean space limits the problem to the particular case in which the previously defined number $\bar{n}$ of annihilated photons is zero. There is thus produced a continuous escape of photons outside the system [*champ expérimental*]. This makes it clear that if the stable level of an atom is its lowest energy level, it is because the photons virtually contained in this atom are then fully dispersed.

Analogous considerations are implied in quantum theory concerning the width of spectral lines. In the testing of one form of the law of decay it is admitted that, when $t \rightarrow + \infty$, the system *atom + photon* tends toward a state of equilibrium in which the probability of the state *excited atom + annihilated photon* is zero, while that of the state *nonexcited atom + free photon* is equal to 1. This is actually the case if the system exists in an unlimited Euclidean space; but if the same system were enclosed in a reflecting container with a finite volume, the state of equilibrium, attained asymptotically for $t = + \infty$, would be a well-defined superposition of the two states considered to be possible.

It goes without saying that all of the above considerations, which are quite schematic, should be gone into more deeply, in greater detail, and made mathematically precise. Here our only goal was to point out the nature of the connection which we believe to exist between the principle of the exclusion of advanced electromagnetic waves and the law of increasing entropy for a photon gas. It also goes without saying that the essential condition for this identification, forbidden in classical theory, was the introduction of these elementary entities, *photons*.[4]

8. *The irreversibility of radioactive disintegrations.* On this subject, we will repeat almost verbatim what has just been said concerning the *Brehmstrahlung*. Given a process of disintegration which transforms a parent nucleus into a daughter nucleus and one or two light elements (electron, positron, neutrino, neutron, photon, alpha particle), *the reciprocal process of synthesis exists with the same quantum probability*. If, in fact, the radioactive processes are always *disintegrations*, and never *syntheses*, it is essentially by virtue of the macroscopic law according to which the probability of the system daughter nucleus + 1 or 2 light elements occurring before the system corresponding parent nucleus is absolutely negligible: the population of parent and daughter nuclei, and that of the one or more light constituents, is not a population in statistical equilibrium, for light constituents are continuously escaping from the system.

It has thus been shown exactly why it must be said, however paradoxical this may seem, that *the irreversibility of radioactive transformations is a macroscopic phenomenon.*

In short, the trajectories of radioactive nuclei are represented

---

4 In all of the preceding it is clear that we do not adhere to the pre-quantum theory of the irreversibility of radiation proposed by Wheeler and Feynman [16, 5]. Macroscopically, there is a radical dissymmetry between the future and the past in the phenomenon of the exchange of energy between an electromagnetic system *(charges + waves)* and another system; we have explained this in the text, and it is on this point, we think, that Wheeler's and Feynman's theory is physically inexact.

in space-time as canals which preserve residues of the exceptional fluctuation from which the universe recedes and carry them into the present epoch as the universe becomes more uniform.

9. *The irreversibility of the quantum measure analyzed by von Neumann* [14]. This appears when one studies an ensemble of systems depending on the same Hamiltonian H (t), and described by orthogonal wave functions $\psi_k(t)$, respectively affected by the weighting factor ω_k; it is enough here to recall that the measurement made at instant t on all the systems of the ensemble tends to equalize the various π_k.

To actually show that the irreversibility of quantum measurements is not inherent in the elementary phenomenon but is imposed by the macroscopic character of the measuring apparatus and the observer, we imagine that a series of measurements M_p of the ensemble is carried out, a series ordered in time in the following unusual way: the result of each measurement is recorded in turn, but in order to examine them it is necessary to wait until the n measurements $M_1, M_2, \ldots M_n$ are completed. If the n results are examined in the natural order $1, 2, \ldots n$, von Neumann's theory applies in the usual manner to the predictable retarded waves created by $1, 2, \ldots n$; by contrast, if these results are examined in the reverse order $n, n\text{-}1, \ldots 1$, von Neumann's theory will likewise be applied to the postdictable advanced waves created by n, $n\text{-}1, \ldots 1$, so that no objective irreversibility will have appeared.

But the type of experiment just described is entirely artificial, and its use would constitute a waste of information. In fact, each measure M_p depends on the result of the preceding measurement $M_{p\text{-}1}$; together they constitute an example of experimental reasoning in Claude Bernard's sense. We will now see how the logical sequence of the terms of this experimental reasoning entails their temporal ordering because of the involvement of the macroscopic character of the apparatus and of the observer.

Let $T_{p\text{-}1}$ be the mean instant of the measurement $M_{p\text{-}1}$, and $t_{p\text{-}1}$ be the instant in which the observer is aware of it. $T_{p\text{-}1} < t_{p\text{-}1}$ by virtue of the law of retarded actions: *the observer sees in the past.* Now let t_p be the mean instant in which the observer obtains the

97

measurement M_p: $t_{p-1} < t_p$ by virtue of the law of psychological time: *the observer's mind necessarily explores the temporal dimension of the universe in the direction of retarded actions*. Finally, let T_p be the mean instant in which the measurement M_p is taken: $t_p < T_p$ by virtue of the law of retarded actions: *the observer acts in the future*. Finally

$$T_{p-1} < t_{p-1} < t_p < T_p, \qquad \text{Q.E.D.}$$

To sum up, if there is in fact a total disparity between the well-known predictable divergent wave and the postdictable convergent wave which can be introduced symmetrically, this disparity is essentially a macroscopic phenomenon. The flow of their psychological time impels observers in the direction in which the predictable wave is propagated, and this is what permits them to find the wave through one measurement, to lose it during the projection of a new measurement whose result is only probable, and to rediscover it again through the carrying out of this measurement, a bit like a cat playing with a mouse which is running in and out of mouseholes. But the same sort of discontinuous study of the postdictable wave is forbidden by the law of psychological time, which does not permit experimental reasoning in the inverse direction of time; it is for this reason that, in complete opposition to the concrete character of the predicted wave, the postdicted wave is only a vain abstraction, hardly valid for the experiment which has been made, only a phantom which cannot be resuscitated.

BIOLOGICAL AND PSYCHOLOGICAL CONSIDERATIONS

10. *Logical succession and temporal succession in abstract reasoning*. It can easily be demonstrated that in abstract reasoning the logical sequence is ordered in the same way as the temporal sequence. If one attempts to reverse the temporal order of the terms in an actual case of reasoning (and not in a semblance of reasoning created by memory), it is no longer the proposition itself

which is being dealt with, but one of its reciprocals. Let it be noted in passing that the precautions we must take in formulating different reciprocals provide a timely reminder that the system under consideration is part of a much vaster system, and that the way in which the part is included in the whole must be taken into account.

Now, when I reason, it is difficult to resist the impression that, according to certain rules accepted in advance, I set up certain thought-experiments whose results I must then establish. Moreover, the cerebral work is accompanied physiologically by the usual symptoms of the dissipation of energy.

We do not have to take sides here for or against the thesis of a complete psycho-physiological parallelism; it is sufficient to point out that almost all authors accept a minimum of psycho-physiological parallelism, and it is hard to see how it could be otherwise once the brain is recognized to be a material condition of thought.

The preceding remarks, which point out a certain similarity between theoretical reasoning on the one hand and experimental reasoning and its interpretation in terms of quantum physics (§ 9) on the other, are consistent with the cautious form of parallelism. They suggest that the efforts of the brain at work might well have a real analogy with quantum measurement, that is to say, might consist in the manipulation of microscopic entities by a macroscopic apparatus. It is therefore the macroscopic character of the whole apparatus of the brain which imposes on logical reasoning the condition of revealing itself only in the progressive course of time.

11. *Retarded actions and memory*. If I am shown a target pierced with a hole I conclude that it is not in its original unmarked condition and that a bullet has penetrated it; by no means do I come to the conclusion that a projectile is going to come through the hole and make the target intact again. This is an application of the principle of retarded actions to the very brief interaction of two systems: the target and the bullet.

In conscious life, the psychological trace of past events is well known, and is termed memory; the absence of any psychological trace of future events is also well known, and is termed ignorance of the future.

These remarks, like those of section 10 above, are made within the framework of a psycho-physiological hypothesis which, if not complete, is then at least partial. It does not seem absurd to imagine that if thought has a physiological concommitant in the brain, then memories are related to the material effects which sensations cause the brain to undergo.

12. *Negative entropy* [1] *and biology.* On earth, a great many of the interactions producing irreversible physical evolutions are due to life. The physicist opens the tap separating two different gases. The duck on a pond maintains a divergent wake.

This negative entropy, in the words of Léon Brillouin [1], is not created by life, for life sustains itself through natural negative entropies. For its own sustenance, animal life disrupts the metastable equilibrium of the chemical compounds prepared by plant life. And plants store the solar energy which otherwise would be dissipated. Like radioactivity, life is one of the canal-like systems in which the original heterogeneity of the world is conveyed through time until an instant in which it belatedly shatters.

We have just seen life destroy or create metastable equilibriums in the same way that a hydraulic engineer drains a mountain lake or dams a torrent. Indeed, an entire network of distribution of negative entropy is represented by a living organism, and also by the evolutionary line which has produced it. How could this extremely complex network, whose very existence represents a negative entropy, have been created at the expense of the natural tendency toward dissipation of energy? Biology replies that millennia have been necessary and thus suggests a comparison with human industry, whose power is augmented by its own accomplishments. But here the comparison with radioactivity ceases to be valid: what is the source of the tendency of vital negative entropy to persevere in being and to renew its forms?

In his highly interesting study of Maxwell's demon and of the new definition of entropy permitted by cybernetics, Brillouin demonstrates 1) that Maxwell's demon cannot function in a gas in thermodynamic equilibrium because the radiation being that of thermal equilibrium, the molecules are invisible and 2) that if Maxwell's demon wishes to see the molecules, he must possess a luminous source at a temperature higher than its surroundings and equivalent to a reserve of negative entropy; the information which he draws from the functioning of this source permits him to diminish the entropy of the gas, from which follows the comprehensive schema:

> Negative entropy → information → negative entropy

But Brillouin demonstrates that the final negative entropy is always less than the initial; it is therefore quite possible for the demon (or a robot constructed *ad hoc*) to diminish the entropy of the gas, but at the cost of a still greater increase in the entropy of the system source + demon + gas. Brillouin's study therefore makes the remarks at the beginning of section 12 quantitatively precise.[5]

What is essential in the activity of Maxwell's demon (or the robot replacing it) is the absorption in the aperture of rapid molecules coming from the left and slow molecules coming from the right. Expressed in terms of postdiction (§ 6), this action implies the notion of convergent or advanced waves; but, objectively and macroscopically speaking, these waves do not exist, for the demon is obliged to wait until a molecule of the desired kind presents itself. He need not wait at all, however, in order to light his torch. This phantom existence of advanced waves at the macroscopic level must be the principal reason for the slowness of biological evolution; by contrast, once reserves of potential energy have been amassed, nothing prevents their rapid utilization.

Is it or is it not possible to suppose that the demon has the initiative in the maneuvers he executes? The affirmative response is implied by the spontaneous conviction of all men that they have

[5] The present study was almost complete when we first saw Brillouin's papers.

the power to act; indeed, almost all mathematicians and physicists share this conviction, as can be seen by the way they approach a problem: the specialist in theoretical mechanics chooses his initial conditions; the scientist dealing with thermodynamics opens a tap. The radical negative response is contained in Spinoza's celebrated fable of the weathervane. As physicists, we need not take sides; it suffices to describe from without the behavior of a living organism or that of an active man as a persistent tendency to produce exceptional configurations. Whether what our consciousness terms intention or will is a cause or a consequence of this persistence of the improbable is a question which concerns philosophy; nevertheless we wish to make a few modest and hypothetical remarks on this point.

13. *Practical action compared to an argument.* Suppose one is to study a mathematical treatise. The only way to do this is to study the work step by step from the first to the last page. When one is studying the nth proposition it is necessary to keep in mind the virtual presence of everything which has preceded it; otherwise one would understand nothing. It is also necessary to be able to recall explicitly any of the definitions or propositions already encountered. The rest of the work, though already in existence, is, for the student, nothing but a blank page. And, although the work is already written and printed, the understanding of the nth proposition represents an arduous effort: the will of the reader is as painfully strained as that of the plowman who opens a furrow.

Let us try to imagine what the temporally symmetrical operation would be. Initially the reader knows the entire content of the work. He opens it at the last page and works backwards toward the first, erasing step by step the knowledge of the theory which he possessed. The very absurdity of such an idea obliges us to lay down the principle that *the law of rationally acquired knowledge is essentially a law of increase.* This categorical decree bears a strong resemblance to those which we have clarified, in sections 2 and 3, on the basis of phenomenological thermodynamics and of statistical mechanics.

This being the case, may we attempt to reverse the order of

terms in our consideration of section 10, and to deduce temporal succession from logical succession, rather than the contrary? The description just given of the mastery of an already completed mathematical theory presents incontestable analogies with the awareness that we have of our own vital life, since events, once they have taken place, fill the four-dimensional framework of Minkowski space: conscious action, as described by Bergson, with its attention to life in the present moment, could be compared to the rational study of a book of mathematics, with its effort to logically comprehend the proposition being studied at the moment. It is necessary to remember, however, that the quantum tie between the future and the past is no longer deterministic but probabilistic; the logic according to whose rules the evolution of things is sketched in Minkowski space is certainly not Aristotelian logic, but a probabilistic logic, certain of whose characteristics are already precisely specified [14]. From this perspective, what we subjectively term efficacious volition is certainly bound to the persistence of exceptional fluctuations affecting the physical systems which we term organisms and their surroundings, including both the appearance of these fluctuations and their destruction under the pressure of the environment. We would not agree with critics who might assert that this hypothesis (formulated in extremely vague terms) is the negation of efficacious action, for it seems certain to us that the fact that the problem of voluntary action is seen either from the objective point of view of physics or from the subjective viewpoint of psychology implies the very framework in which the reply will be given. We think that there must be no contradiction between these two points of view, but rather complementarity in Niels Bohr's sense. One thing is certain in any case: the most original intention and the most heroic volition have roots in the past whose force and continued endurance escape spontaneous awareness.

Do they also have connections with the future which consciousness is completely unaware of? Certain authors [11] have produced curious examples seeming to show that unconscious psychology can explore the course of events succeeding those which explicit consciousness has attained, and can do so in the form of clearly distinguished details, though these details are generally (and even, we will understand in a moment, necessarily) symbolic. In the light of our preceding comparison, this operation resembles that of the reader who leafs through a mathematical treatise beyond the point that he has actually studied. Although in doing so he can acquire glimmerings, perhaps revelatory, of the content of the demonstrations which will follow, he cannot have a clear view of all their details, or integrate them exactly into their context. In terms of our example, the difference between unconscious and conscious thought resembles that which exists between the casual reading of a text and its methodical study; similarly the facts of premonition, reported by certain authors, inevitably take an enigmatic form preceding the actual events, which are then clearly recognizable once their symbolic traits are understood. This suggests that such facts do not constitute an absurdity which science or philosophy ought to discount a priori; but, naturally, we take no sides in a matter which is so delicate, and which is not within our province.

NOTES—

[1] Brillouin, Léon, *Journal of Applied Physics*, XXII, 1951, pp. 334–37 and pp. 338–43.
[2] Costa de Beauregard, O., and d'Espagnat, B., *Revue des questions scientifiques*, 1947, pp. 351–70 and pp. 527–48.
[3] Costa de Beauregard, O., *Comptes rendus*, CCXXX, 1950, p. 1637 and p. 2073—*Actes du congrès de physique théorique*, Paris, 1950.
[4] Costa de Beauregard, O., *Revue scientifique*, no. 3305, 1950, pp. 34–40.
[5] Feynman, R. P., *Physical Review*, LXXVI, 1949, pp. 724–59 and 769–89.
[6] Fock, V., *C.R. Acad. Sci. URSS* (Doklady), LX, 1948, pp. 1157–59.
[7] Heisenberg, W., *Les principes physiques de la théorie des Quanta* (Paris, 1932). (*The Physical Principles of Quantum Theory* [New York: Dover, 1950].)

[8] Loeve, M., *Revue scientifique.*
[9] Poincaré, H., *Calcul des Probabilités* (Paris, 1896), 129–30.
[10] Poincaré, H., *Science et méthode* (Paris, 1908), 64–94.
[11] Richet, Ch., *L'avenir et la prémonition* (Paris, 1927).
[12] Riesz, F., *Comm. Math. Helv.*, XVII, 1944–45, p. 221.
[13] Stueckelberg, E. C. G., *Helv. Phys. Acta.*, XIV, 1941, pp. 588–94 and XV, 1942, pp. 25–37.
[14] Von Neumann, J., *Mathematische Grundlagen der Quantenmechanik* (Berlin, 1932). (*Mathematical Foundations of Quantum Mechanics* [Princeton, 1955].)
[15] Watanbé, S., *Revue de métaphysique et de morale*, 1951, pp. 128–42.
[16] Wheeler, J. A., and Feynman, R. P., *Reviews of Modern Physics*, XVII, 1945, p. 157 and XXI, 1949, p. 425.

ROBERT BLANCHÉ

The Psychology of Duration and the Physics of Fields

Remarks by the Editor. Professor Robert Blanché, viewing Bergson's philosophy from the vantage point of nearly fifty years of scientific advance, argues that the sharp dualisms characteristic of Bergsonism are no longer tenable and must be replaced with a new awareness of "complementarity." Bergson above all attempted to establish the continuity of the inner life, which he believed to have been deformed by illegitimate "atomistic" analyses. But in order to stress the continuity of psychological experience, he was forced to make an abrupt distinction between consciousness, whose successive elements are said to "interpenetrate," and the world in space, whose units are described as mutually distinct, atomic. Bergsonism is thus correctly viewed as opposing a psychology of continuity to a physics of discontinuity—the "stream of experience" against nineteenth-century Newtonian physics.

Twentieth-century physics, however, rejects the simple Newtonian picture of discrete mass particles existing in an empty

105

space. Instead, physicists today must attempt to view physical reality in terms of complementary concepts (for example, "wave" and "particle") and therefore as possessing both the continuity of the field and the discontinuous properties of the particle. The psychologist ought to learn from the physicist how to associate seemingly opposed concepts; he would thus discover evidences of both continuity and discontinuity in the life of consciousness. Bergson's "intuition" of psychological continuity, Blanché argues, must be balanced by an equally valid "intuition of the instant."

Once it is seen that discontinuity and continuity are equally real aspects of mental life, both Bergson's sharp distinction between consciousness and the material world in space, as well as the barriers established between the sciences of psychology and physics, are overcome. Bergson's "Heraclitean psychology," though possessed of invaluable insights, thus takes its place in a newer and broader psychology. At the same time, all possibility of reformulating Bergsonism so as to bring it in line with more recent discoveries is lost. Bergson's philosophy constitutes, Professor Blanché concludes, an "implicit axiomatics," no part of which can be transformed without disfiguring the rest. Thus, one must think either as a Bergsonian or as a psychologist. *The following essay by Professor Blanché was originally published in the* JOURNAL DE PSYCHOLOGIE NORMALE ET PATHOLOGIQUE, *XLIV (July-September, 1951). It appears here in translation with the permission of the author and the* JOURNAL DE PSYCHOLOGIE NORMALE ET PATHOLOGIQUE.

THE HERACLITEAN PSYCHOLOGY which flourished toward the end of the nineteenth century instituted not only a psychology of flux but a psychology of continuity and a psychology of duration as well. These three ideas are in fact so intimately bound up with each other in this newer psychology that it is difficult to separate them. Perhaps the most striking trait is an anxiety to reestablish the continuity of the inner life, which had been shattered through an "atomistic" analysis. This continuity is not exclusively that of duration or flux, since it will be observed already, in cross-section, in the instantaneous complexity of consciousness. However, a flux certainly does provide its best illustration. Or, more precisely, this continuity is that of the temporal flux itself. A nameless flux, like that observed in the current of a river, is, in its undivided continuity, no more than an image of true becoming, an image that is a translation into the visual universe. Of its two components, spatiality and temporality, it is from the second that flux derives its continuity; space appears on the contrary to be a principle of juxtaposition, or reciprocal externality, hence of fragmentation. Because a flux, or more generally, any movement whatever, participates at once in both time and space, it lends itself to being considered in two ways, either as a unified totality without real parts or as a succession of discrete positions. Remove the spatial element from the idea of flux and only the pure flow of time will remain in which nothing suggests cutting-up [*découpage*]. The unfolding of a melodic line, rather than the flow of a river, will be the symbol, if one is absolutely necessary, which will most adequately express the *legato* of our inner life. True duration, whose reality we experience in ourselves, is as much *continuity* as *becoming*.

Since these two notions are indissolubly joined, the monopoly which duration possesses over the second assures it a monopoly over the first. In order that the temporal flow should appear to us in the form of a becoming, in order that it should offer us something other than an infinitesimal unique instant, forever renewed and ceaselessly abolished, the present must necessarily already have a certain breadth in which the past is prolonged and the future prefigured. But this lack of ruptures between parts, this anteriority of the whole over the elements which can then arbitrarily be carved out of it, is this not the very essence of continuity? Where this intimate solidarity through interpenetration is lacking, therefore, all interrelation and all becoming will be lacking also. This is precisely the case with things juxtaposed in space. Space is not only external with respect to us, it is exteriority itself, *partes extra partes*. This is why, if it is true that our fabricating intelligence handles only the immobile and the discontinuous easily, there is no reason to be surprised at its feeling so much at ease in the study of the physical world. In constructing its object with halts and points, our intelligence simply proceeds in the direction in which matter has already oriented itself. For matter, ballasted with geometry, tends toward spatiality, *i.e.*, initially toward an existence spread out all at once in its entirety; but space, in turn, in its close connection with numerical multiplicity, tends toward atomicity. Hence to a dynamistic, continuistic theory of duration there corresponds, as a counterpart, a theory of space which presents space not only as a principle of simultaneity but also and inseparably as a principle of fragmentation.[1]

A vast, bipolar system is thus organized in which a multitude of oppositions comes to converge. By maintaining the opposition of duration and extension in constant coincidence with that of consciousness and things, in this system the ancient dualism of spirit and matter, of psychology and physics, is fully reinstated—a dualism which classical psychology was content to transport from the terrain of substances to that of phenomena. In this dualism, ancient as well as psychological, space alone was affected: external things were agreed to endure just as much as consciousness. And the latter, in truth, though it was asserted to be unextended, was always conceived with the aid of spatial representations. Pascal, agreeing in this with the Cartesians, reproached Aristotle's followers for speaking spiritually of corporeal things and corporeally of spiritual. Now, this reproach could with justice be turned against Descartes' followers. Did not Descartes invite this inversion, in fact, by making space continuous and time discontinuous? Henceforth the attempt will be made not only not to think of spiritual things in terms of space but also not to think of corporeal things in terms of duration. "Outside of us, reciprocal exteriority without succession; within us, succession without reciprocal ex-

---

[1] There is indeed in Chapter IV of *Matter and Memory* an analysis which opposes the continuity of concrete extension to the net of spatial threads which science sustains there. But the analogy thus outlined between space and time appears, in the whole of Bergson's work, only as a parenthesis. *Time and Free Will* and *Creative Evolution*, notably, emphasize their dissymmetry.

teriority" (TFW 108; *Essai* 175). Thus, the old ontological dualism is exasperated to the point of becoming one of space and duration: that is, to be sure, that of thing and progress, but also that of juxtaposition and fusion, of the punctual viewpoint and the global point of view. The psychology of continuity is thus affirmed as a counterpart of a physics of discontinuity in which, after motion is geometrized, space is in turn arithmetized.

Now, at the end of the nineteenth century such a physics represents no more than half of the existing physics. If the corpuscular conception of matter is at the point of asserting itself, on the other hand it has not renounced the totalitarian pretensions of the older mechanism: alongside of matter, Augustin Fresnel's light waves and then Maxwell's electromagnetic waves have introduced a new sort of physical reality, one which can no longer be reduced to a juxtaposition of well-localized and mutually exclusive *particles*, but which is characterized to the contrary by the continuity of *fields*, each of which is capable of filling all of space and of coexisting there in superposition with others. And soon a new step will be taken: the two domains of physics, initially separate, will be seen to interpenetrate quite intimately, the undulatory representation imposing itself on the study of material corpuscles just as, a short while previously, the corpuscular representation imposed itself on the study of light waves. The duality of continuity and discontinuity, therefore, ceases to coincide with the duality of psychology and physics, since it divides physics into two great provinces. Moreover, in each of these provinces this duality will be rediscovered as an entirely essential characteristic: the opposition of field and particle will no longer be that of two parts of physics, it will be that of two points of view equally indispensable to the consideration of physical reality.

Physical reality alone? The reflection aroused by this paradoxical conjunction of opposed concepts, which both refer to and exclude each other, leads us to recognize in such a mode of thought not an artificial and exceptional process, to which the physicist is reduced only when constrained and forced, but, on the contrary, a particularly revealing case of a most ordinary and

normal procedure of our mind which—to utilize Bohr's terminology—"idealizes" the notions it handles in order to purify them,
but then finds itself obliged to correct the insufficiency of concepts thus obtained by associating each with a "complementary"
concept. This is a procedure which Bergsonian philosophy had
already perfectly discerned and described. "Concepts . . . ordinarily go in couples and represent two contraries. There is hardly
any concrete reality which cannot be observed from two opposing
standpoints, which cannot consequently be subsumed under two
antagonistic concepts. Hence, a thesis and an antithesis which we
endeavor in vain to reconcile logically" (CM 234; PM 224). But
where discursive intelligence fails, intuition succeeds by dissipat-
ing artificial antinomies. Thus intuition surmounts, for example,
and precisely as regards duration, the seeming alternative of the
one and the many. But where the couple continuity-discontinuity
is concerned, this function no longer succeeds, and the duality is
not overcome. The fundamental intuition of Bergsonism on the
contrary is one in which concepts like duration, life, interiority,
continuity, interpenetration, progress, creation, memory, and
liberty come to coalesce, or more precisely, in which these concepts arise through successive differentiations and solidifications.
And this group of concepts will assume its full significance only
through its relation to a group of antithetical concepts. In order
to be communicated and initially, perhaps, simply in order to be
developed, the philosopher's intuition is required also to be dispersed into concepts. As soon as he speaks of continuity he leaves
the door half-open to an entire system of notions, associated or
opposed, and in the end his entire dualism must pass through this
door.

Nevertheless, when the system of ideas, in which a doctrine is
enclosed and in respect to which it is defined, is modified, the doctrine must itself be affected. One is pleased to note in Bergson's
work and particularly in *Time and Free Will*, passages concerning
time which seem to announce some views of contemporary
physics.[2] It will be no less legitimate to ask whether, inversely, the

---

[2] L. de Broglie, "The Concepts of Contemporary Physics and Bergson's Ideas

actual development of physical concepts does not invite us to revise, on this point, certain theses of *Time and Free Will*. Like the physicist, the psychologist will perhaps be compelled, if he does not wish to be condemned to a one-sided view of his object, to accustom himself to handling the pair continuous-discontinuous instead of attempting systematically to eliminate one of its terms. In any case, recognition of the continuity of duration will no longer be a reason to consider the instant an artificial view of the understanding, due to the intrusion of spatial representations. Just as inversely, spatial divisions will not exclude the continuity of extension.

A first revision would be suggested by the abandoning of a unique, unitary mechanistic physics. Today this is not difficult to imagine: *Gestalt* psychology is charged with this task. Already in the era when *Time and Free Will* expounded its new concept of duration, Baron Christian von Ehrenfels analyzed temporal forms and observed that a melody, a movement, or even any change whatever, possesses a psychological reality independent of the sensory elements which sustain it. Since then the Berlin school, as is widely known, has made systematic use of this notion of *Gestalt*. On the one hand it is applied in the description of all contents of consciousness generally; on the other it is employed beyond the domain of consciousness itself: it is precisely in field physics that such examples can be found. One will join forces here with Bergson in order to drive from psychology, and even from biology, explanations and descriptions "of a mechanistic kind." But precisely because such explanations and descriptions no longer exhaust the possibilities of physics, their exclusion ceases to forbid the possibility of any analogy between physical and psychological phenomena. Just as some decades ago physicists taxed their ingenuity in imagining mechanical models for electromagnetic phenomena, so now electromagnetic models of psychological phenomena are being forged. Spatial representation is reintroduced into the description of consciousness and, with it,

on Time and Motion," *Revue de métaphysique et de morale*, October, 1941 [translated above (*ed.*)].

a principle of distinction. A structure supposes nice differentiations. And if, in the interior of such a form, the forces of cohesion impede the dispersion of the parts from one form to the
other, on the contrary, the change takes place abruptly. Nature
makes jumps. Like the spatial field, the temporal field is structured
and hence subject to such ruptures. The actual indivisibility of a
verse, of a dance step, to which Bergson had already drawn attention, has precisely as its result their isolation in some way from
those to which they are nonetheless related. Caesuras cut up duration. However, discontinuity will not be established again save
within ensembles and does not penetrate to their interiors in order
to dissociate them into elementary individuals: like living beings,
the verse, the dance step, conserve their unity. Still more perhaps
than for Bergsonian philosophy, it is essential to the theory of
form to press the contrast between *organization*, in which the
whole establishes the existence of the parts, and *fabrication*, the
simple assemblage of pre-existing pieces. The sole difference
which here separates the two doctrines is that the dividing line is
displaced: instead of marking the limits of physics, it traverses
physics itself. But wherever there is organized form, *Gestalt*, the
interpretations of point-notions which are brought in must be
absolutely rejected. In this respect therefore, the psychology of
form does no more than confirm the previously employed con-
demnation of all species of mental atomism.

A judgment of perhaps excessive severity. Since the domain of
forms, as is correctly stressed, extends beyond psychology and
biology and includes field physics, one cannot fail to take interest
in what occurs in the latter. The analogies which are drawn from
one science into another are often fruitful, but the speed, we say
rather the slowness, of the propagation of ideas explains the
anachronisms which occur in the establishing of correspondences.
Just as Bergson's psychology of continuity rested on a unitary
mechanistic physics which was then already out of date, so, a
quarter of a century later, the choice between point-element and
field is discussed by *Gestalt* theorists at the very moment when
physicists, from whom their inspiration was initially drawn, begin

to surmount this alternative. The mutual penetration of wave and particle physics forces the scientist everywhere to associate the concepts of continuity and discontinuity and suggests to the philosopher that such an association of complementary concepts actually represents a normal mode of thought and perhaps makes it possible to remove the major obstacle which recently opposed the introduction of "atomistic intuitions" into psychology. Henceforth, in fact, such intuitions cease to form, with the representation of continuity, a true alternative which involves the choice of one disjunct and the rejection of the other. Einstein's photon no more obliges us to sacrifice the discoveries of Fresnel and Maxwell in order to restore the corpuscles of Newton, than the rediscovery, in psychology, of the atomistic point of view necessarily signifies either a return to the doctrine of mental elements and mental chemistry or the renunciation of the precious descriptions owed to the psychology of flux and the psychology of totalities. The example of physics therefore will doubtless furnish an argument which will have considerable weight when our judgment of psychological atomism comes in for revision.

One ought not, it is true, to enter into this terrain save with greatest prudence. The notion of complementarity, which is was necessary for physics to accept at a certain stage of its development, remains suspect. Many good minds consider it to be a simple makeshift: far from resting there, thought only pauses awaiting something better; it halts there a moment to catch its breath, as at a stair from which it will step by a dialectical overcoming. And the probabilistic interpretation of the wave, today accepted by all, or nearly all, physicists, will perhaps provide the means for this overcoming. We endeavor to escape, for our own part, that fatality of time-lag to which in turn Bergson's psychology and the psychology of form seem to testify, and not to bind present-day psychology too closely to a physics which may already be outmoded. In the last analysis, however, whether or not the union of wave and particle is comprehensible, or fails to make clear the way in which these terms are mutually articulated, one thing appears in any case to have been established: in all areas of physics

113

it is necessary to have recourse to two systems of representations and concepts, organized around the two categories of continuity and discontinuity. It is thus proved that the pertinence of the ideas pertaining to one of these systems does not exclude the legitimacy of the antithetical system. This is a lesson which the psychologist has no right to neglect.

A simple analogy [furnished by the wave-particle duality], on the other hand, can provide no more than a suggestion. We will therefore not go so far as to rehabilitate the concept of a "nervous shock" or, more generally, to imagine a *psychon*. But, in the absence of particles of consciousness, is it not at least possible to speak of particles of duration? It is only within a conception in which duration adheres so closely to its content that the two are inseparable, and in which, furthermore, this content is one with the psychological life, that these two questions are considered to be one. To identify duration with the life of consciousness is to make it necessary to describe in the former the kinds of relationships which are conceived to have been recognized in the latter. Then it will be necessary to say that all divisions of duration are caused by the contamination of the idea of space, that the instant, in particular, is only an artificial view of becoming, and finally that physical time, which neither endures nor extends, has no reality save in the mind, as a mongrel concept. But if the apparent continuity of the inner life and the impossibility of revealing constituent elements within it naturally invite those who describe it to accentuate one of the aspects of the temporal medium in which it unfolds, this justifies neither limiting duration to consciousness nor displacing the discontinuous or, more precisely, the point-like [*ponctuel*] aspect of time, on the assumption that this aspect of time is entirely alien to becoming, into space. Instant and duration are two concepts equally necessary to the conceptualizing of time —though, depending on the case, they may be unequally important. Though each excludes the other, each nonetheless requires the other, for neither is capable by itself of describing the flux of phenomena.[3] Men have not attended, in order to suspect this, to

[3] Cf. Octave Hamelin, *Essay on the Chief Elements of Representation* (Paris: Presses Universitaires de France, 1907), Chaps. I and III. René le Senne, in "The

the latest speculations of physics. The manner in which they use their verb forms, whether of *time* or *aspect*, will suffice to show this. The philosophy of duration itself is very near to realizing this necessity. It underlines the originality and irreducibility of duration: you will never attain this, we are correctly told, by adding instants to instants. But cannot this argument, with justice, be reversed? If you divide duration, you will end only with portions of duration, not instants. And this is precisely why, when it is posited that duration in itself exhausts the reality of becoming, space must be utilized in order to engender the instant: since it cannot be furnished by time, it can only be provided by the mathematical point. As if the spatial medium possessed the exclusivity of discontinuity and atomicity!

This is in fact one of the essential theses of *Time and Free Will*, where it is introduced as the necessary counterpart of the reduction of real time to duration. It is also one of the most paradoxical of these theses. It had been customary to see in space and time, as well as in the motion which results from their composition, the very models of continuity: discontinuity is produced there only by our minds when it applies the concept of number, the archetype of discrete quantity. Now, on the contrary, the spatial medium is invoked as the indispensable background before which numerical multiplicity is deployed. On one side, therefore, space and number; on the other, time attracting movement. From space one tends to eliminate extension to consider only the point; or, if one prefers, one tends to reduce extension to a simple collection of points. Yet the same arguments invoked in favor of duration could easily be transposed in favor of extension. Without an elementary memory which binds two instants, there will never be more than one of them; hence no before and no after, no succession, no time (DS 48; DSf 61). Similarly, without an ele-

---

Permanent and the Contemporary Mission of the Philosopher," *Les Études philosophiques*, January-March, 1948, p. 4, writes: *"Real time . . . is the mixture of the continuity of duration and the discontinuity of succession.* The multiplicity becomes successive only on the condition of having duration as its thread [*trame*]; . . . and, by contrast, duration becomes time only by being articulated in succession. . . . Time must be wave and particle at once."

mentary perceptual act which relates two points, there will never be more than one point; hence no right and no left, no juxtaposition, no space. If a consciousness is necessary to effect the synthesis of temporal instants, why should it be less necessary to effect the synthesis of spatial positions? Certainly, several instants cannot exist at the same moment, and this is why a principle of relationship is required to constitute a duration. But neither can several points exist at the same place, and thus is not *another* principle or relationship necessary in order to constitute extension? Inversely, to the juxtaposition of diverse points at the same time, through which a spatial whole is constituted, corresponds the succession of diverse instants at the same place, through which a temporal whole is created. And if one hesitates before the second formula, insisting that a point of time does not merely occupy a spot but fills space, it will not even be necessary to remark that the physicist today refuses to attach any meaning to the phrase "an instant as large as the world"; it will be enough to note, while remaining on the same ground, that the first formula calls for a similar correction, since a spatial point does not merely occupy an instant but fills the entire time. These are simply diverse ways of expressing the differences between time and space. The properties of space and time actually appear in many respects to be symmetrical, if all the required permutations are made in passing from one to the other: and the argument is only half completed when the impossibility of different times existing *at the same time* is raised, and when advantage is drawn in favor of duration, to which no analogous property corresponds in the nature of space. Time therefore no longer excludes the instant, while space no longer excludes extension, in the sense of a dynamic continuity of interdependent parts. Space is not only that which separates, it is also that which unites. Precisely like time it has, to re-employ Whitehead's terms, a *prehensive* character no less real than its *separative* character. In a spatial field, a modification at one point immediately influences the whole, in which a global redistribution is provoked, through an almost instantaneous influence which excites each element as from within in virtue of its very intimate dependence on all others. Naturally, this spatial dynamism retains a spatial character. The solidarity of the parts of extensity is of another character than that of the parts of duration: it is not a matter of a *progress*, in opposition to the static immobility of the instant, but of an *interaction* opposed to the independence of individuals dispersed in space. But though different from the irreversible flux of causality, the simultaneity of reciprocal action nonetheless represents another form of connection between phenomena. As Carnot's principle had done for the second, field physics confirms the importance of the third *analogy of experience*, in illustration of which Kant was able only to invoke the phenomenon of gravitation.

The ties which Bergson attempted to establish between duration and continuity, as between space and discontinuity, ought therefore to be undone. If the quality of continuity is recognized in our inner duration, this by no means authorizes us to conclude that our inner duration is perfectly continuous, without breaks or parts, and still less that this inner duration is the only one to be that way. Doubtless this last thesis, which comes to attribute to space a strongly granular structure, receives a degree of support from the new physics. For a physicist who has renounced viewing space as an empty, pre-existing framework in which physical objects come to be located and for which geometrical properties are to be treated like other physical properties from which they are inseparable, who has renounced, for the rest, defining physical dimensions other than by the measurements that can actually be made of them, the question of the atomicity of space reduced to that of knowing if the precision that we can apply to the measurement of lengths has a lower limit: a question to which quantum discontinuity enjoins him today to reply in the affirmative. But the classic thesis of the continuity of space is thereby completed and interpreted, not destroyed. If the appearance of continuity results from a mass effect [*effet de masse*], it is nonetheless a well-founded appearance, for the statistical consideration of vast ensembles is no less legitimate than that of isolated individuals. Waves, since they are measured, are as much a part of the physical

117

world as corpuscles—though not by the same right; the cloud has as much reality as the raindrop. And above all, the reasoning which holds for space holds also for time, which must similarly be composed of particles of duration. Symmetry, it is true, is not perfect, since classical time is retained as a parameter of evolution. It nonetheless remains true that by engendering space, or, more generally, the dimensions of a field, by discrete quantities, contemporary physics invites us to discover subjacent elementary entities wherever field continuity reigns. This new way of envisaging continuity cannot fail to re-echo in the problem of psychological duration. We do not imprudently extend the analogy. We do not forget that the introspective psychologist has not yet found a means to employ measurement or to safeguard his observations, and that he cannot change the scale of his experience. But we do not forget either that he does not use the same criteria as the physicist for determining his object and that the real is defined for him not as objectively measurable, but as intimately experienced. It will suffice, as soon as discontinuity and even temporal atomicity are encountered in a concrete experience, and the subject of this experience knows how to dispose us so that we may repeat the experience, for the psychologist to accept it in his descriptions of phenomena. It will be insisted, for example, that the history of a consciousness does not always unfold with this curved motion in which each moment prolongs the preceding, that it contains ruptures, beginnings of abrupt changes; all this doubtless prepared by the past, but in the way that an increasing pressure prepares the shattering of the glass: comes the decisive instant, the die is cast. As in a symphony, that favorite example of psychologists of continuity, where changes of tempo are not all accomplished by insensible degrees, where the movement sometimes brusquely stops or starts afresh, where it happens that a *presto* succeeds an *andante* without transition, as by a sudden fiat. The "intuition of the instant" [4] ought thus to be construed to be as authentic as the intuition of duration. Only—and it is here that

---

[4] Cf. Gaston Bachelard, *L'intuition de l'instant* (Paris: Stock, Delamain et Boutelleau, 1932).

118

the teachings of physics ought to be heard—this admission of the psychological reality of the one ought not to be interpreted as a denial of the psychological reality of the other. We do not have to choose between James and Roupnel, Bergson and Bachelard. We accept at once both the instant and the interval. We ought simply to learn how to associate the two representations if we wish to have a comprehensive view of the inner life. Is it not the case that the inner life, with its infinite complexity and its extraordinary plasticity, tolerates the most opposed manifestations, that it is *par excellence*, if there is one, the domain in which contradictions can be realized, and finally that of all scientists it is the psychologist who ought to be the most adept at substituting for the manipulation of the *or* the manipulation of the *and?* If there is something of a paradox here, it is that the psychologist should receive from the physicist, instead of giving to him, such a lesson of complementarity.

Bergson's philosophy forms such a harmoniously interrelated whole; it presents such a choice example of that intimate unity through mutual penetration which it makes the essence of continuity, of duration, and of the spiritual life, that it is all but impossible to detach one of its elements without disfiguring it. Attempt to isolate one of its theses and you make it grimace. This is why the reservations and the criticisms which can be formulated concerning it seem actually to testify to a lack of understanding. In building the immense system of polarization which constitutes its dualism, and in which the pair time-space comes to exist, Bergson ends finally by erecting a sort of implicit axiomatic, in which the meaning of each term is fixed by the relation which it sustains with the whole of the system. "Real duration" will thus be distinguished from the time of which it is one component; "perfect spatiality" will be distinguished from space as the limit toward which it tends; and the first will be decisively bound to, among others, the notions of interiority and continuity, the second to the notions of exteriority and mutual independence. Henceforth, Bergson's theses concerning space and time cease to be contestable, even when they verbally contradict affirmations which we take to

119

be true, since the words, on both sides, no longer signify the same things. It is indeed true that changes in the meanings of terms affect the propositions in which they are used. But it is true as well that what they state no longer concerns duration or spatiality, but only Bergson's idea of them. They are no longer anything more than partial expressions of a vast intuition in which two representations of the world are contrasted in an almost Manichean fashion: on the right hand the stoic vision of a full and harmonious cosmos animated like a great living organism in which everything conspires; on the left the afflicted spectacle of a blind mechanism in which, as in Epicurus' universe, highly independent elements mingle or disperse through chance encounters. If Bergson's theses are deformed by detaching them, in order to challenge them separately, from the totality of the philosophy of which they form a part, they are no less deformed when detached in order to be integrated one by one with an impersonal scientific point of view. The first rule of axiomatic thought is to break communications with the pre-axiomatic meaning of one's terms. When, therefore, one states the thesis of the continuity of inner duration, it is necessary to choose either to think as a Bergsonian or to think as a psychologist. Understood as a thesis of scientific psychology, Bergson's thesis no longer remains isolated and independent; it takes its place in another ensemble, one vaster than that from which it was initially taken. It should not be surprising that changes which take place at one point of this field, however distant, should have an effect on the field as a whole.

RELATIVITY

HENRI BERGSON, ALBERT EINSTEIN, AND HENRI PIÉRON

Remarks Concerning Relativity Theory

Remarks by the Editor. In 1905 Albert Einstein published his first paper on the special theory of relativity. This was followed, in 1908, by Hermann Minkowski's formulation of a "four dimensional space-time geometry" and, in 1914, by Einstein's general theory of relativity, which in 1919 received dramatic verification. Though originally associated with the names of Hendrik Lorentz, Henri Poincaré, and others who had helped to build its mathematical and physical foundations, relativity theory had come (by the time of the exchange between Bergson and Einstein [1922] translated here) to be identified almost exclusively with the work of Einstein.

Duration and Simultaneity (1922) is Bergson's attempt to confront the basic tenets of his philosophy with the philosophically significant conclusions of the theory of relativity. The result of this confrontation is a thoroughgoing criticism of the special theory of relativity, and, in particular, of the relativistic notion of multiple time-series. There is, Bergson holds, only one time-series in the universe—the qualitative temporal series which "living and conscious" beings share in common. The plurality of times presupposed by the special theory of relativity must be construed as illusion or, rather, as the "effects of perspective."

Bergson's seemingly destructive attack on relativity theory understandably has drawn bitter criticism. But it should not be concluded that because Bergson criticizes relativity he is attempting to force science back into the narrow framework of Newtonian physics. Einstein, he insists, has created a "new way of thinking" as well as a new physics; the new way of thinking appears to Bergson uniquely fruitful, and the new physics is indisputably an advance in precision and scope over its predecessor. Further, Bergson insists, relativity theory rests on a more complete and accurate awareness of change. For Newtonian physics all states of motion or rest must be understood in relation to a universal and static "reference system": absolute space, at absolute rest. But relativity theory abolishes this fiction of an overarching static framework. The principle of relativity asserts that no physical system is really any more "at rest" or "in motion" than any other: where there is motion there is, simply, relative displacement; where there is change, an entire physical situation is transformed, without there being any unmoving space in relation to which this change must be understood.

Not only, then, does Bergson view relativity theory as a theoretical and empirical advance over earlier physics: he sees it as coinciding at many points with his own philosophical preconceptions. The difficulty is, however, that certain of the concepts of relativity theory appear to Bergson to be "conventional"; that is, they are useful to the scientist though they do not depict real characteristics of physical nature. Among these are the concepts of multiple time-series and the relativity of simultaneity. But the task of the philosopher, according to Bergson, is precisely to discern what is conventional in science and what is not. This is the basic task undertaken in *Duration and Simultaneity*: to discover what is conventional and what is not, in the relativistic conception of time.

Bergson's explanation of the appearance of conventional elements in relativity theory is the same as his explanation of the appearance of conventional elements in scientific thought generally: that is, it is caused by the science's inability to give a completely adequate description of change, motion, and variability. In the case of relativity theory this basic limitation is caused, Bergson holds, through the introduction of privileged reference systems which are for purposes of mathematical expression *assumed to be at rest*. This artificial but useful introduction of static elements into relativity theory can be explained by reference to an example. Let us assume, Bergson suggests, two physical systems S and S' in motion relative to each other. The principle of relativity informs

124

us that neither of these systems is any more in motion or at rest than the other: we observe only their mutual displacement. But in order to assure the invariance of the equations of the special theory of relativity (the Lorentz transformation), the physicist must make a radical distinction between these two systems. One system is to be transformed into a *reference system;* it is then said to be at rest and to suffer no relativistic effects. The other system is said to be in motion; its time is thereby retarded, in accordance with Lorentz' equations. But the choice of one system as being *at rest,* though unavoidable, is not based on any characteristic of physical nature; and the static viewpoint thereby introduced must be understood as thoroughly artificial: a fiction, but a necessary fiction.

But, having introduced a "conventional" immobility into his calculations, the relativity physicist is then free to introduce it arbitrarily, at will. Again, let us assume systems S and S' moving with respect to each other. If system S is the earth, and system S' a rocket departing from the earth with a high uniform velocity, and if the earth is agreed to be "at rest" (that is, if it is decreed to be a reference system), then the rocket will undergo the well-known relativistic effects: its length will contract, its time will retard, its mass will increase. But it is equally possible to declare system S (the earth) in motion and system S' (the rocket) at rest. When this is done, the relativistic effects will be undergone by the earth, while the length, mass, and duration of the rocket will now be unchanged. Effects, however, which may be introduced and erased by sheer fiat, can not be interpreted as real effects; they are, rather, mere "effects of perspective."

Bergson's essential argument against accepting relativistic space-time effects at face value, however, rests on his belief that, when taken as descriptions of physical reality, they generate contradictory descriptions. Let us again assume our two systems, the earth and the rocket, in motion relative to each other. Let us assume, further, that a real, "living and conscious" physicist is placed in each system. What, Bergson asks, will then transpire? The physicist in the rocket will assert that his system is a reference system, and therefore "at rest": the earth's time will thus seem to him to be retarded. The physicist on the earth will also declare his own system to be a reference system and therefore "at rest": time will seem to him to be retarded aboard the rocket. But can we really believe that the system comprised by the rocket *at the same time* exhibits both the nonretarded time discovered by its occupant and the retarded time imputed to it by the physicist on the earth? Or, from the other point of view, is it possible to believe that the earth possesses not only the nonretarded time discovered by its occupant but, at the same time, the retarded time which it appears to have from the viewpoint of the physicist on the rocket?

Critics will be quick to object that the phrase "at the same time" begs the question at issue. They will further object that unless some acceptable meaning can be given to this phase, the supposed contradiction which Bergson believes he has discovered is not really a contradiction. Bergson's reply is that an unambiguous characterization of the phrase "at the same time" can be derived from the scientist's experience of duration. The physicist on the earth, in our example, *imputes* a retarded time to the rocket; but he *actually measures and experiences* a constant duration in his own reference system. The physicist on the rocket *imputes* a retarded time to the earth; but in his own reference system he *actually measures and experiences* a constant duration. But, all human consciousness being essentially alike and enduring at the same rate, we can legitimately state that all scientists in all frames of reference experience and measure the same time. Borrowing a metaphor from mathematics, we discover that experienced time is a constant in relation to which other aspects of reality are "variable." If Bergson's reasoning on this point is valid, then the contradiction which he believes can be derived from the relativistic retardation of time is quite real and quite serious: it is indeed impossible for the same system to have two different "times" at the "same time." But experience shows us, Bergson insists, that any given system really has only one time: the actually measured and experienced time discovered by the scientist inhabiting it.

In his discussion with Einstein, Bergson is at pains to develop

126

his criticism of relativity theory in terms of the concept of simultaneity. His argument requires three steps. First, Bergson points out that the concept of a universal time is derived by common sense from the extension of the "proper time" experienced in our immediate environment to increasingly distant surroundings. Second, he argues that our most basic concept of simultaneity is derived from our *experience* of two or more events occurring "at an instant": an experience which requires that our consciousness be both one and multiple. The concept of absolute simultaneity is derived, like the concept of a single, universal time, by extending this immediate experience to more and more distant events. Finally, Bergson shows that the "simultaneity" involved in relativity theory is based not on an immediate experience but on the regulation of clocks by means of optical signals. In systems moving uniformly with respect to each other, this type of "simultaneity" is discovered to be not absolute, but relative: two events which appear simultaneous within a moving system will appear successive to an observer viewing them from a system "at rest." This second kind of "simultaneity" is necessary in physics, and relativity theory has gained much by utilizing it. But, Bergson holds, it is dependent on our immediate experience of "absolute" simultaneity, without which we should never have been able to make or utilize clocks in the first place.

In replying to Bergson, Einstein distinguishes between the time studied by the psychologist and the time studied by the physicist. The concept of a universal time is indeed, Einstein agrees, derived from the psychological experience of simultaneity and is a first step toward objectivity. But our capacity to deal with the high propagational velocity of light reveals to us that the concept of simultaneity derived from ordinary perceptual experience leads to contradictions. In relativity theory we discard psychological time in order to attain to the objective time of objective events and thus overcome our originally subjective impressions. There is no "philosopher's time" which is both physical and psychological; there is only a psychological time which is different from the time of physics.

127

To Henri Héron's objection that the "psychological" experience of simultaneity can be in error, Bergson replies that imprecision provides no grounds for rejecting psychological considerations. The laboratory experiments through which Piéron
establishes the imprecision of our perception of simultaneity are
themselves dependent on "psychological observations of simultaneities." *The following interview of April 6, 1922, originally
published in the* BULLETIN DE LA SOCIÉTÉ FRANÇAISE DE PHILOS-
OPHIE *(July, 1922), appears here in translation with the permission of the Société Française de philosophie.*

HENRI BERGSON—I came here to listen. I had no intention of
taking up discussion. But I acquiesce to the friendly insistence of the *Société de Philosophie*.

And I begin by stating at which point I admire M. Einstein's
work, which seems to me to impose itself on the attention of philosophers as well as scientists. I see in this work not only a new
physics, but also, in certain respects, a new way of thinking.

A complete study of this work would naturally treat of the
general as well as the special theory of relativity, the question of
space as well as that of time. Since it is necessary to choose, I will
take the problem which interests me particularly, that of time.
And since it is not possible to speak of time without taking account of the hour, and since the hour is late, I will limit myself to
summary remarks on one or two points. It will be necessary for
me to leave the essential to one side.

Common sense believes in a single time, the same for all beings
and all things. What does such a belief stem from? Each of us
feels himself endure: this duration is the flowing, continuous and
indivisible, of our inner life. But our inner life includes perceptions, and these perceptions seem to us to involve at the same time
ourselves and things. We thus extend our duration to our immediate material surroundings. Since, moreover, these surroundings are themselves surrounded, there is no reason, we think, why
our duration is not just as well the duration of all things. This is

the reasoning that each of us sketches vaguely, I would almost say, unconsciously. When we reach a higher degree of clarity and precision, we represent to ourselves, beyond what can be called the horizon of our external perception, a consciousness whose perceptual field impinges on our own, then, beyond that another consciousness situated analogously with resepect to it, and so on again, indefinitely. All these consciousnesses, being human, seem to live the same duration. All their outer experiences unfold thus in the same time. And since all these experiences, impinging on each other, have, by pairings, a common part, we end by representing a single experience, occupying a single time. From then on we can, if we wish, eliminate the human consciousnesses we have disposed at long intervals like so many resting places for the movement of our thought: there is now only the impersonal time in which all things elapse. Here we have the same reasoning in a more precise form. Whether we remain vague or whether we seek precision, in both cases the idea of a universal time, common to minds and to things, is a simple hypothesis.

But it is a hypothesis that I believe to be well founded and which, in my opinion, contains nothing incompatible with the theory of relativity. I cannot undertake to demonstrate this point. It would be necessary to study much more minutely than I have just done, real duration and measurable time. It would next be necessary to take the terms which enter into Lorentz' equations one by one and search for their concrete significance. Then one would find that the multiple times of relativity theory were all far from being able to pretend to the same degree of reality. As one advanced in this study, it would be seen how the relativistic concept corresponding to the scientific viewpoint and the concept of common sense which roughly translates the data of intuition or of consciousness complete each other and even lend each other mutual support. It is true that it would be necessary, in making this study, to dissipate a very grave confusion, to which certain currently accepted interpretations of relativity theory owe their paradoxical form. All this would carry us too far.

But what I cannot establish as regards time in general, I beg

129

your permission to achieve at the very least a glimpse into, in the particular case of simultaneity. Here it will be seen without difficulty that the relativistic point of view does not exclude the intuitive point of view, and even necessarily implies it.

What is meant ordinarily by the simultaneity of two events? I will consider, for simplicity's sake, the case of two events which will not endure, will themselves not be in flux. Thus posed, it is evident that simultaneity implies two things: 1) an instantaneous perception, 2) the possibility, for our attention, of sharing itself without dividing itself. I open my eyes for a moment: I perceive two instantaneous flashes departing from two points. I term them simultaneous because they are *one* and *two* at once: *one*, insofar as my act of attention is indivisible, *two*, insofar as my attention nevertheless divides itself between them and doubles without splitting itself. How can the act of attention be one or many at will, all at once and all at one time? How can a trained ear perceive at each instant the global sound produced by an orchestra and nevertheless unravel, if it wishes, the notes produced by two or more instruments? I do not take it upon myself to explain it; it is one of the mysteries of the psychological life. I simply observe it and make the remark that in declaring simultaneous the notes produced by a number of instruments, we express 1) that we have an instantaneous perception of the ensemble and 2) that this ensemble, indivisible if we wish, is divisible if we wish, also: there is a single perception, and nevertheless there are many. This is simultaneity, in the current meaning of the word. It is given intuitively. And it is absolute in that it depends on no mathematical convention, on no physical operation like the regulation of clocks. It can never be established, I realize, save between neighboring events. But common sense does hesitate to extend it also to events as distant from each other as possible. It is said instinctively that distance is not an absolute, that it is "large" or "small" according to the point of view, according to the term of comparison, according to the instrument or organ of perception. A superman with a giant's vision will perceive the simultaneity of two "extremely distant" instantaneous events as we perceive that of two "neighboring" events.

When we speak of absolute simultaneities, when we represent to ourselves instantaneous sections of the universe which pluck out, so to speak, definitive simultaneities between events as distant as could be wished from each other, it is of this superhuman consciousness, coextensive with the totality of things, that we think.

Now, it is undeniable that the simultaneity defined by relativity theory is of an entirely different order. Two events more or less distant, belonging to the same system S, are here called simultaneous when they take place at the same time, when they correspond to an identical indication, given by two clocks which are found next to each of them. These clocks have been regulated mutually by means of an exchange of optical, or more generally electromagnetic, signals on the hypothesis that the signal pursues the same trajectory both going and returning. And this is true, without doubt, if one takes up the viewpoint of the observer inside the system, who takes the system to be immobile. But the observer within another system S', in motion with respect to S, takes his own system as a reference system, takes it to be immobile, and sees the first in motion. For him, the signals coming and going between two clocks in system S do not traverse, in general, the same trajectory coming and going; and consequently, for him, the events taking place in this system when two clocks mark the same time are not simultaneous; they are successive. If one grasps simultaneity in this oblique way [*de ce biais*]—and this is what relativity theory does—it is clear that simultaneity contains nothing absolute and that the same events are simultaneous or successive according to the point of view from which they are considered.

But, in posing this second definition of simultaneity, is not one obliged to accept the first? Does not one admit the first implicitly alongside of the second? We term E and E' the two events to be compared, H and H' the clocks placed respectively next to each of them. Simultaneity, in the second sense of the word, exists when H and H' mark the same time; and it is relative, because it depends on the operation through which the two clocks are mutually regulated. But, if such is really the simultaneity between the indications of clocks H and H', is it the same for the simultaneity between the indication of clock H and event E, between the indication of clock H' and event E'? Evidently not. The simultaneity between the event and the indication of the clock is given by a perception which unites them in an indivisible act; it consists essentially in the fact—independent of all regulation of clocks—that this act is *one* or *two* at will. If this simulaneity did not exist, the clocks would count for nothing. Clocks would not be made, or at least no one would buy them. For clocks are only bought in order to know what time it is; and "to know what time it is" consists in observing a correspondence, not between an indication of a clock and another indication of a clock but between an indication of a clock and the moment at which one finds oneself, the event taking place—something, finally, which is not the indication of a clock.

You tell me that the simultaneity intuitively witnessed between any event whatever and this particular event which is the indication of a clock is a simultaneity between neighboring events, closely neighboring events, and that the simultaneity which you deal with generally is that of events distant from each other. But, again, where does proximity begin, where does distance end? Scientific microbes, posted respectively at points E and H, will find the distance separating them enormous, that is, the distance between the clock and the event you declare is its "neighbor." They will construct microbe clocks, which will be synchronized by an exchange of optical signals. And when you come to tell them that your eye established purely and simply a simultaneity between event E and the indication of clock H which is its "neighbor," they will reply to you: "Ah no! we will not admit that. We are more Einsteinian than you, Monsieur Einstein. There will be no simultaneity between event E and the indication of your human clock H, unless our microbe clocks, placed at E and H, mark the same time; and this simultaneity will be succession for an observer outside of our system; it will contain nothing intuitive or absolute."

I raise, moreover, no objection to your definition of simultaneity any more than I raise any objection against relativity theory in general. The observations which I have just presented (or rather sketched, for I would be carried much further if I wished to give them a rigorous form) have an entirely different object. What I want to establish is simply this: once relativity theory is accepted as a theory in physics, everything is not finished. It remains to establish the philosophical signification of the concepts it introduces. It remains to discover at what point the theory renounces intuition, up to what point the theory remains attached to it. It remains to make allowance for the real and the conventional element in the results at which the theory arrives, or rather in the intermediaries the theory establishes between the posing of the problem and its solution. In taking up this task in regard to time, it will be seen, I believe, that relativity theory contains nothing incompatible with the ideas of common sense.

ALBERT EINSTEIN—The question is therefore posed as follows: is the time of the philosopher the same as that of the physicist? The time of the philosopher is both physical and psychological at once; now, physical time can be derived from the time of consciousness. Originally individuals have the notion of the simultaneity of perception; they can hence understand each other and agree about certain things they perceive; this is a first step toward objective reality. But there are objective events independent of individuals, and, from the simultaneity of perceptions one passes to that of events themselves. In fact, that simultaneity led for a long time to no contradiction due to the high propagational velocity of light. The concept of simultaneity therefore passed from perceptions to objects. To deduce a temporal order in events from this is but a short step, and instinct accomplished it. But nothing in our minds permits us to conclude to the simultaneity of events, for the latter are only mental constructions, logical beings. Hence there is no philosopher's time; there is only a psychological time different from the time of the physicist.

HENRI PIÉRON—I would like, in regard to the confrontation between psychological duration and Einsteinian time attempted

133

by M. Bergson, to point out that there are instances in which this confrontation is experimentally realized, when the psychophysiologist studies the impressions of duration, succession, simultaneity by scientific method.

Now, for a long while, astronomers have already recognized that it is impossible to begin from psychological simultaneity in order to determine with precision a physical simultaneity when it is a matter, by the method of the eye or ear, of fixing the position of a star in the reticule of a telescope at the moment of a pendulum's swing. Here is the kind of concrete experience suggested by Bergson in order to show the possible intervention of impressions of duration in the relative determinations of physical time.

We know that it is physiologically impossible to obtain an exact mental translation of a physical simultaneity between heterogeneous sensory impressions. In fact, the latency of transformation of the external excitant in the nervous influx and the propagation time of that influx change with the bodily regions and the sense organs implied without taking account of the complex and irregular cerebral variations. But there is more: we suppose that two symmetrical retinal points receive a luminous impression; it seems that, under these conditions, the perceived simultaneity will be a certain index, within the limits of a given approximation, of physical simultaneity. Now, it suffices for these luminous impressions to have a different intensity in order for this not to be so. I have been able to determine a difference of intensities such that the most feeble luminous excitation, physically preceding the strongest excitation by a few hundredths of a second, is perceived in reality precisely as the later. Thus determinations of psychological succession or simultaneity can in no case be utilized as a measurement of physical time, which requires a spatial translation, following a scientific rule which has justly been illuminated by M. Bergson. It is through the coincidence or the noncoincidence of flashes left by signal-apparatuses on a surface animated with a more or less rapid motion that we judge physical simultaneity in taking account of all the useful corrections. For these measurements of time, as for all the others, it is the visual acuteness which intervenes. And thus the Bergsonian duration seems to me to be obliged to remain a stranger to physical time in general and particularly to Einsteinian time.

BERGSON—I am entirely in agreement with M. Piéron: the psychological establishing of a simultaneity is necessarily imprecise. But, in order to establish this point through laboratory experiments, it is to psychological observations of simultaneities—imprecise again —that it is necessary to turn: without these no instrument readings will be possible.

ANDRÉ METZ AND HENRI BERGSON

Exchanges Concerning Bergson's New Edition of Duration and Simultaneity

METZ: *Einstein's Time and Philosophy*

Remarks by the Editor. In 1923 Bergson, responding to criticisms of his interpretation of relativity, published a second edition of *Duration and Simultaneity* containing three new appendices. In the following article, which appeared in the *Revue de philosophie* in 1924, André Metz develops a threefold criticism of Bergson's newly restated position. Metz's discussion begins with an analysis of the nature of time measurement, which he describes as founded on purely physical facts and not on psychological considerations. If similar physical phenomena repeat themselves under exactly similar conditions, their durations are equal; any repetitive phenomenon (whether mechanical, chemical, or electromagnetic), since it marks out equal durations, may be used as a clock. Though time units pertain originally to the time-measuring instrument, they may be applied as well to the "vital phenomena" (*not* the stream of consciousness) of a nearby observer. In this way is born the notion of an observer's *proper time*. In pre-relativistic physics, widely separated observers in motion with respect to one another cannot have different proper times. But Einstein concludes that the proper times of such observers *must* differ.

Bergson, Metz protests, wishes to show that the concept of contrasting proper times, like the concept of purely relative simultaneity, is an "illusion." A simple example, he says, will show Bergson's error. Let us assume a moving sidewalk[1] on a track. According to Bergson a clock on the sidewalk and a set of clocks along the track will mark the same time at every point of a journey if they have been synchronized originally at a common point. Bergson's argument, however, depends on the assumption that a perfect *reciprocity* exists between the moving sidewalk and the track so that what the observer on the sidewalk can say about the dimensions of the track, the observer on the track can say concerning the dimensions (including the temporal dimension) of the sidewalk. But, Metz insists, Bergson commits two distinct errors. First, he confuses the status of "proper" dimensions in relativity theory with that of "coordinate" dimensions. The reciprocity of systems is not expressed as simply for coordinates as for proper lengths. Second, the true reciprocity of reference systems can be discovered by a simple mathematical operation, which demonstrates that the *coordinates* (including the temporal coordinate) employed to mark the space-time location of the sidewalk from the viewpoint of the track are also "rediscovered" from the vantage point of the sidewalk. Coordinates are never merely "apparent" dimensions.

Bergson is also mistaken in his interpretation of "Langevin's voyager." Let us assume that the track is transformed into the planet earth and the sidewalk into a projectile which leaves the earth in a straight line at high velocity, halts at a midpoint in its

---

[1] Metz actually refers in his example to a *trottoir roulant*, which patrons of the Paris Metro will recognize as a species of moving sidewalk—a sort of "horizontal escalator" connecting certain Metro stations.

trajectory, and then returns. In spite of the fact that Lorentz' equations indicate that the observer on the projectile will have experienced, for example, two years while the observers on the earth experience two hundred, Bergson holds that in both systems the same amount of time will have elapsed. Again, however, Bergson argues on the basis of the assumed *reciprocity* of the two systems. But in this particular case reciprocity cannot be discovered, even on Bergson's own assumptions. The projectile does not have one trajectory, but two: one for the departing journey and one for the return. This means that the equation giving the time (t') required by the departing journey and the equation giving the time (t') for the return journey must be added. When the addition is performed a new equation is produced, which does not involve reciprocity.

Finally, Metz concludes, Bergson fails to account for certain well-known experiments, as well as for the nature of acceleration. The experiments of Armand Fizeau, of Alfred H. Bucherer, and of Albert Michelson demonstrate concretely and with precision that relativistic effects are quite real, and not illusory. The most ordinary experience reveals that Bergson's prized "reciprocity" does not apply to accelerations. *Professor Metz's essay, originally published in the* REVUE DE PHILOSOPHIE, *XXXI (1924), appears here in translation with the permission of the Société des Amis de Bergson. Professor David A. Sipfle and Mary-Alice Sipfle have collaborated with the editor in the translation of this group of articles.*

BERGSON, after a polite controversy with "a most distinguished physicist" (M. Jean Becquerel, professor at the Museum, although he is not identified), has recently published a "second, enlarged edition" of his work *Duration and Simultaneity: With Reference to Einstein's Theory*. Here we find the ideas defended by the author in his first edition made stronger and more precise by the addition of three appendices, where he uses all the resources of his subtle and powerful dialectic to develop his arguments against relativistic physicists.

In his book, Bergson is concerned only with *special relativity*, that is, with the first part of Einstein's work. However, the results which are the most important from a philosophical point of view and are, consequently, the most discussed, are already present in special relativity.

Bergson starts from the "Lorentz transformation," which constitutes the fundamental mathematical expression of special relativity. He establishes it at the very beginning of his book after presenting the classical explanation of Michelson's experiment. But a mathematical formula is not very important unless one fully understands the meaning of the quantities involved. Moreover, the problems posed in relativity theory are far removed from our habitual preoccupations, and one must undertake a thorough analysis of current notions, complicated by new definitions and even new concepts, in order to understand the modifications which Einstein's physical theory can bring about in philosophy.

It is in the temporal, rather than the spatial, order that Einstein's ideas have profoundly affected the most common notions. Indeed, it has long been acknowledged that the way in which a body is located in space is relative to the observer. This is not the case with time, however; the notion of the universal, absolute flow of time seems to us, prima facie, a fundamental datum of the human spirit —a "pure intuition," in Kant's words.

But let us look more closely. For each being, the notion of the flow of time is bound up with the notion of the movements or modifications which the being undergoes. Each conscious being thus considers that there is, for him, a succession, a "before" and an "after," and that there is no possibility of reducing this datum to anything else.

Thus far, the problem of the measurement of time has not arisen. In order to measure time, it is necessary to measure the modifications which the being under consideration has experienced and to find a means of numbering these modifications according to arbitrary units. The following concept, which is an immediate consequence of the principle of sufficient reason, can provide a basis:

"If analogous phenomena are repeated under precisely similar conditions, their durations are the same." [1]

It is precisely this principle which governs the operation of clocks or instruments for the measurement of time: a certain number of phenomena succeed each other under conditions which have been rendered as exactly alike as possible. Thus, in ordinary clocks the movements of a pendulum are maintained, electrically or mechanically, in such a way that each oscillation repeats itself under conditions much like those which preceded it. But other systems can be imagined. Consider, for example, a balloon filled with oxygen at a given temperature and pressure, into which identical grains of phosphorus are thrown successively. If the oxygen is continually renewed, if the apparatus is regulated so that a grain of phosphorus is introduced each time the previous grain finishes burning, we will have a chemical clock. It is also possible to imagine an electromagnetic clock based, for example, on the duration of the electromagnetic vibrations of the light from a cadmium flame ("cadmium line"). Chemical or electromagnetic clocks even have the advantage, from the theoretical point of view, of not being closely dependent on conditions of latitude or altitude for their regulation, as is the case with pendulum clocks (it is known, in fact, that the length of the pendulum which beats the second varies appreciably with these factors).

It obviously can be objected (from the practical point of view) that it is impossible to create external conditions exactly like those given initially. But experiment, with all the cross-checkings it permits, shows us that, at least for many phenomena, such conditions can be approximated very closely and that the approximations worked out in the measurement of time are at least as precise as those which modern physics attains in other sorts of measurement. Furthermore, everything indicates that progress will continue here as elsewhere and that more and more precise measures of time will become available to our descendants through the per-

[1] Time is therefore measured by motion, as an angle at the center [of a circle] is measured by the arc intercepted. The unit of time is a time, and not a "motion," just as the unit of the angle is an angle and not an arc; but time has the same measure as motions, just as the angle has the same measure as the arc intercepted.

139

fecting of apparatuses and methods of correction. We can thus assert that not only do we know what equal durations are, but also we possess the practical means of measuring these durations.

The measure of time of which we have just spoken applies initially to the clock itself, for it is the measurement of the movements (or of the chemical, electromagnetic, etc., modifications) of that clock. By neglecting propagation time, we can apply this measure to the vital phenomena of a sufficiently close observer: it is in this way that the proper time of an observer can be measured.

Thus we can imagine a scientist in his laboratory, whom we will call "Peter," to retain Bergson's terminology. Near him (as near as we wish to imagine) this scientist has a very precise clock, based on a phenomenon which is as little influenced by external events as possible, for example, on the duration of light vibrations of a given line of a certain metal (an electromagnetic clock). He defines a second as the duration of a certain number of these vibrations, determined once and for all. Near his clock (as near as we wish) he studies any physical or chemical phenomenon whatsoever, for example, the combustion of a one gram crystal of octahedral sulphur in an oxygen atmosphere. He finds that combustion has required n seconds. If he repeats the experiment, and if all the circumstances are the same (the means of ignition, initial temperatures, pressure, etc.), he will always find n seconds, in accordance with the principle of sufficient reason. In this way, he will be able to compare durations among themselves within his laboratory and even to establish other clocks on the basis of other phenomena. If these clocks are properly calibrated with the first, all of them will give readings which are always in agreement, as we have just seen. These readings measure the proper time of the laboratory.

It is quite remarkable—and at the same time profoundly reassuring—that this proper time, which relativity introduces as a reality inherent in beings and things themselves, is nothing less than the time of traditional philosophy, Aristotle's "number of motion" (motion understood in the very general sense of change, of whatever kind), so that the preceding explanation is simply the development of Saint Thomas' definition according to Aristotle: *Numerus motus secundum prius et posterius.*

But thus far we have spoken only of phenomena which occur in close proximity to each other. What will happen if we consider two beings in motion with respect to each other? In addition to "Peter," the physicist who is installed in his terrestrial laboratory, imagine another physicist, "Paul," for example, enclosed in a projectile arranged as a laboratory and traveling at a great speed in relation to Peter. Paul has, moreover, a clock based on the same vibrations as Peter's and constructed in the same fashion; and he studies the same phenomena under entirely similar conditions of temperature, pressure, etc. Everyone, relativist or not, admits that Paul will discover the same numbers as Peter. If Peter's gram of sulphur burns in *n* seconds according to Peter's clock, Paul's gram of sulphur burns in *n* seconds according to Paul's clock. In the immediate vicinity of the observer Paul, there is a proper time of his projectile, valid for the measurement of all the phenomena which occur around Paul, just as there was around Peter a proper time for his laboratory.

But can Peter's and Paul's clocks be compared? Yes, if, for example, a certain time after having moved away from him, Paul again passes into Peter's immediate vicinity. If we suppose that Peter and Paul synchronized their clocks the first time they passed, we will be able to see whether their clocks still read the same at the second encounter, that is, whether the proper times of the two beings Peter and Paul have been equal.[2]

Now here is where relativity theory differs from the previous theory of universal time. The latter asserts that the two clocks will mark the same time. Einstein's theory, based on precise experiments, rationally interpreted, shows us, on the contrary, that Peter's and Paul's clocks will differ according to the path taken.

It can be objected that Peter's and Paul's clocks can be compared with each other not only when they meet but also at any

---

2 Fundamentally, it is simply a matter of knowing whether Paul's round-trip is a sufficient reason for his proper time (*numerus motus*) to differ from Peter's.

other moment, through signals or any means of transmission what-soever. These physical means permit us to realize, in a very precise way, our natural idea of simultaneity at a distance.

Indeed, each of us believes that he can record any datum which takes place at a distant point (and which he knows about through the intermediary of more or less rapid signals) as simultaneous with an event of his own history, for example, by recording the arrival of the signal and by correcting for the propagation time,[3] or by any other means equivalent to this. Before Einstein, it had been believed that this simultaneity had an absolute sense, that is, that two events termed "simultaneous" for one observer were necessarily simultaneous for everyone.

Einstein arrived at a different result by starting from an experi-mental fact which had been known for several years but had never been explained in a manner consistent with the rest of our knowl-edge. This fact is the *isotropy of the propagation of light*, that is, the fact that the *velocity of light* (and of electromagnetic waves) *is the same in all directions* for any observer, provided that he is not accelerating with respect to the fundamental "Galilean sys-tem," by which we understand the system defined by the center of gravity of the solar system and the directions of the so-called "fixed" stars.[4]

At first glance, this isotropy for all observers seems absurd, for if one observer (unaccelerated) verifies it, it certainly seems that a second observer, traveling with a uniform translational motion in relation to the first (and therefore also unaccelerated), will neces-sarily notice a difference between the velocities (measured with respect to him) of light in different directions. This is not the case, however; the isotropy is firmly established, not only by Michel-

[3] This is merely one of several possible ways of proceeding, but we single it out because it corresponds to a certain conception of simultaneity at a distance, and *it is this conception which is considered in the rest of this article, as it is in the whole of relativity theory.*

[4] By extension, a "Galilean system" is defined as any rigid system (any system of solid bodies immobile with respect to each other) having a uniform transla-tional motion with respect to the first. The "unaccelerated" observer belongs to a particular "Galilean system."

son's experiment but also, and especially, by all the experimental verifications of electromagnetic theory (Maxwell's theory).

Starting from this experimental result, Einstein demonstrated, by the now famous argument of the track and the train (which has been completely distorted by certain popularizers), that two events which are simultaneous for the observer on the track cannot be simultaneous for an observer on the train. He has done this by using a criterion of simultaneity[5] which agrees completely with the natural concept of this notion (as independently conceived by each of the two observers).

It must be noted that this dislocation of simultaneity occurs only for events which take place at points *distant* from each other; in fact, the simultaneity of two events which coincide—"coincidence at once spatial and temporal" or "absolute coincidence," as

[5] In his little book *Relativity, the Special and General Theory* Einstein presents things differently: following the classical method in mathematical physics, he explicates his theory as if it were posed a priori and, in particular, presents the criterion of simultaneity at a distance as being a definition; it is only after having established in this way all the mathematical consequences of the theory that he has recourse to experimental verifications. But he has often insisted on the fact that the time of "relativity" is *exactly the same as ordinary time* from the point of view of "simultaneity" as it is from the point of view of "duration." He thus escapes the reproach formulated by Jacques Maritain (*Revue Universelle*, April, 1922), who believes Einstein's definition to be arbitrary and different from the natural concept. One could not say as much for Hans Reichenbach (*Revue Philosophique*, August, 1922), who asserts the possibility of "dealing with simultaneity in an entirely arbitrary fashion," which is absurd.

Another mode of exposition, less classical but more convincing, consists in starting from experimental results and showing *that in interpreting them rationally one is necessarily led to the ideas and formulae of Einstein's relativity.* This is the method which has been followed by André Metz in *La Relativité* (Chiron, ed.).

Einstein's criterion is as follows: two events are simultaneous if an observer equidistant between the two events perceives them through the intermediary of light *at the same time. Simultaneity at a distance* is thus reduced to a *coincidence at once spatial and temporal,* and hence absolute, on the retina of the observer (the two retinal images are *superimposed*). Furthermore, since the velocity of light is the same in all directions for this observer, the criterion clearly conforms to the natural concept of simultaneity.

Einstein therefore escapes another objection, also made by Maritain (*Revue Universelle*, April, 1922), of having introduced the term to be defined into the definition. The simultaneity which is being defined is *simultaneity at a distance,* while the "at the same time" which figures in the definition refers to an *absolute coincidence,* already known.

the relativists say[6]—is an indisputable fact, which must be admitted by all observers if it is established by any of them. Moreover, it can be said that two events which meet in time and space are in reality two merged events, two events which are one. The dislocation becomes greater as the spatial distance between the two events increases.

The same dislocation does not occur for observers at rest with respect to each other. If a group of observers at rest with respect to each other is termed a "reference system," it can be demonstrated that in this system two events which are "simultaneous" with a third are simultaneous with each other, and that simultaneity thus defined is valid for all the observers of the system.

But it is not valid for other observers who are in motion in relation to the first. If, therefore, it is possible to define (by thus extending the proper time of one of the observers to the others) a *time* which is valid for the entire system, this time will have no validity at all for observers in motion with respect to the first, either from the point of view of duration or from the point of view of simultaneity. And the expression, "The events which take place in the world at the moment when I speak," has no meaning unless I specify the "reference system" I have chosen. Similarly, when the physicist introduces into his equations a "time t" or a "time zero," he must state what is to be taken as his frame of reference.

Let us note, in passing, that the errors of some popularizers[7] must be avoided. These writers believed, in effect, that the dislocation of simultaneity was due to the fact that the external world is known to us through the intermediary of light; it is thus, in a way, a consequence of the means of transmission of our perceptions which we have chosen. This manner of presenting things is incorrect. The formulae which produce the retardation of time are the same for an observer using a different criterion of simul-

---

[6] The so-called theory "of relativity" thus results in a certain number of absolutes, such as *proper time, proper dimensions* (which we will examine a little later), and *absolute coincidence*. That is because reasoning must be based on something, and behind a relative there must necessarily be an absolute to support it.

[7] Daniel Berthelot, Théophile Moreux, Gaston Moch, Charles Nordmann, etc.

taneity, provided that his criterion is also consistent with the natural concept of simultaneity.

Actually, we have established the fact that certain signals (electromagnetic and luminous signals)[8] possessing a certain velocity c (300,000 kilometers per second) are transmitted with the same velocity in all directions, whatever the velocity of the observer who measures them (provided that he is not accelerating with respect to a Galilean system); this property, solidly established by a number of corroborative experiments, clarifies the nature of real time and space for us and forces us to acknowledge the properties indicated earlier, which can be summed up as follows:

1) *As concerns duration:* If any two moving objects depart from one point and, after having followed different paths, meet again, their proper times, actually measured on the two moving objects themselves, can be different from each other. And this is true, even though the event of departure and that of arrival (the meetings of the two moving objects) are both spatially and temporally coincident, and therefore indisputably and absolutely coincident.

2) *As concerns simultaneity:* Two events spatially separated from each other and simultaneous for an observer (who makes measurements in conformity with his natural concepts) remain simultaneous for all observers at rest with respect to the first; but they are no longer simultaneous for an observer in motion with respect to the first. Simultaneity at a distance is indeed a reality, but a reality which depends on the observer.

It is clear that the time of which the relativists speak, insofar as either duration or simultaneity is concerned, is really physical time, ordinary time, and not a scientific monstrosity[9] created by more or less arbitrary conventions.

---

[8] If other signals are propagated with the same velocity, they are necessarily endowed with the property of isotropy: the consequences do not depend on the fact that it is light which is involved.

[9] Lucien Fabre's expression. Fabre's error is quite widespread among the popularizers. This is also, to a certain extent, Bergson's error.

• But Einstein has not limited himself to showing that simultaneity is relative and that the measurement of durations depends on the path followed; he has given precise mathematical formulae making it possible to pass from the measurements made in one frame of reference to those made in another. He has termed these equations the "Lorentz transformation," although he himself made an important correction in the equations which Lorentz had derived[10] and it is under this name that they are now known.

In order to understand the significance of the quantities involved in these formulae, let us take a simple example. Consider a rectilinear moving sidewalk, moving with a constant velocity on a track which is part of a Galilean system (hence the sidewalk itself is part of another Galilean system). We can choose an origin on the track at A and measure lengths on the track from this point. In addition, let us place stations B, C, D at equidistant intervals on the track, each furnished with a clock.

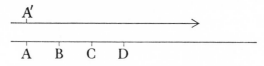

Figure 1. The moving sidewalk and its track.

We assume that these clocks are set, using Einstein's criterion of simultaneity (applied by observers in the system defined by the track), by a standard clock placed at point A; all these clocks, which are "in agreement" for all observers on the system track, indicate the proper times of their stations.

At A', carried along with the moving sidewalk, there is a clock based on analogous phenomena which serves to give the time of the system sidewalk; all the other clocks of this system will have to be set (using Einstein's criterion, applied this time to the sidewalk system) by clock A'. We will suppose, to take a point of departure, that clock A' is directly opposite A at time *zero* of clock A, and also reads *zero*. At this point, let us note that, since

[10] Lorentz has acknowledged this in *Das Relativitätsprinzip*, where he shows that he accepts Einstein's ideas completely.

Einstein's criterion gives different results for the observers on the track and for those on the sidewalk, the clocks on the sidewalk, which at the track's time *zero* happen to be opposite certain of the track's clocks, are not in agreement with these latter (save for those at point A) and that the disagreement increases as clocks farther and farther from A are consulted (supposing that these observations are all made at the track's time *zero*).

Given this, if an event takes place on the track' (for example, a breakdown of one of the supports of the sidewalk), the event will be noted, from the point of view of "time and space," by the observers on the track: thus, for an accident occurring at C, they will note that it took place at distance AC, twice the distance AB from the origin and, reading the clock placed at C, they will state their reading, thus completing the indication of the *distance* through the indication of the *time*. But the observers on the sidewalk can also make measurements of space and time as if their sidewalk were at rest (this is what is called "taking the sidewalk as a reference system"): thus the observers will have found a certain distance from A' and a certain time for the event in question.

While the distance from the origin x and the time t are given in the first system (the track), the corresponding "coordinates," the distance from the origin x' and time t' of the second system (the sidewalk), are given by the *Lorentz transformation:*

$$x' = \frac{x - vt}{\sqrt{1 - \dfrac{v^2}{c^2}}} \qquad t' = \frac{t - \dfrac{v}{c^2}\,x}{\sqrt{1 - \dfrac{v^2}{c^2}}}$$

where v represents the velocity of the sidewalk in relation to the track and c the velocity of light.

In this way, we have just discovered the "coordinates on the sidewalk" x' and t' as a function of the "coordinates on the track" x and t. The inverse problem may be posed, and the following formulae are derived from the first two by a very simple calculation (a resolution of equations of the first degree):

147

$$x = \frac{x' + vt'}{\sqrt{1 - \frac{v^2}{c^2}}} \qquad t = \frac{t' + \frac{v}{c^2} x'}{\sqrt{1 - \frac{v^2}{c^2}}}.$$

When x' and t' are applied to the two quantities x' and t' which have just been found by means of the first two quantities (x and t), x' and t' will allow us to again derive *the same* x and t with which we began. The second differs from the first only by the substitution of $-v$ for v (a substitution which is entirely justified by the fact that if the sidewalk is considered to be at rest, the velocity of the track is $-v$), and this important property is called the *reciprocity of two reference systems related by the Lorentz transformation.*

It must be stressed that these formulae were derived exclusively for the case in which the two reference systems (track and moving sidewalk) are "Galilean"; indeed, the experimental facts on which they rest are true only in this case. It is therefore not permissible to use the Lorentz transformation beyond the limits of the case for which it was established (barring justification by means of previous calculations based on this case).

An interesting effect, termed the "apparent contraction of lengths," can be deduced from the Lorentz transformation. Let us see what this involves.

Suppose we wish to determine, from the track, a length placed on the sidewalk in the direction of its movement—for example, the distance separating two successive reference points marked on the sidewalk; let us call these the anterior and posterior reference points. Since the sidewalk is in motion with respect to the track, the way the mathematical physicist goes about measuring this length is "to make t = a constant"; to translate this into ordinary language, let us say that this is accomplished by placing a graduated ruler along the track and by reading the division of the ruler which the anterior point passes at the moment the posterior point passes zero. In practice, this is not convenient; but quite apart from the difficulties involved in actually doing this, we see that by this procedure we make measurements which are simultaneous with respect to the track (this is properly what is termed, to make $t = $ a constant). Now, since simultaneity does not have the same meaning for the observers on the track as for those on the sidewalk, it is not surprising that by using this procedure we find a different length from that obtained for the same distance (the distance between the anterior and posterior points) by the observers on the sidewalk.

The observers on the sidewalk simply take the standard rulers which they carry with them and lay them down along the distance to be measured, acting (in conformity with the concept of the dimension of a body) as if the sidewalk were at rest. The length which they obtain in this way is what is called the proper dimension of this portion of the sidewalk; it is an intrinsic property of this part of the physical object, just as the proper time considered at the beginning of this article was an intrinsic property of clocks, or of moving objects carrying clocks with them.

The measurement obtained by the observer on the track, who makes calculations which are simultaneous in his own frame of reference, is less than the "proper dimension" found by the observers on the sidewalk itself. This is why the effect thus produced is termed the "apparent contraction of lengths." Years earlier, the physicists Hendrik Lorentz and George FitzGerald had found that this contraction was involved in the negative result of Michelson's experiment,[11] but they did not see all of the even more important consequences for time (simultaneity and duration). As a result the "contraction of lengths" seemed an unjustifiable hypothesis invented for the needs of a specific instance. After Einstein's analysis of the notions of duration and simultaneity, the

[11] But one must take care not to believe (as some journalists do) that Michelson's experiment is the sole basis for relativity theory. In fact, relativity theory explains a large number of previously known facts which until then had been interpreted only by the aid of *ad hoc* (and even, in certain respects, improbable) hypotheses. All these facts constitute so many *experimenta crucis* in favor of relativity; they are Fizeau's experiment concerning the propagation of light in water, and the experiments of Bucherer, and Guye and Lavanchy on the increase in the mass of high speed electrons.

contraction becomes a result which fits logically into the structure of relativity.

Moreover, if the people on the sidewalk also measure the lengths of the track from their point of view through observations simultaneous with respect to the sidewalk, they will find smaller numbers than those representing the proper lengths of the portions of the track considered. Hence, the lengths of the track seem foreshortened for the observers on the sidewalk, just as the lengths on the sidewalk seem foreshortened for the observers on the track.[12] Here again there is reciprocity between the track and the sidewalk.

This apparent contradiction is deduced, we have said, from the Lorentz transformation by means of a series of appropriate reasonings and calculations. But we must beware of the belief that the coordinates x or x' which occur in these formulae are the seemingly contracted lengths to which we have just referred; x and x' are the results of real measurements, which are related to each other in the manner we have explained above. Furthermore, x and x' are not always related in the same way with respect to size, as is the case with "apparent length" and "proper length": while apparent length is *always* shorter than proper length, x can be larger or smaller than x', depending on the circumstances. And if an event is defined by x and t (distance and time) in the track frame of reference, it is possible that the corresponding coordinate x' will be found to be smaller than x; but then, as has been shown above, in speaking of x' and t' and applying the Lorentz transformation, one obtains the same x and the same t with which one began, thereby deriving an x which is greater than x'.

In other words, the *reciprocity of frames of reference* is not expressed, in ordinary language, as simply for *coordinates* as for *apparent lengths and proper lengths*. This is because coordinates are never *apparent* dimensions, that is, *virtual images* or dimensions which the observers *attribute* to the lengths of another sys-

12 We are concerned here with lengths in the direction of motion; lengths measured perpendicular to the direction of motion are not modified.

tem by a sort of perspective;[13] they are always the dimensions themselves, as they are actually measured.

Bergson, who considers himself a relativist like "Einstein himself," believes that he is able to maintain "a unique time and an extension independent of duration . . . in Einstein's hypothesis taken in its pure state" (p. vi). In other words, he wishes that the times actually measured by the observers of two different systems (each considered in its turn as "living and conscious") would always be the same.

He nevertheless admits the Lorentz transformation, which he himself derives in Chapter I. But he tries to demonstrate to us that what is involved in these equations is an "unreal or fictitious time," stating that this "time cannot, under pain of contradiction, be perceived by a consciousness, real or imaginary" (p. 66). And he takes up again the example of Langevin's voyager, an example which had previously occasioned heated discussions. Langevin's example concerns a traveler who leaves the earth and travels at a uniform and very high velocity, only 1/20,000 less than the speed of light. After one year of his own time, he turns around and returns to the earth. It is proved by means of the Lorentz transformation that when this traveler returns, his clocks appear to be slower than those on the earth. In the example chosen, this retardation is such that the traveler, who has lived *two years* in all (going and returning) according to his clocks (and according to all the phenomena which take place in his projectile, including the vital phenomena of the observer), discovers on his return that the earth has aged by *two hundred years*.

Bergson believes that he can demonstrate that "the same time is involved" for the voyager (whom he calls Paul) as for the observer remaining on the earth (whom he calls Peter), since, as he says, motion is reciprocal and "the two persons are interchangeable."

This is completely erroneous. Paul's motion, which includes an about-face in the middle of his trajectory, is not reciprocal

13 The italicized expressions are Bergson's.

with that of Peter, who has remained constantly within the same Galilean frame of reference. There are a certain number of errors here which must be avoided; in order to take account of these, let us again consider our moving sidewalk and our track, which give a physical meaning to the famous "frames of reference." If Bergson has placed his traveler Paul in a projectile, we can make one further supposition and place his projectile on our sidewalk, with the condition that the sidewalk is given the same speed. We will then suppose that the projectile, with Paul and his clocks, is simply carried along with movement of the whole sidewalk. Let us refer to figure 1 (p. 146) and suppose that each of the distances AB, BC, CD equals 1,800 million kilometers. Paul has set his clock (the one at point A', where the projectile is located) by the clock at A at the moment he passes A (at instant *zero* on the track). At this moment Paul's clock and Peter's clock agree, each reading zero hours, zero minutes; the "spatial and temporal" coincidence which occurs at the "origin-event" can be illustrated by figure 2.

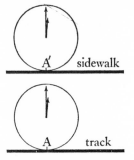

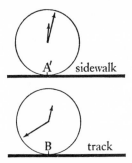

Figure 2. Encounter of A and A' at the origin-event.

Figure 3. Encounter of A' (the point on the sidewalk where Paul is located) with B.

When Paul arrives at B, 1,800 million kilometers from A, he will encounter a clock of the system track which reads *one hour and forty minutes* (*i.e.*, one hundred minutes). But the observer at point B will see (like Paul himself) that Paul's clock reads only *zero hours and one minute;* the clock at point B thus advances ninety-nine minutes over Paul's, as is shown in figure 3.

Do not believe that Paul, "reciprocally," sees his watch *advance* by ninety-nine minutes over that of the observer at *B*; this would be a false interpretation of reciprocity. The Lorentz transformation, whether the first set of equations or the second is taken, will give the *same* result (that of figure 3) for the coincidence of *A'* and *B*; and since the observer at *B* sees Paul's watch retard by ninety-nine minutes in relation to his own, Paul will see his own watch retard by ninety-nine minutes over that at *B*. This is an absolute event, independent of the observers, characterizing the encounter of *A'* and *B*.

But in that case, it will doubtless be objected, what becomes of reciprocity? Well, it does exist, and this can be demonstrated precisely and rigorously. To see this, let us put forward the following proposition:

PROPOSITION 1: *If the observers previously stationed along the course to be taken by the moving sidewalk in the track frame of reference compare Paul's clock with their own clocks (synchronized in the track frame of reference), they will find that Paul's clock seems to be more and more retarded with respect to their clocks as he passes them one by one.*

What is the reciprocal of this proposition? Is it the following?

PROPOSITION 2: *Paul sees the clocks which he passes one after the other in the track frame of reference retard progressively in relation to his own?*

No, and proposition 2 even contradicts proposition 1; if the first is *true* (in conformity with the Lorentz transformation), the second is *false*.

If we look closely, we see that in proposition 1 we are concerned with several clocks in the track frame of reference, compared to a single clock in the sidewalk frame of reference. It is then necessary, if we are to have the true *reciprocal* of proposition 1, to place on the sidewalk behind, and at fixed distances from *A'*, a series of clocks *B'*, *C'* . . . , which are synchronized with Paul's clock (according to the criterion of simultaneity, applied to the sidewalk while it moves), as indicated in figure 4.

153

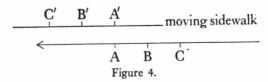

Figure 4.

If then Paul (who might just as well consider himself to be at rest) consults the observers whom he has placed at B', C' ..., and who note the differences between Peter's clock and each of theirs at the moment they pass him, Paul will say:

PROPOSITION 3: *Peter's clock retards progressively in relation to the clocks successively encountered in the sidewalk frame of reference.*

It is this third proposition which is the reciprocal of proposition 1. It is *true* if the first is *true;* it expresses relations between objective data—between realities, not appearances.[14]

But, Bergson asserts, if Paul is considered during the whole of his round-trip journey, "Paul living and conscious obviously takes his projectile as a reference system: by this very fact, he immobilizes it. Now the projectile is at rest; it is the cannon, with the earth attached to it, which is moving through space. Everything that was said about Peter must be repeated about Paul; since movement is reciprocal, the two persons are interchangeable. If a few moments ago, looking into Peter's consciousness, we witnessed a certain flow of time, it is exactly the same flow of time which we are going to discover in Paul's consciousness. If we said that the first flow of time lasted two hundred years, the other will last two hundred years as well. Peter and Paul, the earth and the projectile, will have lived the same duration and aged similarly" (DS 74; DSf 103).

This entire argument is based on the reciprocity between Peter's system (the track or the earth) and Paul's system con-

---

14 Thus it should not be said (though it is to be seen nevertheless in many articles or elementary works on relativity) that "the clocks of a system in motion appear slow in relation to the clocks of a fixed system," for the fact of being fixed or in motion changes nothing in the objective realities; depending on the manner in which the data are made precise, the preceding phrase may be true or false. It should be said: *any one of the clocks of a system retards progressively in relation to the successively encountered clocks of the other frame of reference.*

sidered throughout the whole of his journey, out and back.

Now, there is reciprocity between Peter's frame of reference (the track) and Paul's (the sidewalk) on the journey out into space; this is a property of the Lorentz transformation, which is validly applied in this case. If, after a year's journey, Paul makes an about-face, there is again a reciprocity between Peter's system (the track) and Paul's system (*another* moving sidewalk, if one wishes, but surely not the same one) *considered during its return trip*, the reciprocity being understood in the rigorous sense that we have considered above. Indeed, the Lorentz transformation still applies, but it is not the same in the second case as in the first because the relative velocity is no longer the same (it has changed sign).

Reciprocity is not applicable, however, if these two trips are considered as a whole. To obtain a valid formula in this case, one must take the equation giving t' for the first trip and the equation giving t' for the second trip and add their results. But one then has a second, more complicated equation, which does not involve reciprocity.[15]

To approach the problem from the other side, the equations can still be applied if we suppose that Paul is at rest during the first year of his journey (that is, if we take a system connected with Paul, or the moving sidewalk, as our frame of reference) and then apply the equations (in a modified form, of course) during the second year by choosing a second frame of reference connected with Paul. And the same results (not the inverse results) will be found: two years for Paul, two hundred years for the earth. Changing the point of view does not change the objective observations.

As for applying the Lorentz transformation as it stands to Paul, on the assumption that he is at rest during the whole two years of

[15] The properties of Galilean frames of reference in Einstein's theory are entirely analogous with those of *straight lines* in plane geometry. Consequently, to extend to a set of two successive trajectories in Galilean frames of reference the properties of a single Galilean frame of reference is equivalent to attributing to a set of two straight lines the properties of a single straight line (a shorter path, for example); in other words, this amounts to saying that one side of a triangle is equal to the sum of the other two sides.

his own proper time, we have no right to do so, for these equations have been established for the case of a *single* uniform and rectilinear motion with respect to a Galilean frame of reference. Paul's entire motion in no way possesses these characteristics. To say that "the two persons are interchangeable" is to apply a property of the Lorentz transformation to a case for which it is not valid.

But Bergson does not wish to consider that Peter and Paul both might be "living and conscious" at the same time. He wishes, at all costs, to consider either Peter or Paul as the living and conscious subject; and in this case the other, with his rulers and his clocks, becomes "imaginary" or "fantasmic." When Becquerel[16] points out to him that the observers of both systems nonetheless note real times (the proper times of their clocks) for the same events, Bergson replies by restating his original position. "If one takes a standpoint outside of relativity theory," he repeats three times, there is no disadvantage to reasoning in this way; but for a relativist, "Paul en route" can be "neither living nor conscious": he is simply "a phantom, an empty marionette," and "everything that physics will tell us about Paul's observations en route must be understood as observations *which the physicist Peter attributes to Paul*...." What time, therefore, does Paul's clock really indicate? "Exactly the same time as Peter's clock," Bergson replies.

Thus, according to Bergson, the time t' indicated by the Lorentz transformation is not the real time marked by Paul's clock, but a phantom. We have seen above that this interpretation is incorrect. According to the equations, t' is actually the time indicated by Paul's clock, and it can be read without any difference of interpretation, either by the observer in Peter's frame of reference or by Paul himself.[17] To say that t' is something else is to commit a real sophism, based on a grave confusion of terms.

Furthermore, the Lorentz transformation is not based on mere

16 Whose letter is cited on pp. 246–50 in the second edition, without the author's name.

17 We arrive at this result, therefore, even if we consider each of these observers to be living and conscious *in isolation* (as Bergson demands). Moreover, since we are dealing with objective verifications, *truth does not depend on the point of view chosen.*

156

speculation. It is founded on a certain number of experiments, and the quantities which it involves cannot be taken in a different sense from that which they have in these experiments.

In the first case, an observer (Peter) ascertains that the "phase velocity" of luminous phenomena in water is 225,000 kilometers per second if he is at rest with respect to the water. He imagines another observer, Paul, in motion with respect to the same liquid, and he calculates that Paul must find a different velocity for the propagation of luminous phenomena, according to the Lorentz transformation. Is this an illusion which will be dissipated (as Bergson claims) as soon as Paul becomes living and conscious? *No.* We can put ourselves in Paul's place (this is the object of Fizeau's experiment) and verify, as living and conscious beings, that the velocity measured is the one Peter calculated by means of the Lorentz transformation.

Another example: an observer (Peter) measures the mass of a certain number of electrons and finds a certain value m; then he imagines another observer, Paul, in motion with respect to the electrons and calculates, as a consequence of Lorentz' equations, that Paul must find a greater value for the mass of the same electrons. Is this an illusion which will be dissipated (as Bergson claims) as soon as Paul becomes living and conscious? Not at all. We can put ourselves in Paul's place (this is the purpose of Alfred H. Bucherer's as well as Charles-Eugène Guye's and Charles Lavanchy's experiments) and establish, as living and conscious beings, that the mass measured is the one Peter had calculated as a consequence of the Lorentz transformation.

Finally, if an observer (still Peter) measures the velocity of light rays in all directions around him, he finds that this velocity is the same (there is isotropy). If he imagines another observer, Paul, in motion with respect to him, he calculates according to the Lorentz transformation that Paul must also find the same velocity in all directions. Is this, again, an illusion which is going to be dissipated as soon as Paul becomes living and conscious? Not at all, for the Michelson experiment shows us that light really is isotropic for Paul, living and conscious, just as Peter had calculated.

Many other facts are explained similarly by Lorentz' equations —the real equations, and not those which Bergson has interpreted in his own way. To be sure, the journey in a projectile, which would make it possible to convince the most skeptical critics, has not yet been accomplished. But the experiments which we have mentioned (as well as all those which verify Maxwell's theory) amount to quasi-certainty on the subject of the result of this journey. And above all, since the Lorentz transformation is based on these experiments, it shows us how the quantities which figure in them must be interpreted.[18]

But it is difficult, even for an anti-intellectual, not to attempt to be logical with himself; and Bergson, who has based his entire philosophical system on "pure duration" and on the excellence of "intuition" (which he understands in an extremely broad sense), is anxious to save universal time. The second and third appendices of the second edition attempt, in spite of everything, to justify the reciprocity between Peter and Paul, a property which does not apply (as we have seen) when Paul makes a *round-trip* journey with a change of velocity in the middle.

It is this change of velocity, or acceleration with respect to a Galilean frame of reference, which introduces the dissymmetry between the two observers. For Bergson, on the contrary, "the acceleration itself is reciprocal, and hence the systems S and S' are interchangeable." To prove this to us, he repeats in other words, upon several occasions, that "only one of these observers is living and conscious."

Here, again, we must be clear about what is at issue. Is it simply a matter of saying that if Paul is accelerated with respect to Peter (that is, changes velocity with respect to Peter, who is considered to be at rest), Peter is, reciprocally, accelerated with respect to Paul? This much is clear, but given this obvious truth, the issue remains unsolved.

Or is it a matter of claiming that, if Peter remains in a Galilean

18 Otherwise, it would be better to state frankly that one does not accept these equations.

system[19] and if Paul undergoes accelerations with respect to Peter, *nothing* will distinguish Peter from Paul from the physical point of view? And that everything which Peter says about himself or Paul, Paul will have to say about himself or Peter? This is indefensible, and the most commonplace examples refute this assertion: if Paul is in an automobile which carelessly crashes into a thick wall, and if Peter is at rest, protected behind the wall, Paul will be killed as a result of the abrupt change of velocity which he has just undergone, and Peter will continue his existence as a "living and conscious" physicist. In general, any moving object which undergoes a sudden acceleration with respect to a Galilean frame of reference is subjected to inertial forces whose effect is real and easily observable. These forces distinguish the accelerated from the nonaccelerated observer with certainty and without real reciprocity.

It matters little that a philosopher might construct a sort of philosophical relativity in which there is no longer any sort of absolute and in which acceleration is reciprocal. This sort of relativity does not interest us, for it is contrary to experience. Einstein's theory "of relativity," which is a physical theory taking account of real phenomena, has nothing in common with Bergson's theory, which is inapplicable to the real world.

One might be tempted to believe that the second part of the theory, that is, general relativity, reconciles Einstein with Bergson by removing all the restrictions of the first. This is not so. The general theory of relativity assimilates gravitational forces with inertial forces. It replaces the notion of uniform and rectilinear motion with the notion of a space-time geodesic. But it no more eliminates the real existence of acceleration than it abolishes the absolute.

For Einstein's theory of relativity does not abolish the absolute. Like any physical theory which takes account of real facts, it postulates the absolute and, in the last analysis, calls upon it. To

---

[19] That is to say, as we have seen, that PETER is in uniform translation (or at rest) with respect to the center of gravity of the solar system and the directions of the fixed stars.

be sure, it pushes it farther back than we had previously thought. But why should this be surprising? Science constantly progresses, and precisely because of its progress, of its increasing precision, it is called upon from time to time to demonstrate to us that the means employed until then do not reach the intrinsic properties of things as simply as was believed and that, in order to discover these properties, a few additional corrections must be introduced. But the physicist, insofar as he reasons as a physicist, cannot prevent himself from believing that intrinsic properties of things do exist, or at least he reasons and acts as if he believes so. Even if, in another capacity, he asserts that he is an idealist or subjectivist, this is an affirmation which he leaves aside when he acts as a scientist, just as the psychologist who claims to be a determinist continues to reason and to act in his practical life as if he believed himself to be free.

With the appearance of Einstein's theories we have witnessed one of these cases where the absolute is pushed back. Certainly, on the basis of a superficial examination of the novel aspects of the new mechanics, subjectivists could believe that they had found a confirmation of their theses. They saw affirmed there that certain entities ("space" and "time"), considered until then to be objective properties of the external world, were henceforth to be considered as "relative to the observer"; they did not realize the fact that, behind the properties which were becoming relative, others were rising up to restore the absolute, which science needs in order to establish its foundations.

What, then, is the position of Einstein's theory in relation to philosophy? It is a *physical* theory, verified through many experiments, but it touches on certain philosophical problems, especially the problem of knowledge. We will examine relativity theory more closely from this point of view.

It is generally admitted today that most of our perceptions are a function not only of the nature of external objects, but also of the relations of our perceptual organs to these objects, so that many of the properties which we attribute to these objects by the testimony of our senses are not intrinsic properties of the bodies.

Thus taste, odor, and even color are not found as such in bodies, but are in reality manifestations of certain relations between external objects, the interposed media, and our senses. Nevertheless, in the case of the concepts of the *dimensions* of bodies and the *time* in which phenomena endure, it appears that these concepts actually do correspond to real, intrinsic properties of the external objects themselves.

Does Einstein's theory of relativity destroy this conception? Not at all. It affirms the absolute reality of the intrinsic properties of beings and of things; these properties are precisely their "proper dimensions" and "proper time," that is, the dimensions and the time as measured by an observer who remains in the immediate vicinity of the objects considered and who operates in conformity with his natural concepts.

But it also affirms, as a logical consequence of precise and rationally interpreted experiments, that these proper dimensions and times cannot be arrived at as simply as was once believed—at least by observers in any sort of motion with respect to the objects in question. Finally, it shows us that absolute space and universal time, of which we have a kind of intuitive idea, must disappear as such and give way to notions which are more complex, and which involve a certain number of corrections, if we wish to arrive at the intrinsic properties of things.

Universal time is probably one of the mental habits—Bergson would undoubtedly say intuitions—which it is difficult to change. But if it is necessary to choose between these habits and reason, shall we condemn reason? We would be wrong to do so.

Indeed, intuition, in the broad sense in which Bergsonian philosophy understands it, is, in the realm of knowledge, what the reflexes are in the realm of action. Moreover, just as there are "instinctive" (innate) reflexes and "habitual" (acquired) reflexes, so there are natural intuitions (it is these which are properly termed intuitions) and quasi-intuitions stemming from mental habits. The one and the other are, like the reflexes, molded on life, as Bergson says; it follows that they are valid for the ordinary cases which vary little from the circumstances in which we

161

ordinarily live. But, just as instinct errs when entirely new circumstances abruptly arise, so intuition (or better, quasi-intuition) teaches us falsely when we trust it beyond the limits of our ordinary vital needs.

In order to criticize this quasi-intuition, we can appeal only to reason, which, beginning with sensible experience and rational principles, leads us more slowly, even more clumsily—but also more surely—toward truth. A sound philosophy can proceed with certainty only on the basis of reason, which relies most heavily on its principles and to a lesser extent on the results of experience as its points of departure. And it is a sound philosophy of this kind which is applied, consciously or not, by all physicists and indeed all scientists when they function as scientists.

This raises an important question. Do not universal time and absolute space constitute a part of the very foundation of "rational principles"? No, for there are no rational principles except those which follow immediately from the definition of terms. Now, what is space? What is time? Do they have an existence in themselves? No, space does not exist apart from the objects which are found in it; it is a construction of the mind on the basis of these objects. And time does not exist apart from the movements (or, more generally, modifications of àll kinds) which occur in these objects.

But until now it had been believed—in line with certain habits of the mind, and in conformity with certain experiments pushed to a certain degree of approximation—that the different times, each defined by the proper duration *(numerus motus)* of a being, all coincided in such a way that between any two events all observers would note the same interval of time. It was also believed, in the same way, that simultaneity had an absolute meaning. More precise experiments, rationally interpreted, demonstrate to us that these are only approximations. Although they are quite sufficient for the needs of our practical life (and this is why they seem quasi-intuitive), these approximations are no longer sufficient if greater precision is required or if we are to study velocities which are much greater than those to which we are accustomed.

As has often been pointed out, and quite rightly so, this is analogous to the relativity of verticals. Each of us has a natural notion of the direction *vertical*, a notion which is indispensable to us in practice. It is completed by the quasi-intuitive certitude that all these verticals are parallel to each other. We find it almost impossibly difficult to imagine that men should be able to walk "upside down." This quasi-intuitive certitude corresponds to an approximate truth, quite sufficient for the needs of the material life, but it becomes an error if one tries to apply it to very precise measurements or to measurements made over great distances.

Strictly speaking, *since time and space have no independent existence apart from the beings and things found in them,* Einstein's results contain nothing absurd, nothing contrary to a sound philosophy. They indicate that observers in motion with respect to objects must make one more correction in addition to those formerly required if they want to know the intrinsic properties of objects. This correction is due to the fact that their motion is different from that of the objects in question and that consequently they are in a poor position to judge the properties of these objects directly.

This necessary correction should not surprise us any more than the classical correction which an observer situated in the air must make in his perceptions in order to determine the dimensions of a body in the water. Since the observer and the object are not in the same medium, a correction must be made which, moreover, would disappear if one of them were to move from one medium to the other. Similarly, corrections due to the relative motion of the observer and the object disappear when the observer moves at the speed of the object or inversely; in this case the measurements represent the intrinsic properties of the bodies.

The philosophical bases of Einstein's theory become quite clear if one appeals to the principles of traditional philosophy. To the principles, but not the details, for the great thinkers of antiquity and the middle ages drew certain consequences from Aristotle's physics (and particularly his astronomy) which can no longer be allowed. Thus they admitted that all terrestrial "motions" (all physical, chemical, mechanical, or other modifications) were directed by the movements of the first heaven or "empyrean heaven," from which they concluded that these motions were capable of serving as a measure of time for all beings. Just as Aristotle's astronomy (though quite remarkable for its time) is no longer accepted today, the conclusion drawn from it no longer has any value. This is precisely what Father Sertillanges[20] has pointed out about the philosophy of Saint Thomas. Father Sertillanges, though not yet familiar with Einstein's theories, asserts, in the chapter entitled "Relative Time and Absolute Time," that "To believe in absolute time today is an unnecessary act of faith. . . . Let us simply say that such pretensions must be renounced: the relative surrounds and drowns us. . . . We must be content to measure time as we measure lengths, with the units borrowed, as they are, from the relative fixities which surround our lives. . . ."

Therefore, the theory of relativity agrees perfectly with the bases of traditional philosophy. This is not to say that they are bound to each other to such an extent that should a new advance challenge Einstein's work, in the precise form in which it now exists, we would have to abandon traditional philosophy. No, it is not necessary to attempt to establish a sort of *concordisme* between philosophy and science which would necessitate continual adaptations on the part of the former and soon make it the slave of the latter. But scientific progress can be useful to philosophers by forcing them to reflect more profoundly on certain problems and thereby to enlarge philosophy. Thus the philosopher will learn from the new physics that the notions of "space" and "time" are not necessarily absolutes when they are extended by the mind beyond beings and things themselves. But he will have to take care not to consider Einstein's formulae to be rigorously exact. To be sure, these formulae represent phenomena far better than those

[20] *Saint Thomas d'Aquin*, by Reverend Father A. D. Sertillanges (Paris: Alcan, 1930), II, 49–50.

previously used, but this is not to say that future breakthroughs will not necessitate further corrections in matters of detail. Let us simply say that relativity theory may not be the definitive truth, but it constitutes a step—a giant step—toward the truth and as such, for those who study it closely, could only confirm the eternal principles which govern all science and philosophy.

Finally, if we regard it as a whole, this theory can teach us yet one more thing: it has been imposed by experiment and, on the other hand, it constitutes a rational synthesis more powerful than any other ever known, encompassing, so to speak, all the sciences previously studied. There is here a manifestation of the rational character of the world, made all the more striking because it is imposed on us by the facts and not by our reason. In spite of ourselves—in spite of the resistances of quasi-intuitive habits—we are gradually led to connect everything we know through ever closer logical bonds. It becomes increasingly clear that we need a Reason, beyond our world where everything holds together logically, to control this world—not an inert reason according to which things come about (for then something or someone else above this intelligence would still be needed), but an acting Reason, the first cause and real cause of the entire universe.

BERGSON: *Fictitious Times and Real Time*

Remarks by the Editor. Metz's criticisms were quick to provoke a reply. The May-June, 1924, issue of the *Revue de philosophie* contained the following response by Bergson, titled "Fictitious Times and Real Time." In replying to Metz, Bergson counters, in turn, with three basic objections. The first concerns the problem of the reciprocity of reference systems, as exhibited in the example of "Langevin's voyager." The second involves Metz's denial of the reciprocity of acceleration. The third involves the experiments which Metz believes are capable of establishing the retardation of time.

In dealing with the example of Langevin's voyager, Bergson

reiterates the argument of the first appendix to *Duration and Simultaneity*,[1] attempting to make clear a simple distinction which he believes Metz has failed to grasp. If a projectile departs from the earth at a high uniform velocity, and then returns at that same velocity to the earth, it is possible to declare either the earth or the projectile a "reference system." But whichever system is made into a reference system, and thus immobilized, the other system will seem to undergo a temporal retardation. What Bergson wishes to make clear is that, from the vantage point of the immobilized system, not only is the temporal retardation of the system in motion an illusion, but the observer represented as existing in that system is "fictitious." In explaining this distinction, Bergson refers to the common experience of observing a person of normal stature at a distance. Under these circumstances the observed person appears reduced to diminutive proportions; yet we do not confuse this dwarf-like image with the real person, or claim that the real person is a dwarf. But just as we make corrections to account for the effect of ordinary perspective, so we should correct for the perspectival effects (effects which may be described as due to the "perspective of velocity") involved in relativity theory. And when we do so we distinguish between the real observer, actually measuring and experiencing a real duration, and a "fantasmic" observer in motion relative to him, whose imputed duration is neither real nor experienced. It must be stressed here, to avoid confusion, that just as two people viewing each other at a distance observe each other as "reciprocally diminished in size," so two observers in systems in motion with respect to each other both see each other's times as retarded. But relativity theory requires that one system be selected as reference system and all calculations made from its vantage point. As soon as this is done, Bergson asserts, we are dealing with one real observer and one observer-as-represented, one real and one purely conventional time.

In failing to make this distinction, Bergson insists, Metz fails to understand the complete reciprocity which exists between refer-

[1] All three appendices are translated in the Library of Liberal Arts edition of *Duration and Simultaneity* (New York: Bobbs-Merrill, 1966).

ence systems for relativity theory. Metz sees very well that the observer who departs from the earth, halts, and then returns to the earth from a point midway in his trajectory, actually occupies two reference systems; he also sees that this fact establishes a dissymmetry between him and the earth-bound observer, who occupies only one reference system. But it is equally possible to choose the rocket as reference system and assert that the earth is in motion. If this option is taken, the observer on the stationary rocket will occupy only one reference system while the observer on the earth will in turn occupy two. The systems of the observer on the earth and the observer on the rocket are therefore perfectly reciprocal, for the same dissymmetry can be accorded to the double journey of each. But in both cases it is a fictitious or "virtual" observer who is viewed as making this double journey.

The attempt to prove, by mathematical means, that space and time coordinates will be measured as identical on each of two systems relatively in motion also fails, and for the same reason. To establish his mathematical proof of the reality of temporal retardation, Metz must be able to assert that the velocities of the two systems in question *have opposite signs*. But this purely mathematical dissymmetry cannot be discovered in the case where one system is declared to be at rest, while another is declared to be in motion. A system which is "at rest" cannot be described as moving with a negative velocity. Metz has actually assumed two systems in motion, neither of which is a reference system, both of which are viewed from the vantage point of some other reference system. But it is the relations between this reference system and the other two systems which must be considered.

Metz also hopes to show that Bergson's account of acceleration is faulty; but his argument against the "reciprocity of acceleration" not only does not take account of the distinction between real and merely represented reference systems, it also depends for its explication on a very poorly chosen example. Rather than dealing with an automobile which strikes a thick wall, Metz should have considered two systems of identical structure which strike each other. In the latter case it is perfectly clear that in the en-

167

counter of the two systems, acceleration can be asserted of one system as well as of the other. Moreveor, the damage to the occupants of both systems will be equally drastic.

Finally, the experiments to which Metz appeals cannot be taken as proving the reality of relativistic space-time effects. For whether we are dealing with the velocity of light in water (as in Fizeau's experiment), the mass of electrons (as with Bucherer), or the isotropy of the speed of light (as with Michelson), we must distinguish between the system decreed to be motionless and the system decreed to be in motion; in the first there is a real observer who measures real dimensions, in the second a virtual observer who measures dimensions which are not real. When this distinction is made, the experimental evidence falls into its true perspective. *Bergson's reply to Metz follows. Originally published in the* REVUE DE PHILOSOPHIE, *XXXI (1924), it appears here in translation with the permission of the Société des Amis de Bergson.*

To the editor:

I N AN ARTICLE on "Philosophy and Einstein's Time" published in the next to last issue of the *Revue de philosophie*, André Metz raised several objections to the argument found on pages 72–80 of my book *Duration and Simultaneity*. These objections are all variations on the same theme, which involves a grave error. The error is instructive, however, and deserves to be examined more closely. This is what I will attempt to do.

The objections are three in number. The first refers directly to the paradox of the "journey in a projectile." Another, which I will dispose of next, concerns reciprocity of acceleration in a more general sense. A third, finally, includes the arguments by which Metz believes it possible to establish the retardation of time through experiments made within a system to which a retarded time is attributed by virtue of the Lorentz transformation. I am surprised that Metz has not pressed this last objection still further. It is the most interesting of the objections, and the only one which is based on anything new. Except in form, the other two do not differ from those raised by Jean Becquerel, to which I have already replied in the three appendices to *Duration and Simultaneity*. Apparently my reply was not clear enough, since Metz has evidently not understood it. Therefore I am going to begin by examining it again, adding a few supplementary explanations. In any case, it is in the first objection that the fundamental error appears most clearly.

I. Let us recall the paradox of the "journey in a projectile." The physicist Peter is at rest on the earth beside the cannon which has just propelled Paul toward a star at a velocity of 259,807 kilometers per second. The Lorentz transformation seems to indicate that Paul, having been returned from the star to the earth with the same velocity, will have lived only two years if two hundred years have elapsed for Peter during the same interval.

But, as I said, if one carefully examines the Lorentz transformation equations, the manner in which they were obtained, and the significance of the terms which comprise them, it is clear that Paul's two years are only years *attributed to* Paul by the physicist Peter. The Paul who lives in a slower time than Peter's is therefore a "fantasmic" being; he is the image which Peter obtains when he follows the rules of perspective constituted by the Lorentz transformation. A real Paul, actually measuring a real time, would be a physicist Paul, taking his projectile as a reference system and consequently immobilizing it. He would thus live the time of a rest system, that is, the two hundred years which Peter was living. I say "was living" because Peter is no longer living as soon as Paul, who until then is merely imagined, becomes "living and conscious." He moves, he drags the earth with him at the velocity which Paul possessed, and, insofar as he now occupies a retarded time, immediately becomes a representation in Paul's mind. In brief, Peter and Paul are like two persons of normal stature who see each other diminished by distance. Each of them is reduced to a midget in the eyes of the other. No one will conclude from this that the one or the other has actually become a midget. The midget is "fantasmic"; it is the man of normal dimensions who is real. Since, moreover, the faculty of observing and *seeing* belongs to

169

the real person, and consequently to the man of normal dimensions, it is clear that the midget can only be something which *is seen;* he does not see. The same is true for Peter and for Paul. Insofar as Paul occupies a time which is slower than Peter's, he is observed and does not observe; he is only an image. Paul could undoubtedly become an observer; from an image, he would become a reality. But then he would no longer be in a retarded time. His time would be the time of an observer, and hence Peter's.

This is the argument. It is based on the perfect reciprocity of the two systems which are brought together here; no matter what kind of movement is attributed to them. Furthermore, the demonstration of this reciprocity has nothing to do with any particular application or interpretation of the Lorentz transformation. It is independent of all applications and interpretations. It is based on the simple fact that it is impossible to adopt two frames of reference at the same time in relativity theory; consequently, it is impossible to suppose two real "living and conscious" physicists at the same time. It is possible to immobilize whichever of these frames of reference one wishes; but as soon as one has chosen a frame of reference, one has thereby located the real physicist, the one who lives and measures time. The other will become a physicist whom the first will no doubt represent to himself as alive and measuring time, but a physicist merely conceived as living, conceived as measuring, in a time conceived as retarded. As soon as the real physicist tries to transport himself into the moving system in order to actually measure its time, he immobilizes it and measures in it a time which is certainly no longer an *attributed* time, but which is then no longer a retarded time; it is the same time as that of the system which he has just left. Since this system is now in motion, it is now assumed to exist in a time which is, in its turn, retarded. This is the essential point, to which I will return in a moment. Metz has not grasped this, and this explains his entire article. He does show that, in order to apply the Lorentz transformation to the case in which Peter is at rest and Paul is traveling in a projectile, it is necessary to suppose that Paul, having arrived at the star, jumps into a new projectile which was traveling in the opposite direction, that is, jumps into a new (virtual) frame of reference. Peter, as observer, remains in a single system, while Paul, who is observed, successively occupies two; the dissymmetry between them is absolute. So much for the evidence. But it must be added that the time of Peter, as an observer, is a real time, actually measured by a real physicist; the retarded time is that of Paul in motion, Paul who does not take himself to be a reference system (who undoubtedly *could* take himself as such at any instant, but who would then immobilize himself), Paul, finally, who is found to exist.as a physicist only in Peter's mind. This time is thus an attributed time, a fictitious time. If Paul is made the real physicist immediately after his departure, his projectile immediately comes to a stop and becomes a single system while Peter's system departs and returns, splitting into two systems just as Paul's did, and is found in its turn to exist in a retarded time which is henceforth only an attributed time; once again there is dissymmetry. In brief, if we find a dissymmetry between Peter's and Paul's respective systems in the first case, we discover an exactly corresponding dissymmetry between Paul's and Peter's systems in the second. It is these two disymmetries which are perfectly symmetrical to one another, and it is this which consititutes the reciprocity. This reciprocity, I repeat, is perfect from the moment the one physicist is supposed to be in one or the other of the two frames of reference. It cannot even be asserted that the velocity of Paul, taken to be in motion, and that of Peter, taken to be in motion, have contrary signs; to speak in this way would be to refer the two systems to a third, in which the real physicist would be. If one makes this new hypothesis, the actually measured, perceived real time is in the third frame of reference, and the two other times, equally or unequally retarded, are henceforth only times attributed to Peter and to Paul by the real physicist who represents them to himself.

André Metz points out that Peter's frame of reference is a "Galilean system," and that Paul's is not. But if we begin with this, and if we then note, with Metz, that the Lorentz transformation applies only to Galilean systems, we will merely con-

171

clude from this that there is no paradox in the journey in a projectile, that Paul will not return two years older to find that Peter has aged two hundred years, for the very simple reason that a traveler subject to Lorentz' equations cannot turn around. This conclusion is, strictly speaking, unavoidable. The universe of the special theory of relativity is a theoretical universe in which Galilean and non-Galilean frames of reference do not coexist. They are all in uniform translation, and Paul, once he has left Peter, has left for good. If we want Paul to return, we must use an artifice and suppose that Paul's system (*as observed*, for if he were really an observer, and not merely represented as one, he would be at rest) splits in two at a given moment, and that the dissociated part merges with a new system in uniform translation which moves in the opposite direction with exactly the same velocity. Thus we are actually dealing with three frames of reference in uniform translation. But we will find these same three frames of reference if Paul is the observer. His system is then at rest, and it is the former system, Peter's, this time being observed, which is divided into two. Here again there is no irreducible dissymmetry, except for the physicist placed in a fourth system into which neither Peter nor Paul will enter; and this is the very physicist Metz becomes when he argues as he does on pages 71–78 of the *Revue de philosophie* [pp. 151–57 of this book (ed.)]. But then the real time is that which Metz perceives and measures where he is, and this time is neither Peter's nor Paul's. As for the variously retarded times in which Peter and Paul grow older by virtue of the Lorentz transformation, these are times merely attributed to physicists who are merely imagined. We are therefore led to the same conclusion. Metz's argument concerning the irreducible dissymmetry between Peter's frame of reference and Paul's is valid when Metz is in neither Peter's system nor Paul's, but then each of these two times, Peter's and Paul's, is a fictitious time. If, on the contrary, he successively places himself in the respective systems of Peter and of Paul, the time of each of these frames of reference in turn is actually perceived and actually measured. But in this case there is perfect reciprocity; it is the same two retarded times which are successively attributed to the systems where Metz is not, the same two real times which belong in turn to the frame of reference in which Metz is actually located.

We are thus always brought back to the same point. To speak of reciprocity between Peter and Paul is not to apply the Lorentz transformation in any way at all, legitimately or illegitimately. It is simply to confirm that in relativity theory, a real observer, actually measuring a real time, is an observer who takes himself as a reference system and who is henceforth immobile. Consequently (assuming initially, for the sake of simplicity, that the universe is reduced to the systems of Peter and Paul), it is impossible here to make real observers of Peter and Paul at the same time, since this would be to deny their reciprocal displacement after having affirmed it. It is necessary to choose; and then the retarded time, which is that of the moving observer, is only a time attributed on the basis of the Lorentz transformation by the immobile observer to the observer who is in motion with respect to him, and who is henceforth only assumed to observe. Once again, when a man of normal stature seen from a distance looks like a midget to me, he is unreal insofar as he is a midget, unreal insofar as he has the dimension I perceive. This does not prevent him from being real insofar as he is a perceiver; but, insofar as he is a perceiver, he is of normal stature. He may perceive me as a midget; I am then unreal insofar as I am a midget, though I do not cease to exist and to be what I am. If we are both made into midgets, it is because a third person has been introduced who perceives himself from no distance at all, and who alone is real because he alone retains his size and he alone is the observer. It is the same for Peter and Paul. After mentally eliminating the rest of the universe, we can re-establish any frame of reference whatever, locate a third person there—for example, ourselves—and then observe Peter and Paul from this new point of view. Neither the one nor the other, insofar as they fit this new description, is any longer an observer; both are observed. Granted that their systems no longer correspond symmetrically, neither of the retarded times which we now assign to them is a real time.

Let us recapitulate. The first objection falls of its own weight, and the argument on pages 71–78 is invalid because Metz does not distinguish between a real observer, actually making measurements in his system, and an observer *represented by him as real*, to which he *attributes* certain measures by transforming, according to a certain rule, the measurements which he himself has made. If I want to actually measure Peter's time, I must enter Peter's frame of reference; I must become Peter. If I want to actually measure Paul's time, I must take Paul's place. Having occupied in turn their respective frames of reference, I find that my two successive views of the whole of the two systems are perfectly symmetrical to one another. If I remain outside of both (and this is what Metz supposes in pages 71–78), the dissymmetry is evident, and Metz's argument is valid; but then both persons, Peter and Paul, are simply represented as observers by me, and I am the only real observer. Their times undoubtedly become more or less retarded in relation to mine, but these are fictitious times attributed by virtue of the Lorentz transformation and are not actually measured. Furthermore, I would be the first to admit that relativity theory, as a physical theory, does not have to distinguish between the real observer and the observer who is represented as real. In *Duration and Simultaneity* I have shown how and why relativity theory is obliged to put the actual and the virtual on the same plane. But the task of the philosopher, who wishes to know to what extent Einstein's times are real times, that is, times capable of actually being perceived and measured, is precisely to re-establish this distinction. This is the goal of *Duration and Simultaneity*.

André Metz errs when he believes that in this book there is another theory of relativity, distinct from that professed by physicists. The physics of relativity, and only that physics, is studied in *Duration and Simultaneity*. But it is studied in order to answer the philosopher's question, not the physicist's. The question is to know what can be perceived and what is condemned to remain merely conceptual, what is an actually measured, real time and what is an attributed time, an auxiliary time, an unreal time. It is quite possible that some relativistic physicists who have contributed to the development and even the creation of relativity theory may have difficulty in admitting this distinction. It is possible to be an eminent physicist without being trained to deal with philosophical ideas. Philosophers, no less than others, need to be reminded of this. But it is pointless to argue here about the physicist's special competence: the question is no longer concerned with it. Moreover, whether it is a matter of physics or philosophy, the appeal to authority is useless.

I could continue this discussion further if it were really necessary, but I would merely be paraphasing what I have already said in the appendices to *Duration and Simultaneity*. I would like to go a little further and point out more clearly the exact point that Metz missed. Apparently, he has not seen why it is not possible, on the hypothesis of relativity, to attach "living and conscious" observers to several different systems at the same time, why only one system—that one which is actually adopted as a frame of reference—contains real physicists, why the other systems are consequently inhabited only by physicists *which the real physicists represent as* real, and particularly, why the distinction between the real physicist and the physicist *represented as* real is of great importance in the philosophical interpretation of this theory, while philosophy previously had no need to concern itself with this problem in order to interpret physics. The reason for this is quite simple.

From the standpoint of Newtonian physics, for example, there is an absolutely privileged frame of reference, an absolute rest and absolute motions. The universe is thus composed, at each instant, of material points, some of which are at rest while the others are moving in a completely determined manner. This universe therefore contains *within itself*, in space and time, a concrete configuration which does not depend upon the physicist's point of view. All physicists, no matter what moving system they belong to, refer back, mentally, to the privileged frame of reference and attribute to the universe the configuration that it would have if it were thus perceived from the absolute standpoint. If, therefore, the physicist *par excellence* is the one who inhabits this privileged frame of reference, there is no need here to establish a radical distinction between this physicist and the others, since the others proceed as if they were in his place.

But in relativity theory there is no longer any privileged frame of reference. All systems are equivalent. Any of them can be set up as a reference system which is henceforth immobile. With respect to this reference system, as with the Newtonian, all material points in the universe will be found either to be immobile or to move in a determined manner, but this will be true only for this particular frame of reference. If we adopt another, the immobile will move, the moving will become immobilized or change velocity, and the concrete configuration of the universe will have radically changed. However, the universe could not have these two configurations at the same time; the same material point is not both at rest and in motion. A choice must therefore be made, and from the moment you choose a definite configuration, you establish the physicist belonging to the frame of reference from which the universe takes this configuration as a living and conscious, really perceiving physicist. The other physicists, as they appear in the configuration of the universe chosen in this way, are consequently virtual physicists, merely conceived as physicists by the real physicist. If you confer reality on one of them (insofar as he is a physicist), if you suppose that he perceives, acts, and measures, his system is no longer a virtual frame of reference, no longer merely conceived as capable of becoming a real frame of reference; it is a real frame of reference, and thus is at rest. You are dealing with a new world-configuration, and the physicist who was real a moment ago is now only represented.

Langevin definitively expressed the essence of relativity theory when he wrote, "The principle of relativity, in its special as in its general form, is at bottom nothing but the affirmation of the existence of a reality independent of frames of reference, in motion with respect to one another, from which we observe changing perspectives. This universe has laws which can be given an analytic form independent of the frame of reference through the use of coordinates. Although the individual coordinates of each event are dependent on the frame of reference, it is nonetheless possible to express these laws in an intrinsic form, as geometry does for space, thanks to the introduction of invariant elements and to the construction of an appropriate language." [1] In other words, the universe of relativity is as real, as independent of our mind, as absolutely existent as that of Newton and of the ordinary man. But, whereas for the ordinary man and even for Newton, this universe is a collection of things (even if physics is limited to studying the relations between these things), Einstein's universe is simply a nexus of relations. The invariant elements which are here taken to be constitutive of reality are expressions containing parameters which can take on any value and which do not represent times and spaces any more than anything else, since, in the eyes of science, only the relation between the parameters will exist, and since there is no longer any time and space if there are no longer any things, if the universe no longer has any configuration. In order to re-establish things, and consequently time and space (as is necessarily done whenever one wishes to obtain information about a particular physical event, perceived at particular points of space and time), it is necessary to restore a configuration for the world, but one will thus have taken a standpoint, adopted a frame of reference. The system chosen becomes, moreover, by that very fact, the central system. The very essence of relativity theory is to guarantee to us that the mathematical expression of the world which we will encounter from this arbitrarily chosen point of view will be identical to that which we would have found by taking up any other point of view whatsoever if we conform to the rules which it has laid down. If you retain only this mathematical expression, there is no time any more than anything else. If you restore time, you re-establish things, but you have chosen a reference system and the physicist who will be attached to it. No other can exist for the moment, though any other could have been chosen.

[1] "Le principe de Relativité" (conference faite à la Société française des Electriciens).

Relativity theory, therefore, could not admit an absolutely and definitively privileged system. This is the heart of the theory. This is to say that Metz is mistaken concerning the role of the "fundamental Galilean system" in the special theory of relativity. It is indisputable that the Lorentz transformation was established for systems in uniform translational motion. And it is no less incontestable that, in order not to remain in the purely abstract, in order to give a physical and concrete meaning to the words "uniform translation," in order to determine in fact what is uniform translation and what is not, we must refer to the "fixed stars" and in particular to the sun, which is one of them. This simply means that in view of the enormity of the distances, the reciprocal displacements of the stars are, for us, practically equivalent to immobility. But a physicist carried by a projectile "in the direction of a fixed star" would after a certain time, notice that there was neither "fixity" nor "direction," since the star would move with velocities which he could not determine and in a direction which he could not define. Moreover, he would have made the same observation regarding any other visible star toward which he had been propelled. Since the immobility of his former "sky," which we shall suppose he has left behind, has now been dissolved into movements of every kind, it is quite another system of "fixed stars" which rises up before him beyond the old one, a system which now serves to define uniform translation for him. Hence his former "fixed stars" played a purely practical role and possessed nothing of that absolute immobility, or, moreover, of that absolute motion, uniform or varied, which some thing ought to possess in the world so that an absolute character—of some kind—could be attributed to either the rest or the motion of any of our physical systems.

Furthermore, considerations of another kind would lead even more directly to the same result. It would be sufficient to point out that the existence of gravitation makes the real universe one in which Lorentz' equations apply, strictly speaking, only during infinitesimal periods of time. In these infinitely short periods motions are theoretically uniform and, in this sense, absolutely uniform, since their uniformity has nothing to do with division of things into systems which are or are not "Galilean." But this division, we repeat, is itself entirely contingent, entirely subordinate to the practical necessities which make it necessary for us to stop at a certain degree of approximation.

II. That it is difficult to exorcise the phantom of absolute spatial motion, I would be the first to agree, and I have explained why. This same difficulty might also explain Metz's error concerning "the reciprocity of acceleration." Let us turn to this next objection.

The argument of the second appendix to *Duration and Simultaneity* could be summed up as follows. Let us consider acceleration in the case of translational motion (the case of rotation is examined in the following appendix). Take two systems, S and S'. One of the following two alternatives must be true: either the real physicist decides to take account of only these two systems and consequently places himself in one or the other, or he locates himself in a third, which we will term S''. On the first hypothesis, there is perfect reciprocity between S and S': if the physicist is in S, system S is immobile and system S' draws nearer to him or goes further away with successive accelerations; if the physicist is in S', it is S' which is at rest and S which approaches or retreats while undergoing exactly the same accelerations (once again one cannot even say that the accelerations of S and S' possess contrary signs, for this would be to take a position in a third system S'', which is not allowed by the hypothesis). Moreover, whether he is in S or S', the real observer, in each case occupying a rest system, effectively measures the same real time: in both instances, the observer represented by him in the moving system passes through the same series of diversely retarded times. These are fictitious times, which the merely represented observer is assumed to measure.

Let us now turn to the second hypothesis. The real observer is in S'', which is then at rest, and therefore it is in S'' that time is actually perceived and measured. It is quite evident that at a given moment one will generally find different velocities in S and

179

S' and, consequently, two different times, both slower in relation to those of S''. But both of these times will now be attributed times. Hence, if one wishes to deal with real times, then acceleration creates no dissymmetry, and if one wishes to consider the acceleration of one of the two systems to have actually created an irreducible dissymmetry between them, then one is no longer dealing with real times.

It is always the same point that Metz misses—the necessity of placing a real observer somewhere. Even so, he seems to have wished to vary the form of his argument at this point, for he appeals to the changes which acceleration can cause within a system. "If Peter remains in a Galilean system," he asserts, "and if Paul undergoes accelerations with respect to Peter, is it true that nothing will distinguish Peter from Paul from the physical point of view? And that everything which Peter says about himself or Paul, Paul will have to say about himself or Peter? This is indefensible, and the most commonplace examples refute this assertion: if Paul is in an automobile which crashes into a thick wall, and if Peter is at rest, protected behind the wall, Paul will be killed as a result of the abrupt change of velocity which he has just undergone, and Peter will continue his existence as a living and conscious physicist." Is it necessary to demonstrate that this argument is invalid? First, the two systems which come together are assumed to have different internal structures (on the one hand, Paul and the automobile, on the other, Peter with the wall and the ground), whereas, to know whether they are interchangeable from the point of view of acceleration, time, etc., we obviously must begin by attributing the same configuration to them. Then psychological elements are unconsciously allowed to intervene, for example, Paul's habit, when he is in the automobile, of looking at things from the social point of view, which is that of the road, and not from his own point of view, which is that of the inside of the automobile. It is because he mentally puts himself at the former standpoint that he says that he is in motion. We obviously must not take his habits and memories into consideration. Let us therefore create a blank in his memory: Paul is inside a system which he

naturally takes as a reference system and which he therefore supposes to be at rest. A shock occurs. He will probably know that
an acceleration has just taken place, but this acceleration could
just as well have arisen outside his system. As a matter of fact,
whether an automobile is flung against a wall or a wall is flung at
an automobile, in both cases the result is identical.[2] Instead of an
automobile and a wall, suppose there are two systems with the
same configuration, Paul in one and Peter in the other. If Paul is
reduced to pieces by the impact, no matter how hard Peter tries
to convince himself that he occupies a Galilean system, he will be
smashed into identical pieces. The fixed stars will not be able to
save him. But let us leave all this aside, for one could quibble over
the details. The essential reason the argument invoked proves
nothing against the "reciprocity of acceleration" is that Paul no
longer forms a single system, either in himself or in relation to the
car, while crashing into the wall. Whether his body is pulverized
or only shaken up, the material points of which it is composed
immediately cease to have the same relations among themselves
and with the car. They constitute multiple systems, S'', S''', etc.,
moving at velocities which are different from each other and
different, also, from that of system S', to which they belonged. In
the eyes of the physicist in S, they therefore have proper times
t'', t''', etc. The reciprocity between S and S'', between S and
S''' is, moreover, complete, as it is between S and S'. This is the
point on which I insisted in the second appendix of *Duration and
Simultaneity*. If we install the real physicist, I said, in S'', S''', etc.,
one after the other (he could not be in several at once), in each
of these he will rediscover and live the same real time t which he
has just left in system S, and will then attribute to system S the
merely represented times t'', t''', etc., one after the other. The
reciprocity is therefore quite complete, provided that one compares two systems to each other and does not set up as one system
what is actually a collection of systems. It is true that we have

---

[2] It goes without saying that the same holds for the car's vibrations. They
cannot inform Paul of his "movement," if he has really taken the automobile for
his reference system, since the vehicle is at rest for him, and each vibration becomes a shock due to an external cause.

successively placed our observer in one or the other of the two systems to be compared. If he were in neither system, symmetry would generally disappear; the two systems under comparison would take on differently retarded times. But neither of these two times would any longer be a real time.

III. I come now to the last point: the supposed verification of temporal retardation through experiments performed within a moving system to which the Lorentz transformation is applied. Metz mentions three experiments to support his claim. I will examine each in turn.

The first is Fizeau's experiment. "An observer, Peter," we are told, "ascertains that the phase velocity of light rays in water is 225,000 kilometers per second if he is at rest with respect to the water. He imagines another observer, Paul, in motion with respect to the same liquid, and he calculates that Paul must find a different velocity for the propagation of luminous phenomena, according to the Lorentz transformation. Is this an illusion which will be dissipated as soon as Paul becomes living and conscious? No. We can put ourselves in Paul's place (this is the object of Fizeau's experiment) and verify, as living and conscious beings, that the velocity measured is the one Peter calculated by means of the Lorentz transformation."

In other words, Metz reasons thus: "I am the physicist Peter, immobile before Fizeau's apparatus, in which water is in motion. I can suppose another physicist Paul, immersed in the water or moving along with the current. According to *Duration and Simultaneity*, the time of the physicist Paul would be retarded fictitiously, since this retarded time would only be an attributed time. Now it happens, on the contrary, that in this case I can myself verify the retardation of Paul's time experimentally, since the observation of the interference lines shows me that Paul's velocity is added to the velocity of light according to Lorentz' formula for the composition of velocities. Hence the retardation is not fictitious."

I reply: In order to measure Paul's time as he measures it, it is necessary to be in Paul's place, in the water. Now, in the water,

182

Paul, living and conscious, takes himself for a system of reference. He is at rest, and the water is at rest with him. In his eyes, it is you, Peter, who are in motion. But he reflects: "Peter believes that he is immobile, therefore he sees me as moving, therefore he judges my time to be retarded, therefore he calculates the velocity that he has attributed to me and the velocity of light according to Lorentz' formula. Indeed, it is this supposition of Paul's which you, an existent physicist, are verifying when you observe the interference lines. Thus you are verifying a temporal retardation which a fictitious moving Paul, whom you suppose for an instant to be real and at rest, would say to himself that you are attributing to him, and not a temporal retardation which a real Paul observes and measures, since, insofar as he is a real physicist, actually measuring time, Paul is motionless and immobilizes the water with him. This is to say again that a retarded time is simply an attributed time, and that the only real time is either your own or else the time, identical with the latter, of a physicist who would immobilize the water with him and would see you—now a virtual and merely represented physicist—in motion.

I proceed now to the second experiment. According to the theology [sic] of relativity, the mass of a body moving with a translational motion should appear to an immobile observer to be increasing in proportion to its velocity. The demonstration of this point rests entirely on the fact that the body in motion is found to have a retarded time with respect to the observer. Thus we are told that if it could be established experimentally that the mass of a body actually increases with its velocity, it would have been proved that the retardation of time is not merely attributed to the body by the immobile observer; it actually does take place. Now it is just this objective increase of the mass of electrons through their velocity which experiments such as Bucherer's reveal. But this is the same case we have just examined all over again. All we need to do is repeat what we were saying about Fizeau's experiment. The time measured by an observer Paul, attached to the electron, if this observer were capable of actually measuring time and if he were consequently real, would be the time of a motionless system, with respect to which the real and motionless observer of a moment ago—let us call him Peter—would now be only a virtual observer, since he would be in motion. Hence Paul would not find himself in a retarded time; but he would say to himself that Peter, if he were to become a real and motionless observer, would attribute this retarded time to him, *i.e.*, to Paul, who has become a virtual and moving observer. Thus when Peter, as a real and motionless observer, observes an increase in the mass of the electron to which the moving Paul is attached, he in no way confirms a retardation of time which a real observer would find in the electron; he merely confirms the retardation which this observer would say was attributed to him, by virtue of Lorentz' equations, by another observer moving with respect to him, who would consider himself to be at rest. No more here than in Fizeau's experiment does a real observer verify from without, I mean from his immobile standpoint, a temporal measurement which would actually be made by a real observer in the moving system.

There remains one final experiment invoked by Metz, the Michelson-Morley experiment. "If," he asserts, "an observer Peter measures the velocity of light rays in all directions around him, he finds that this velocity is the same (there is isotropy). If he imagines another observer, Paul, in motion with respect to him, he calculates according to the Lorentz transformation that Paul must also find the same velocity in all directions. Is this, again, an illusion which is going to be dissipated as soon as Paul becomes living and conscious? Not at all, for the Michelson experiment shows us that light is really isotropic for Paul, living and conscious, just as Peter had calculated."

The fallacy in this argument is obvious. Paul is supposed to be in motion and performing the Michelson-Morley experiment. By observing the lines of interference, he establishes the equality of the two double trajectories, longitudinal and transverse, of the light ray. Are we therefore to believe that he establishes the applicability of the Lorentz transformation to his own system?

It is clear that he does not and cannot establish this applicability, since he does not and cannot apply the equations to his own system. Insofar as he is a real observer, living and conscious, actually performing the experiment (and not insofar as he is a fictitious observer, who is simply assumed to do so), he takes his own system as a frame of reference. This system is therefore immobile, and it is just the immobility of his system which the Michelson-Morley experiment demonstrates to him, not a temporal retardation or a dislocation of simultaneity which would verify the Lorentz transformation. Paul is not in motion unless you introduce a new observer, Peter, who is in turn "living and conscious," with respect to whom Paul moves; but, insofar as he is in motion, Paul is henceforth only a represented physicist; he passes his role on to Peter. The retardation of time and the dislocation of simultaneity are then no doubt produced in Paul's system for this new observer Peter, who, until now, was supposed by Paul to be in motion, who, until now, was simply represented as an observer by Paul, and whom you have just made into a real observer by immobilizing him. But it is no longer in Paul's system that the real observer (who is now Peter) performs the Michelson-Morley experiment, but in his own; and what he verifies by observing the lines of interference is not the applicability of the Lorentz transformation, but, again, just the immobility of his system. In short, the Michelson-Morley experiment never establishes anything in the system in which it is performed, except the immobility of that system; and this experiment establishes the Lorentz transformation only insofar as an observer within this moving system imagines a moving observer, who, taking himself to be at rest, would observe the system in which he has just performed the experiment to be in motion and would conclude from this that the experiment confirms the formula.

I have analyzed the three experiments invoked by Metz. I could cite others of the same kind whose analysis would lead to the same result. Furthermore, it would be in the philosopher's interest to speculate on these experiments, but the lesson to be learned from them has no relation whatsoever to the conclusions which André

Metz believed it was possible to draw from them. I have limited myself to examining these conclusions in this letter, which is already much too long.

Yours truly,

H. Bergson

METZ AND BERGSON: *Concluding Statements*

Remarks by the Editor. Bergson's and Metz's dispute concludes with the following brief "ripostes," which appeared in the July-August edition of the *Revue de philosophie.* In the first, Metz reaffirms his criticism of Bergson's position, insisting that the philosopher's arguments are in no way compatible with Einstein's theory of relativity. The examples of Fizeau's experiment and Langevin's voyager actually establish the existence of a real temporal retardation. To see this it is only necessary to understand the true function of observers in relativity physics. But this Bergson does not do.

Bergson's reply is short and pointed. Besides asserting that relativity theory, while requiring registering instruments, does not require observers to observe what they register (a conclusion Bergson rejects), Metz has made no new point. Moreover, Metz does not take account of a single one of the confusions which have been pointed out to him. Under such circumstances it is useless to proceed further.

In a final note, added by the journal editor, Metz charges that Bergson has surreptitiously modified the roles of the observers participating in the examples under discussion. Einstein himself has written, lamenting the philosopher's error. Bergson, Einstein asserts, forgets that the simultaneity of two events which affect a single being is "something absolute, independent of the system chosen." *The following exchange, including the note added by the editor of the* REVUE DE PHILOSOPHIE, *appears here in translation with the permission of the Société des Amis de Bergson.*

186

ANDRÉ METZ'S REPLY: In many respects I greatly admire the defense of his ideas which Bergson has forwarded to the *Revue de philosophie*, and which appeared in its May-June issue.

But the considerations developed by Bergson in *Duration and Simultaneity*, as well as in his article in the *Revue de philosophie*, can in no way be defended as an interpretation of Einstein's theory.

Basic to this theory there is, in fact, the following fundamental question:

If two perfect, perfectly regulated clocks, entirely in agreement between themselves and originally contiguous, are separated and then meet again after having followed different trajectories, *is it possible that these two clocks legitimately indicate different times*, which depend on the movements executed?

To this question, Einstein's theory replies: YES, and this reply is of greatest importance, since it destroys the ancient notion of "universal time," always measured between two events by means of the same number.

In his book Bergson's reply to the same question is: NO.[1]

The two theories are therefore *contradictory*, and contradict each other concerning the statement of a *physical* fact.

The fact (which no one contests) that when one considers an "observer," he alone is real and the others "observed" are only "representations" in his mind—this fact can no more be involved in the answer to the above question than it can enter into the verification of any physical fact whatever.

Moreover, in Einstein's theory it is a question only of comparing two *clocks* supposed to be perfect to each other. It is true that for the sake of convenience authors of works on this issue have often introduced "observers" who are assumed to perceive the phenomena. But these observers can just as easily be replaced

---

[1] If the consequences of the first reply are developed (after the introduction of a certain number of conditions), one discovers the theory of relativity. If the consequences of the second are developed, one finds *and one can only find* the theorems of classical mechanics (which, for high velocities, have been experimentally invalidated).

by recording instruments, and whether or not they are "living and conscious" is irrelevant.

In his reply,[2] Bergson has endeavored to interpret in his own way the arguments which I have presented[3] concerning the experiments of Fizeau, of Guye, and of Michelson. But the Peters and Pauls introduced by Bergson are not the same as mine. I will therefore return to my argument concerning Fizeau's experiment in order to present it definitively.

I posit an initial observer, Peter, at rest with respect to the water (it is essential that he *be* at rest and that he remain at rest with respect to the water). This observer measures the phase velocity of the light in the water and finds 225,000 kilometers per second. He then imagines a second observer Paul (unreal, fantasmic), moving at velocity v with respect to the water, and he calculates, according to Lorentz' equations, that this observer must find another value, W, if he fictitiously measures the phase velocity of the light in the water.

We can now measure the phase velocity of light in the water with respect to an observer in the water, in motion with respect to it. This is precisely the object of Fizeau's experiment. In this experiment the observer Paul, now real, now moving with respect to the water,[4] finds for the phase velocity *precisely the same number* W which Peter calculated previously and attributed to the fantasmic observer Paul.

The same number! That is the essential point.

Let us apply this result to the problem of Langevin's voyager. First we have an observer Peter, real and at rest with respect to the earth, who propels a projectile at very great speed so that after having turned around in the middle of its trajectory it returns to the earth again after two hundred years of terrestrial time. He

---

[2] *Revue de philosophie*, May-June, 1924.
[3] *Ibid.*, January-February, 1924.
[4] An observer *at rest with respect to the water* is thus compared with an observer *in motion with respect to the water;* this is essential, since the formula for composition of velocities, derived from the Lorentz transformations, is applicable only in this case.

imagines a fictitious observer, Paul, enclosed in the projectile, and he calculates, according to the Lorentz transformation, that this unreal observer must measure two years of his own proper time between his departure and his return to the earth.

If Paul now becomes real, the number which he actually measures is exactly *equal* to the number which Peter had calculated and attributed to the fantasmic observer, Paul. *Two years* are therefore measured by the observer enclosed in the projectile when he is real, while *two hundred years* elapse on the earth between his departure and his return.

The example of Fizeau's experiment is, moreover, not mine; it was suggested to me by Jean Becquerel, whose faithful disciple I have the honor of being. It is particularly convincing because it presents the so-called theory "of relativity" in its true light. Indeed, it is seen to be an explanation of experimental phenomena, a *theory of reality*. This is its true character, and if relativity theory is not this, it is nothing at all.

BERGSON'S LETTER TO JOURNAL EDITOR: You have been kind enough to forward to me André Metz's note. Although it is entitled "Reply to Bergson," I have searched in vain for a word of reply to the twenty pages of critical reflections which I had addressed to the *Revue*. Metz believes that registering instruments are sufficient, with no need for an observer to observe what they indicate. This is the only new point which I have found in his note. Except for this, he limits himself to repeating what he had said concerning the two clocks and also Fizeau's experiment, without taking account of the mistakes which I pointed out to him. To speak as he does of the real and the represented observer, to fail to see in this a distinction which is indispensable for Einstein's theory *and only for this theory*, is necessarily to be completely unaware of the nature of the difficulty. Not only the meaning of my reflections, but also the meaning of my book has totally escaped him. Under these circumstances I can do nothing.

NOTE ADDED BY JOURNAL EDITOR: Following this reply by Bergson, André Metz requested us to add that he believes he has "fully understood Bergson's theory, which *dislocates* the concrete structure of the universe without even retaining the *absolute* of spatiotemporal coincidence, which is essential to any physical theory."

According to him, "Bergson's theory cannot take account of the facts (the experiments of Fizeau, etc.) which have justified the introduction of Einstein's theory, since the objections derived from these experiments have not really been refuted by Bergson, who, in his reply in June, had *modified* the roles of the *observers* who took part in the examples of the article which appeared in February."

He adds, finally, that Einstein himself, after examining Bergson's theories, wrote him concerning this subject: "It is regrettable that Bergson should be so thoroughly mistaken, and his error is really of a purely physical nature, apart from any disagreement between philosophical schools. . . . Bergson forgets that the simultaneity (like the nonsimultaneity) of two events *which affect one and the same being* is something absolute, independent of the system chosen" (letter of Albert Einstein to André Metz, July 2, 1924).

GÜNTHER PFLUG
Inner Time and the Relativity of Motion

Remarks by the Editor. In this essay, a passage from his book *Henri Bergson: Sources and Consequences of an Inductive Metaphysics*, Professor Günther Pflug explores the basic philosophical concerns underlying Bergson's criticism of Einstein's special theory of relativity. Among these are Bergson's unwillingness to admit the existence of a temporal process in the external world, his belief in the "absoluteness" of willed motion, and his attempts to find an absolute system of reference within the concrete experience of the individual. All of these assumptions seem to Bergson to be denied by relativity; *Duration and Simultaneity* is the philospher's attempt to re-establish their validity.

In attempting to show that there can be no concrete conception of duration or motion, as existing in the outer world, Bergson is led to the conclusion that the concept of motion must derive from some experience more basic than that of change of place. To show this he utilizes Henry More's argument against Descartes' theory that all motions are relative. (If one person is seated and at ease while another is flushed from the effort of running, More insisted ironically, surely the first person is really at rest, and the second "absolutely" in motion.) Physicists immediately objected to Bergson's restatement of More's thesis, since this thesis would make the concept of motion dependent in part on "psychological" considerations. Bergson's reply to these objections, however, is to show how it is possible for the scientist to transfer his conceptions of "inner" processes into the "outer" world by extending his experience of motion and duration, as they appear in the context of his near surroundings, to the entire universe. The difficulty with this process is, however, that in the end it makes the scientist's conceptions of the world purely fictitious. What is really experienced, *i.e.*, our own stream of consciousness, our near surroundings, is "absolute"; whatever is merely conceptualized is "relative." Hence the natural "relativity" of scientific thought.

When applied to Einstein's physical relativity theory, Professor Pflug points out, Bergson's theory of the relativity of all scientific concepts reveals several weaknesses. First, it forces Bergson into a strange agnosticism concerning the temporal dimensions of physical systems which are merely represented and not experienced. Second, it leads Bergson to isolate the "inner consciousness" of individual men. Each man, the philosopher holds, experiences only his own duration, yet must view other persons simply as objects of experience; each individual must then construct an interpersonal time which he can share with others. But it is difficult to see, on Bergson's grounds, how the existence of this unique, interpersonal time can be substantiated. *Professor Pflug's essay was originally published in his* HENRI BERGSON:

QUELLEN UND KONSEQUENZEN EINER INDUKTIVEN METAPHYSIK
(1959). It appears here in translation with the permission of the
author and Walter de Gruyter & Company, Berlin.

THE PROBLEM OF THE NATURE of motion cannot be solved if
the inner and the outer worlds are sharply separated, as they
are in *Time and Free Will*. Bergson had already seen this very
clearly. Moreover, a concept of reality had always seemed more
important to him in his investigations than any particular theory
of motion. From the beginning he had been willing to reject
developing solutions, and *Matter and Memory* had opened up an
entirely new way to resolve the problem.

Nonetheless, both the problem of the nature of motion and that
of the distinction between the inner and the outer world continued to develop under the surface of Bergson's thought. In spite
of persistent efforts he had not been able to resolve the question
of whether time is simply a pure inner category—the point at
which his theory of motion had broken down. Decades later, after
Bergson had transposed temporality from the sphere of psychology into that of metaphysics, the difficulties of *Time and Free
Will* appeared in an entirely different guise, as Bergson, in the discussion of Einstein's theory, was forced to fall back on time as a
purely psychical category. In this discussion, which involved him
in an unending dispute with Jean Becquerel and André Metz,
Bergson attempted a conclusive proof of the absolute subjectivity
of time.

The reason for Bergson's having taken sides over such an extremely specialized scientific theory may well have been Langevin's researches, which made the paradoxes of relativity theory
extremely clear. These researches, which formed the kernel of the
dispute with Becquerel and Metz, contradicted the temporal
theory of *Time and Free Will* in two ways. Not only was time
shown to be linked to an external physical process involving the
speed of systems, but the strange division between simultaneity
and succession was erased and the possibility of their mutual in-

terchange established. Both conclusions touched the essential features of Bergson's bifurcation of inner and outer, the first, in which he made time (the most essential category of the inner world) independent of the external world, the second, in which he sharpened still further the peculiar distinction between spatiality and temporality which laid the basis of the distinction between simultaneity and succession. Both, moreover, in striking at the separation of inner and outer, struck also at the possibility of a metaphysical experience in general. It was no wonder then that Bergson, in spite of his widely modified interests and the remoteness of the entire complex of *Time and Free Will* from physical-mechanical problems, should have taken up the problem again.

The point of departure for Bergson's investigations was his interpretation of the Lorentz transformation, which was itself the starting point of relativity theory. In taking the transformation to pieces, Bergson was at pains to analyze both complex mathematical calculations and a complex observed phenomenon in order to be able to return from the observed elements of relativity theory to an absolute time. In so doing he took up the concept of the relativity of observed phenomena, and outstripped the science of his time, in that, appealing to Descartes, he hypostatized the relativity of all movement, including circular and accelerated motion. Thus, skipping over the real problems that result for both uniform and irregular motion in the Cartesian scheme of relativity (touching on them only through his remarks on Ernst Mach's observations concerning the relationships of masses), he moved to a concept of motion in which the outer world is more and more reduced to a concept of point of view.

In discussing relativity theory Bergson's primary goal was to undermine the notion of a concrete concept of motion in the external world. Yet, when he succeeded in producing an explication of the Lorentz transformation showing that the physical concept of motion is a pure concept of outer experience in phenomena, he found that his explication was not unequivocally complete, if it could be applied mutually to any given phenomenon. The possibility thus dawned on Bergson that the concept of motion might arise from some other complex of facts than the experience of change of place.

In classical physics the relativity of rectilinear motion was limited by the assumption of a general medium in which the universe was supposed to be located. The classical theories of the ether as a motionless stuff uniformly filling the universe opposed any thorough relativizing of motion. By the beginning of the nineteenth century, however, the investigations of George Airy and François Arago had already revealed significant weaknesses in this physical hypothesis, and after Albert Michelson's and Edward Morley's experiments had conclusively shown the indefensibility of the theory of the static ether, the demonstration of the absolute relativity of uniform motion was complete.

If Bergson now wished to annul these developments in nineteenth-century physics, he somehow had to try to win back the standpoint of the ether theory, *i.e.*, to find within the possible systems of motion some reference system which could be considered at rest. Toward this end Bergson was at pains to utilize Henry More's objection to Descartes' concept of motion. More attempted to make the phenomenon of inner effort the graduator of the system to be distinguished as at absolute rest (DS 34–35; DSf 38–39).

Straightaway, the defenders of relativity theory misunderstood this aspect of Bergson's critique and spoke of More's argument as a mere folly.[1] These thinkers posed two objections to More's concept of motion. First, they saw it as restricted to willed motion and could find no transition from the feeling of effort to a theory of motion in general which is in any way capable of bridging the gap between More's criterion and the complex of mechanical motion. Second, however—and this reproach strikes More's conception more deeply—the concept of motion thus formulated is limited to a system of two bodies in the earth's gravitational field. Effort, which for More designates the motion of two bodies with reference to each other, is not the reciprocal

1 Jean Becquerel, André George, André Metz, Arthur d' Abro, Charles Nordmann.

194

expression of the relative motion of both bodies but, on the contrary, simply signifies the necessity within a system of overcoming the earth's attraction. True, in an ideal two-body system changes of motion are caused by impulse, though it remains impossible to state in which of two bodies moving rectilinearly with respect to each other the causal impulse is located. Effort thus appears limited to a special case of the general problem of motion, one which conceals more than it clarifies.

This being the case, it seems rather odd that Bergson should, in his encounter with Einstein, have taken further pains with More's argument. Nonetheless it was because of the physicists, who had attacked Bergson for this reason, that his position relative to More was essentially modified. More's argument therefore was of no use to him in finding a criterion for the absoluteness of motion; Bergson's goal was above all to disclose the ontological ground of concepts of motion: he believed he had found this in the feeling of effort. The self-moved man in More's example becomes red-faced from effort, but this is already a phenomenon of the external world and in no way distinguishes his actions from locomotion. This union of effort and motion already presupposes a prior experience of one's own effort, an experience which makes possible the interpretation of the outer appearance of becoming red as an expression of physical effort. The salient point is thus the reasoning by analogy or sympathy which allows one to infer from one's own efforts those of other human beings. The essence of Bergson's argument is, therefore, the contention that the concept of motion must be traced back from locomotion to effort. Outer experience alone cannot constitute this concept, whose essential features are indebted to inner experience. In *Duration and Simultaneity* this dichotomy receives its obvious expression in the division of concepts of motion into those of transport and those of propagation (DS 40; DSf 48).

Bergson thereby reached, in contrast to More, a position opposed to that of the physicists. Motion is no longer simply a physical concept but in a very evident degree a concept of inner reality. This is true even of the meaning of transport, which, in its rela-

195

tivity, makes concrete specification quite difficult. All assertions that the ontological foundation of motion lies in inner phenomena remain for so long without a fruitful effect on the discussion that no one general relation is established between effort and motion. Moreover, this relationship stands in contradiction to the most advanced physical principles.

Bergson thus broke off the discussion of More's phenomenon with the remark that the physical concept is purely outer: "We do not have to take account of absolute motion in the construction of science: we do not know where it is produced, save exceptionally, and even then science should not concern itself with absolute motion, since it is not measurable, and science has measurement as its function. Science cannot and ought not to retain any part of reality save that which is homogeneous, measurable, visual, spread out in space. The motion it studies is therefore always relative and can consist only in a reciprocity of displacement. While More spoke as a metaphysician, Descartes marked with definitive precision the scientific point of view. He even went beyond the science of his own time, beyond Newtonian mechanics, beyond our own, formulating a principle which was reserved for Einstein to demonstrate" (DS 35; DSf 39–40). The entire detour into an ontological formulation appears from this point of view, however, as a blind alley.

Yet the discussion was nonetheless not fruitless. It produced the assertion that the source of motion in inner phenomena is a fundamental fact. Motion is thus split into two components: a core of real experience and a nominalistic fiction. Each external motion is by its very nature not connected with reality. The description of a process in the external world by means of a concept of motion is a purely nominalistic act, one which is to be decided by questions of viewpoint. Nonetheless, the external world is not thereby entirely understood as having a share in the concepts developed in consciousness—as in, for example, the concept of motion. *Time and Free Will* already spoke of transition regions in which inner and outer meet (TFW 126; *Essai* 94). *Duration and Simultaneity* took up this notion again explicitly relative to the discussion of time, depicting the process by which an inner concept is carried over into the external world (DS 46; DSf 57). Bergson considered the derivation for yet a third time on the occasion of Einstein's lecture before the Société Française de Philosophie in 1922, at which time he described the relations between inner and outer world in the following way:

"Common sense believes in a unique time, the same for all beings and all things. What does this belief arise from? Each of us feels himself endure: each duration is the actual flowing, continuous and indivisible, of our inner life. But our inner life includes perceptions, and these perceptions belong at the same time to ourselves and to things. We thus extend our duration to our immediate material surroundings. Since these surroundings are themselves surrounded, and so on indefinitely, there is no reason, we think, why our duration should not just as well be the duration of things. This is the reasoning which each of us expresses vaguely, I would almost say unconsciously. When we submit it to a higher degree of clarity and precision, we represent to ourselves, beyond what can be termed the horizon of our perception, a consciousness whose perceptual field overlaps our own—and beyond that consciousness and its perceptual field another consciousness situated analogously with respect to it, and so on, indefinitely. All these consciousnesses, being human consciousnesses, seem to us to live the same duration. Hence all their outer experiences unfold in the same duration. And since all these experiences, encroaching on each other, have, by pairs, a common part, we end by representing to ourselves a unique experience, occupying a unique time.

At this point we may, if we wish, eliminate the human consciousnesses which we have distributed in place after place as if they were so many relays for the motion of our thought: there remains only the impersonal time in which all things flow. Thus we have the same reasoning in a more precise form. Whether we remain vague or seek precision, in both cases the idea of a universal time common to consciousnesses and things is a simple hypothesis." [2]

[2] *Bulletin de la société française de la philosophie*, XXII (1922), 103.

The possibility of contact between the two worlds thus makes possible the transfer of inner concepts to the outer world and even permits the extension of these concepts from nearby surroundings, in which they are to this extent real (insofar as the outer world is at the same time the perceptual field of the content of consciousness), to the entire universe, which is given for consciousness as a mere possibility for thought. Nevertheless, this transition from real surroundings given in consciousness as a real image to the whole expanse of the universe accomplishes a basic emptying of concepts and thereby a turn from real experience to hypothesis. Concepts borrowed from the inner world pass in this way from the real structures of concrete images to purely fictitious dimensions of human thought.

With this theory of transitions between inner and outer experience—the first concrete theory of its kind since Victor Cousin—Bergson developed the initial basis for his discussion of relativity theory, which makes relativity theory a fiction of human thought. All concepts of pure thought have their source in inner experience, but both of the basic concepts of Einsteinian relativity, the concepts of time and motion, are relative when sundered from the concrete details of a unique act of perception. Every general theory of outer being is therefore relative since it cannot dispense with the concepts of duration and motion and since it must give up the relationship to concrete images and overstep the horizon of consciousness.

In his initial statement of a nominalistic theory of relativity Bergson believed he had at the same time grasped the essence of Einsteinian relativity.[3] In addition, he had found the solution to the paradoxes outlined by Langevin: the relativity of thought, which is at the root of Langevin's studies, is rectified through the constancy of real experience. The return of speculative concepts to concrete experience thus does away with relativity.

This philosophical procedure, when applied to relativity theory, undermines its basic premise, the reciprocity of standpoints. Classical physics had already created the concept of uni-

3 *Ibid.*, 103–104.

form rectilinear motion by positing the relativity of moving and immobile systems; Bergson developed by means of More's example a criterion of absolute rest and, simultaneously, an absolute system of reference which—at least for uniform rectilinear motion—had been lost through the Michelson-Morley experiment. That is, the system in which the real, living observer existed was distinguished from all other systems by means of the real perceptual horizon of the observer. Within this perceptual horizon time and motion were real, experienced dimensions, while beyond this horizon another observer could always be a mere fiction of the real observer's and thereby live a fictitious motion in a fictitious time.

Bergson thereby created what relativity could not find in the Lorentz transformation—an absolute system of reference. True, in order to establish this conclusion he found it necessary to go beyond the arguments of physics, which—as in Langevin's investigations—no longer dealt with any real consciousness. Nonetheless, it did not undermine Bergson's position to include such a standard within his own viewpoint. "Certainly nothing prevents us from supposing, at a given moment, that the reference system is itself in motion. Physics has often had an interest in doing so, and relativity readily makes this assumption. But when the physicist puts his reference system in motion, he actually provisionally chooses another, which becomes immobile in turn. This second system, it is true, may then be put in motion mentally without thought necessarily taking up location in a third. But then it oscillates between the two, immobilizing them in turn through comings and goings so rapid that it can give the illusion of leaving both in motion. It is in precisely this sense that we speak of a 'reference system' " (DS 41; DSf 49–50).

In this actual system at rest the concepts of time and motion possess a reality entirely different from that which they have in the actual system in motion. Here with his real time is the concrete observer for whom the experience of outer motion will be mediated by a kind of inference by analogy whose starting point is the inner passage of consciousness. The time of other system is, to the contrary, only real so long as it has some part in the inner time of the concrete observer by the fact that the system is a perceived reality. If the system falls outside the perceptual horizon, it becomes a mere thought-possibility, and its time becomes fictitious also—that is, conceivable by the concrete observer, but no longer capable of being experienced by him.

Langevin's investigations are thereby stripped of their paradoxes. What becomes of the projectile and its time after it leaves the earth if it is shot into space at half the speed of light is a question which cannot be posed. If the observer remains on the earth, the projectile actually possesses no real time. If the observer is placed in the projectile, the earth loses its own time, and the Lorentz transformation once more bypasses real time and deals solely with a fiction. Of course the observer can in each case construct a valid time concept for the other system which may then be subjected to the Lorentz transformation, but this time will have no reality: it will be fictitious. But concerning the state of the projectile in the individual phases of its flight, the actual observer on the earth can give just as little information as can be given at any time concerning the path of a light ray in Michelson's and Morley's experiment (DS 17ff; DSf 13ff).

Here, however, one of Bergson's more persistent difficulties arose, one which scientists were quick to criticize.[4] Bergson attemped to get out of a difficulty through a flight into agnosticism, only to heighten the difficulties of his position. In pursuing the question of the ultimate relations between inner and outer for the entire range of experience—including the experience of other minds—he tried to mesh both with precision; but in the most critical phase of his discussion he chose to evade the problem through a general agnosticism concerning the experience of the external world and thereby deprived himself of the possibility of discussing relativity theory.

Nevertheless, by such means Bergson developed his starting point quite rigorously: the entire reach of human experience is to be divided into two parts, what is immediately experienced and

[4] André Metz, *Relativité et relativisme. Bergson et Bergsonisme*, 38.

200

what is merely conceptualized. On these terms, however, the latter does not remain inaccessible to possible experience. Living beings constitute, as it were, the center of the reality around them; the objects lying within the horizon of this center come to be immediately experienced, and those which lie beyond its boundary meanwhile remain merely represented. Man's capacity to move, however, makes it possible to push back this horizon, thereby permitting the objects of the world to take part in this reality. Or, to take up the terminology of *Matter and Memory* again: every object becomes an image in two ways, in relation to consciousness and in relation to other objects. Through this concept of reality, which agrees essentially with Berkeley's,[5] Bergson had, through distinguishing real content from perceived and imagined objects, maintained the possibility of introducing a concept of relativity into his system. In this concept of relativity he utilized the application of concepts of inner experience to imagined objects though he did not thereby provide an unequivocal proof, but gave them the status of questions of standpoint. In this way he reached the first level of his discussion of physical relativity. The further lesson provided by this philosophical concept of relativity is that the philosophical form is the prototype of Einsteinian relativity. He therefore had to trace physical relativity back to philosophical relativity as he understood it. Thus Bergson took his stand. He had to demonstrate that the relativity of time and the relativity of motion cited by physicists disappear within the observer's horizon of time and consciousness and there regain their old constancy.

This demonstration, however, ran into a basic difficulty in the Michelson-Morley experiment. For this experiment can, by postulating two further observers, modify the turning points of the light rays so that its three critical phases enter into the observer's consciousness. Thus the relativity of phenomena, which is for Bergson simply a product of mathematical reckoning, can in this way become perceived, apart from any formula. Bergson had al-

[5] On Bergson's relations to Berkeley, see abstract of lectures in the *Annuaire du Collège de France*, 1908, p. 89, and 1909, p. 76; further, MM 3; MMf 3.

ready seen this difficulty clearly enough and because of it had developed an agnosticism according to which the possibility of a threefold observation from three distinguishable standpoints is denied. The question of coordination is thus brought into the foreground, and the comparison of clocks by three observers is revealed to be an insurmountable barrier.[6] This turn toward ontological problems in the midst of physical-technical questions seems at first strange. Nevertheless, the consequences that Bergson drew from it were sufficient for his demonstration. In this way he isolated one of the three observers, who is the only one who is real for himself, while both others, who are outside his horizons, are for him fictitious.

This methodological agnosticism is only the manifestation of an ontological problem which lies still deeper. If the difference between the inner and outer world is in fact a basic ontological distinction, then an insurmountable barrier will exist between individual men. To be sure, Bergson implicitly assumed that his own theory of inner experience is valid for all men. This, however, in no way obviates the fact that each man's inner experience is perceptible by him alone. Other men are also located in the external world and consequently coincide essentially more with outer objects than with individual selves.

Bergson always developed his philosophical viewpoints on the basis of the sciences. This procedure had instilled in him a clear attitude toward objective concepts, according to which the distinction between observer and observed closely parallels that assumed in the Cartesian Cogito. According to this distinction, the human being passes from the limit of his own self in introspection to the status of an object in vision. Even at those points at which Bergson pushed forward to a social philosophy—for example, in *The Two Sources of Morality and Religion*—the scientific attitude toward the object, determined by the positivistic sociological school of Alfred Espinas and Émile Durkheim, was maintained. The circle of understanding, the antinomies of historical science, which in Germany at least from the time of Fried-

[6] *Revue de philosophie*, XXIV (1924), 253.

rich Schleiermacher have been vital philosophical problems and which at the time of Bergson's own achievement remained a point of great concern for Wilhelm Dilthey, lay completely beyond Bergson's horizon. The problem of "other minds" was quickly done away with by hypostatizing an argument from analogy.

The discussion of relativity theory thus shows a basic weakness in Bergson's way of distinguishing inner and outer. The attempt to anchor essentially ontological concepts (such as time-concepts) in introspective experience destroys the unity of transcendental consciousness which Bergson—who was nonetheless striving after a general theory—perhaps tacitly presupposed. The great advantage of Bergson's approach, its capacity to find a starting point in what is really perceived, is bought at the price of the isolation of consciousness. Time, which thus becomes an individual's time-consciousness, entirely loses its connection with the time processes of other men. With this loss each individual consciousness is forced to impute to other human beings a time that is experienced not by them but by his own consciousness. Factual difficulties would become infinite if these times should coincide.

Langevin's research had extricated the individual times of different observers from their coordination [*Koordinierbarkeit*]. This thesis, which proceeds from an entirely different time-concept, was thus at least in agreement with the physical theories of time. At this point Bergson took up his position on the problem of different lived times.

The first part of Bergson's answer is surprisingly consistent: the second observer in Langevin's research is not real; his time is not an experienced, but a fictitious time. He is simply an imaginary dimension of the first observer. With this solution the problem of other minds is again repressed. The other human being is thus reduced to an object of one's own experience. From this point on, Bergson could defend the unity of both his own relativistic approach and Einstein's. Physical considerations thus remain in the imagination alone; the dimensions appearing in Lorentz' formulae are merely fictitious.

André Metz and Jean Becquerel, however, sharpened the ques-

203

tion through different retorts. They raised the question as to what it is that the two observers in Langevin's experiment know to report when they come together again after the completed experiment. Here the questionable problem of the two time experiences is made concrete and transposed at the same time into an experience of the outer world. Bergson did not hesitate in giving his answer to this question:

> In vain then does Peter, attached to the immobile system we term the system of the Earth, desire to interrogate Paul—there, at the moment when he will re-enter the system—concerning his impressions of the voyage: for this Paul has observed nothing and has had no impressions, being nothing more than one of Peter's representations. He vanishes, moreover, the instant he reaches Peter's system. The Paul who has had impressions is a Paul who has experienced during the interval, and the Paul who has experienced during the interval is a Paul who is at each instant interchangeable with Peter, who occupies a time identical with Peter's and who has grown old just as quickly. . . . It is for Paul simply as an object of representation and reference that four hours (represented) will have moved past while eight hours (experienced) will have elapsed for Peter. But Paul, as conscious, and hence as referrer, will have experienced eight hours, since it will then be necessary to apply to him everything we have said concerning Peter (DS 169–70, 171; DSf 254–55, 257–58 [1st Appendix]).

This interpretation of relativity admits of a double interpretation. The phrase "which occupies a unique time" suggests that Bergson nonetheless presupposed a general time in which life evolves, over and above individual physical times—as was implied in *Creative Evolution*. Such an interpretation involves two difficulties, therefore, one philosophical and one physical. On one side there is experience, whose introspective starting point can be developed into a universal time concept. The physical definition of time does not produce the difficulty, which is produced instead by the introspective method, taken to be psychologically adequate. If it is not possible, with Cousin, to make psychical principles constitutive of the external world, there is no possibility of arriving from this position at an ontological thesis. The gap, however, which Bergson had placed between the inner and the outer world cannot here be closed; consequently, what the "identical time" may be, psychology can no longer say, and ontology—since it cannot encounter the real time-concept—can give no information.

On the other hand, the physical consequences of this position also remain extreme. The two observers, on meeting again, must make statements contradicting the physical calculations. Reality and physical theory are placed in absolute opposition. Both will have lived the same time, though neither will have supposed this according to the physical theory. The theory holds, then, only so long as it is not verified. Bergson's discussion was scarcely undertaken with the hope of achieving this result, and the interpretation of "unique time" only entangles the problem in more contradiction and difficulty.

A second interpretation of Bergson's standpoint is possible, by way of the concept "interchangeable." The objection, to which Becquerel had already alluded,[7] that it is not possible to deny physics a double observation, will be met by making the two observers identical. On this interpretation Paul's return coincides with Peter's, and one is in reality dealing with a single person under two aspects.

This thesis is much to be preferred as a way of avoiding physical difficulties since it dispenses with discrepancies between experience and physical theory. The Lorentz transformation holds in all cases, but always for the second observer alone; and the suitability (*gemä β*) of Bergson's special "viewpoint-on-reality" is always merely fictitious. Here the world divides into two components, an inner world and an outer world in general. On the theory that all observers are identical, each other inner world coincides with the particular consciousness of anyone, and the Lorentz transformation is valid without exception for the entire outer world. Here the system in which the living observer exists,

---

[7] Jean Becquerel, "Rezension de Durée et Simultanéité," *Bulletin scientifique des étudiants de Paris*, March, 1923.

and which is always at rest, introduces the temporal deformations which the Lorentz transformation henceforth assumes occur only in the system occupied by the fictitious observer. The fictitious times are purely represented times; the sole lived time is absolute. This interpretation, though it involves a superior attitude of tolerance, places a greater burden on the philosophical component of Bergson's argument. Lived experience—which Bergson believed to be radically threatened by Einstein's theory—by no means supports the identification of two observers. Moreover, this identification does not seem to be consistent with the practical experience of the perception of others. Certainly for each consciousness there exists one and only one inner world; but this does not yet establish an ontological argument for the identity of all these inner experiences.

The essence of this discussion of Einstein's theory of relativity, which in 1922 seemed like a falling back to Bergson's initial position, was thus entirely neglected, along with all the possibilities of widening the psychological approach of *Time and Free Will* provided by *An Introduction to Metaphysics* and *Creative Evolution*. Instead, the discussion returns to the original psychologism and develops the problem of other minds. Granting the basic thesis of the psychological sources of time—a thesis concerning which Becquerel expressed no reservations—for Bergson there remains the difficulty of the transition from introspected time experience to the concept of a concretely existing time, one which exists at least in transcendental consciousness, if not at all in the outer world. To what extent this time concept requires access to the physical world the discussion of *Duration and Simultaneity* cannot make clear.

The question of reality was also further sharpened by this discussion. Bergson's theory that being is being-as-it-appears (in the usual restricted sense of immediately conscious being) leads to a distinction between the real and the fictitious, which also holds for physical theory. At each step the question is earnestly put: What worth do the assertions of physics have when the distinction is made between real and fictitious dimensions? It is certainly possible to doubt Langevin's thesis, as has been the case with many well-known physicists. However, if his thesis is to be explained as correct but unreal, the problem ought not to be over-simplified, and at this point the problem necessarily accords a new importance to the question of the reality of the external world.

In spite of these problems Bergson could not, in *Time and Free Will*, renounce a rigorous solution of the problem of time, on the basis discussed above. It is precisely on this basis of a time lying entirely in the inner world that he will develop his theory of freedom and thus lay the foundations for a metaphysical investigation. We have already seen that in the nineteenth century in France the concept of metaphysics was so closely bound up with the question of freedom that the entire struggle between positivism and spiritualism could have been limited to this one problem.

The second great point of difference, the status of the organic, with its inherent antithesis of causality and finality, which in the middle of the century became a vital issue dividing the two points of view,[8] may itself be reduced to the initial opposition between determinism and indeterminism.

Nevertheless, in *Time and Free Will* Bergson refused to place the problem of freedom, which has been broached by him there, within the full scope of the scientific discussion. Whether there is freedom in nature—whether, for example, the development of species, self-preservation, the capacity for regeneration, irritability, or ontogenesis are to be considered seriously to be causal or finalistic phenomena—remained entirely beyond Bergson's interests. The problem he posed was precisely defined. It led him, fresh from the data of positivism, to the clarification of an initial question: Is there really, in the whole of the experimentally accessible world, any phenomenon which justifies the hypothesis of a metaphysical freedom?

In putting this question Bergson conceded an important point to those who would argue the determinism of the external world on

---

8 Cf. the description of the struggles between animists and vitalists by Félix Ravaisson Mollien in *La Philosophie en France au 19ᵉ siècle* (Paris, 1867), 178ff.

the basis of causality, though this concession was accompanied by a protest against an excessively scientific ethics (TFW 153ff; *Essai* 115ff). However, in contrast to Boutroux he did not raise the question of the existence of freedom in the outer world. Moreover, he did not attempt to reconcile the concept of freedom, like Fouillée, with the representation of natural causality. He acknowledged for his own part the validity of science's pretensions to an integral causality in nature. His solution of the problem of freedom depends upon the exclusion of an area of being from the sphere of the natural science. This initial approach, therefore, justifies his desire to effect a rigorous separation of "outer" and "inner."

This concept of freedom as arising from the inner world must involve a struggle against the investigations of positivistic psychology, just as in order to survive, the inner life must subjugate a strict causal theory, whether of associationism, psychophysical parallelism, or motivational causality. In each case Bergson argued that the psychological theory in question subserves a concept of homogeneous time, a time which is at bottom space. Similarly, the reproach which he directed against the positivist's psychological theory is that it spatializes psychological time and hence makes quantitative dimensions out of the qualitative flux of psychological events. Only thus has this psychology been able to coordinate psychologically measurable dimensions, hypostatize an atomic mental structure, or place individual psychic relations alongside each other on one homogeneous level of time (TFW 145; *Essai* 109).

J. F. BUSCH

Einstein and Bergson, Convergence and Divergence of Their Ideas

Remarks by the Editor. In this brief essay, the outline of a talk given at the tenth International Congress of Philosophy (1949),

208

Professor J. F. Busch seeks to reconcile Bergson's and Einstein's contrasting standpoints. While the philosopher and the physicist are both empiricists, their respective empiricisms represent complementary aspects of scientific thought. Once the close interrelations of Bergson's "method of intuition" and Einstein's "method of intelligence" are explored, the way will be open to the understanding of the concept of "positionality," which combines the essential features of both methods.

Both Bergson and Einstein, as empiricists, attempt to discern the basic characteristics of "nature." Each, however, attempts to do so through a different image of the world. The world of the empirical metaphysician (Bergson) is qualitative; the world of the positivist (whom Busch treats as very close to Einstein) is quantitative. Neither world is to be preferred to the other since the researches of the positivist and the empirical metaphysician both achieve an equal empirical dignity. The interplay of these two worlds explains why nature should appear to us as having both qualitative and quantitative aspects.

The labors of neo-positivism have made clear what is involved in the method of intelligence. Positivism construes nature essentially as a network of quantitative relations, a network whose basic features are capable of being axiomatized. But positivism's axiomatic is always imperfect and incomplete, and the constant coming-and-going between entities and relations involved in the improvement and broadening of this axiomatic directs us towards a "nature" in which terms and relations are not artificially distinct, a nature relative to which the artificial rigidity of our thought tends to dissolve. In short, the quantitative relationships (e.g., physical laws) which positivism attempts to axiomatize are shown to be dependent on an awareness of qualitative relations.

The progress of modern scientific thought is thus marked by a series of interactions between intelligence and intuition. Yet these interactions may also be expressed as the growth of a single experience, the "experience of pure presence." Beginning with Euclid and continuing with Archimedes, Galileo, Michelson and Morley, Busch traces the development of scientific knowledge, showing at each step how man's conception of pure presence has enlarged and developed, at each step gaining a greater "tension" between intellectual and intuitive apprehension. Basic to the experience of pure presence is the fact of positionality. The organism, in taking position before a world, implicitly applies both intuitive and intellectual modes of apprehension. *Professor Busch's essay, which follows, was originally published in the* PROCEEDINGS OF THE TENTH INTERNATIONAL CONGRESS OF PHILOSOPHY *(1949). It appears here in translation with the permission of the author and the North-Holland Publishing Company.*

I. ANY RAPPROCHEMENT between Einstein's and Bergson's ideas demands that a point of contact be established between the method of intelligence and the method of intuition. This point can be found in the fact that both declare themselves to be empiricists. The empiricist chooses a domain of reference termed "nature" from which it seems possible to him to extract the image of a "world." For the radical positivist this world is only an artificial superstructure; for the empirical metaphysician it is an infrastructure possessing a special dignity. For both, the difference in no way implies a different evaluation, since their results possess an equal, specifically empirical dignity which gives them a sort of index of authenticity. Nature seems to favor intelligence no more than intuition; and both of these two methods, insofar as they are empirical, can achieve knowledge of nature by means of their images of the world, a nature which is the representative sign of the milieu in which man sees active existence unfold in front of him. There is also room to ask if it is not this nature which would always be in process of construction through a primordial activity of man, who would feed it with data corresponding on one side to material needs and on the other to the vaster needs of the human spirit. Thus would be explained nature's property of being the realm of the qualitative and of the quantitative, and it would allow us to suppose that everything which science extracts from nature always bears the mark of this mixed realm, henceforth termed the mark of intuitiveness and rationality, science insofar as it is empirical viewing nature in its totality and thereby gaining its index of authenticity. It is to be noted that Bergson, though celebrating the exercise of pure intuition, has many times admitted that it is rarely encountered.[1] In nature there would be the intrinsic unity of the level of life, attained in science through a process of rhythmic interweaving of the two worlds which the understanding for reasons of expediency loves to distinguish, each helping to call forth the other, both thereby gaining the index of authenticity, neither going to the limit.[2]

In order to demonstrate this thesis it would be necessary to disentangle this rhythmic process. This should not be hard to do since rational science has already made a decisive analysis of its own properties in neo-positivism.

II. Neo-positivism's construction of the object is well known. Nature is taken to be a multiplicity of entities in relation, and the world is posited through a play of axioms, which through a coming-and-going connect these relations to entities. Only the former are considered capable of being the object of investigation; the latter enter the picture only as a function of the relationships. This axiomatization is therefore the fundamental sorting out of nature, and it is the intelligence which is at work in defining, by means of axioms, fundamental notions which thus bear the mark of imperfection. But already in this initial phase intuition plays its part, for it is precisely in the coming-and-going between entities and relations that rational rigidity tends to dissolve, directing us toward the common source of entities and of relations, a nature in which it is possible to distinguish them without being able to isolate them. The axioms which are supposed to yield quantitative diagrams are thus shown to be dependent on quality. This role of intuition is increased through the fact that in the axiomatics we find a tendency toward totality. The intelligence here perceives only a totality resulting from a combination; in the light of intuition nonetheless we see here the tendency to suppress

---

[1] Cf. Joseph F. Busch, *Bergson of het betoomd élan* (Amsterdam, 1939).
[2] Cf. Bergson's treatment of the problem of "endosmosis."

rigidity: one must see them dissolving themselves in order to take possession of that nature in which our conscious life unfolds. This totalizing function of axiomatics is brought to light in a series of Gaston Bachelard's remarkable works culminating in *The Philosophy of No*.[3]

III. Max Planck notes that in physical science only three notions are necessary—space, time, and "something moving." These notions can immediately be brought together in the concept of a "point in motion." This is what Poincaré (seconded by Einstein) will define in terms of nature: it will be the foundation of the fundamental notion of voluntary muscular sensations. Perhaps even neo-positivists would have no objection[4] to speaking of this as the observer's "taking position" with respect to an "exteriority." In that case the guideline (cf. the terminology of P. Janet) of physical science will be the "guideline of pure presence." From this "experience of pure presence" physics receives its index of authenticity. The development of this experience and this index can be explained in the following stages.

1. Euclid, basing his thought on Democritus' notion of empty space, places in this empty space the point, which is fixed at absolute rest, but whose position is manifested immediately as an invitation to juxtaposition, space then becoming something other than an empty receptacle, since it is the relation between points which will define position. Presence becomes the fundamental notion founded on a totality of potential relations.

2. With Archimedes the point at rest gains the status of a point in equilibrium. The tie which defines positions possesses a tension. Pure presence begins to develop the germ of "the event." It is shown to be superadded to geometrical constructions. It invites us to choose among these constructions those which will make us able to dominate it. Space becomes the domain of rigid constructions through which one puts himself in search of presences which, taken in a momentary equilibrium, can be put to our service in time.

---

[3] Gaston Bachelard, *La philosophie du non* (Paris: Presses Universitaires de France, 1941).

[4] Cf. A. Ramsperger, *Philosophy of Science* (New York, 1942), *i.v.*, solipsism.

3. Galileo discovers "the supreme affinity of motion and time." The geometrical representation of motion is a symbol in which space and time come together. Thus is born the space of the infinitesimal calculus. Celestial bodies in their orbits exhibit the sort of rigid constructions through which can be interpreted the sequence of events in a spatio-temporal composite which is defined through an order of presences in equilibrium in a space which is transformed with time.[5]

4. It is through Michelson's and Morley's experiment that, in Einstein's theory, this "space" is brought to its greatest tension. This tension will be manifested to such a degree that even the method of Archimedes and of Galileo, heretofore fundamental to rational science, is no longer capable of resisting (cf. the work of Bachelard). Relativity demands the reduction of all the notions of science to others which will be an amalgam of the current notions of space, time, things, motion, velocity, energy, cause, and effect. It is presence which demands hegemony. The primary qualities blend into the secondary ones. Thus is born the pure "phenomenon" which, for the first time in the history of exact science, is none other than nature, i.e., "that which is produced on a foundation." Through a hyper-rational analysis, presence thus acquires an ontological dignity. Space becomes the space of the tensor calculus; it is the metrical field.[6]

IV. Even when it is agreed that this presence is related only to the artificial existence of the physical object, the notion will give an unexpected richness to the fundamental thesis of the taking of position, which Bergson describes in the "experience of the instant" (false recognition). Einstein's conception defines its tangential property. Since it conducts us to the limits of the *metodo resolutivo e compositivo*, pure presence defines the being for which the world is produced and which is here produced tan-

[5] Cf. the *metodo resolutivo e compositivo* of Galileo and Archimedes.
[6] The examination of these data cannot be carried out without continual reference to the works of Alfred North Whitehead, though it is very difficult in Whitehead's case to accept any particular notion without accepting his whole position.

gentially, thereby bringing about an essential weakness that requires the support of intelligence and intuition.

It is remarkable that a special concept has been created to describe this situation in the writings of Helmuth Plessner.[7] He takes the essential category of the living being to be the taking of position, the fact of being produced, and he thus terms its basic property *Positionalität*, which can be translated positionality, if it is permissible thus to put this expression into international circulation. Positionality, then, is the characteristic the living being has of finding itself placed *en centralité* with respect to the world and itself. It is because of this fact that there is for it a "without" and a "within." Through this notion Plessner hopes to find a means of surmounting the Cartesian dualism from which, until now, the life sciences have not been able to free themselves.

W. BERTEVAL
Bergson and Einstein

Remarks by the Editor. Bergson's criticisms of static views of motion, W. Berteval suggests, in many respects parallel Einstein's criticisms of basic features of Newtonian physics. Both Bergson and Einstein 1) reject the concept of absolute rest as a sort of absolute zero from which all velocities are to be calculated, 2) attempt to deal more adequately with what transpires *between* the beginning and the end points of a motion or a period of time, and 3) insist that physics starts from a "moving" reality which is by its very nature complex. From this last consideration both the philosopher and the physicist conclude that rectilinear motions are artificial simplifications of real motions, which, since they result from the interaction of contrasting forces, are curved. But

---

[7] Helmuth Plessner, *Die Stufen des Organischen und der Mensch* (Bonn, 1928).

214

this is to say that for Bergson as for Einstein regularity is a limiting case of the complexity of things, while such a simple abstraction as Euclidean space is incapable of fully representing the flux of matter.

Berteval closes his discussion with a highly speculative comparison of the manner in which Bergson and Einstein attempt to conceive the regularity of nature. Bergson, it is true, criticizes the mechanical regularity and immutability exhibited in scientific laws; yet at the same time he discovers another *order* of phenomena in the constancy of resolution and the sustained harmony of human personalities which have become fully self-aware. He thus implicitly distinguishes between the complex harmony of the will and the simple regularities of matter, and his criticisms of mechanical views of the world are really directed against attempts to derive the former (willed action) from the latter (mechanical regularity). Rather, Bergson insists, we must see that mechanical regularity is derived from the complex harmony of the will. This duality and this derivation, Berteval holds, are also present in certain aspects of Einstein's thought. For Einstein, physics is based not on the mechanical regularities of matter but on the behavior of light. The speed of light is constant, and in this respect immutable; in another respect, however, light must be considered as constantly and infinitely accelerating. This changing constancy of light is for relativity physics absolutely basic, and all real motions must be conceived as degradations of it. Thus the simple regularities of matter must be derived from the complex regularity of light-propagation, and Einstein opposed any attempt to derive the latter from the former. *Professor Berteval's essay, originally published in the* REVUE PHILOSOPHIQUE, *CXXXII (January–March, 1942–43), appears here in translation with the permission of the author and the* REVUE PHILOSOPHIQUE.

WITH THE MODESTY of truly great minds, Bergson thought he had done nothing for modern thought but simply fill in a gap. Modern thought, he believed, has grasped only the outline of time and has allowed its essence to escape. By limiting itself to the observation of successive states, modern thought has neglected the most important thing, that which is between them and which constitutes the reality of time: namely, duration. This duration, which we can perceive immediately, manifests itself in and around us through an unceasing creativity: no two instants are identical.

When we attempt to gain a profound knowledge of reality, we reduce it to laws, that is, to something fixed, always identical. But, in this world we are concerned only with similarities, and the more we endeavor to understand the world, the more we allow its diversities to escape us. Nothing is left for us to do but to acknowledge these diversities. There is no way to explain them. Why do they exist? It would seem that they need not have existed. There are distinct objects where there might just as well have been nothing, and all reality seems to us as if it has added itself, through some miraculous grace, to a possible nothingness. All that it is possible to establish about the states of this reality, apart from their existence, is their greater or lesser degree of divergence. Science is thus reduced to calculating the relations between things and their relations to the whole of things, beginning with an initial zero.

Against this procedure, however, Bergson protests strenuously: science always calculates only the differences between successive states. But when you look into yourself, that is, into the only being of which you have immediate knowledge, do you encounter these marked differences and these successive states? Or do you not, rather, find an absolute continuity, a reality perpetually changed yet always the same? And when you observe the world around you in the light of this discovery, do you not rediscover this continuity in the form of an incessant impetus, an *élan vital?* This is precisely what science has neglected, and what must be re-established. It is a curious fact, however, that, while Bergson insists above all that metaphysical arguments should rest on intimate experience and biology, here is a man, with whom Bergson is partially in disagreement, who provides him with new arguments, derived immediately from mathematics and physics.

Einstein appeared at the moment when Michelson's experiments concerning the trajectory of light rays had involved physicists in an undeniable contradiction: the discrepancy calculated for the trajectory of light rays was not produced. Einstein discovered that the error lay not only in the way we interpret nature but also in the way we calculate motion. Until Einstein offered his explanation, physicists had reasoned as follows: if motion is translated by figures, these figures ought to express absolute quantities added to a zero of absolute motion, and hence to an absolute immobility.

But, Einstein asks, where can this absolute immobility be found? When we say that an object is immobile, we mean that it is immobile with respect to the earth. But the earth moves with respect to the sun, while the sun can only be declared immobile relative to a system that is itself relative to another. When many systems are present, which will we take for mobile, which for fixed? All this is pure convention; there is no immobility save with reference to some other thing. It had been believed possible to speak at least of the immobility of the ether. But it was the immobility of the ether which Michelson's experiment had presupposed, and the experiment failed.

The absolute zero therefore does not exist, and hence absolute numbers, deprived of any foundation, are mere phantoms.

This is the starting point of the theory of relativity; and, remarkably, this is what Bergson had already expressly stated in his critique of the concept of successive states. You consider, he insists, only the extremities or stopping points of a motion; but then, since you do not take account of what transpires between them, you can accelerate or decelerate the motion indefinitely without changing your calculations. These calculations do not, therefore, take account of reality in which the speed of motion plays a very important part, a speed of which you have precisely the feeling in duration. Well: here Einstein's theory makes an advance by showing that this incomplete way of viewing things influences not only our calculations but our perception itself. Our perception is distorted precisely because we continue to confuse

217

motions which have different velocities. Let us briefly consider Einstein's demonstration: when I say of two objects that one moves while the other does not, I can admit indifferently that the first moves with respect to the second or the second with respect to the first. That is, I can just as well relate myself to one as to the other. But what has been forgotten is that, depending on which of these reference systems is adopted, my mode of measurement changes. In fact, velocity is measured by the time required to pass through a trajectory, as measured by synchronously regulated clocks. If I want to establish the velocity of a train by means of the times at which it passes through two stations, it will be necessary that the clocks at these two stations mark exactly the same instant. Now, let us suppose that these clocks are furnished with chimes loud enough to be heard from the other station. A man standing on the tracks at the center of the distance to be traversed (that is, in the first reference system) will hear them simultaneously. But who does not see that for a man placed at the center of the second reference system (that is, the moving train), the clocks no longer strike simultaneously, since one approaches to the extent that the other recedes. Or, if you want to arrange things so that the passenger on the moving train hears both simultaneously, you must slightly displace your clocks, thereby modifying the length of the trajectory and all your measures of length. Until the present time, however, space and time measures had always been considered uniform, regardless of the reference system adopted. But what does this say if not that, here again, as Bergson had observed, only the extremities of the trajectory or the time taken to traverse it had been considered, while no account had been taken of what transpired between them? Only, finally, it is no longer possible to accept an incomplete notion of reality because mathematically false results follow from its generalization—as Michelson's experiment proves.

These errors are negligible in practice. Thus they are not revealed until one deals with enormous distances, as in astronomy, or with unexpected velocities, as with cathode rays. But, then, it had to be recognized that one was dealing with approximations so long as one was using numbers based on a zero which can only be arbitrary. And it is here that we rejoin Bergson again: zero represents nothingness, and Bergson has demonstrated most convincingly that an absolute emptiness is inconceivable. What do I mean when I state that that bottle is empty? That is contains no wine. But it contains air. And if I empty it of air? It will always contain space. What I term nothing is really the absence of something; I always assume some other thing has taken its place. To conceive the absence of everything is absolutely impossible.

Well, the zero, it turns out, introduces obscurity and error into mathematics as well. All mathematics is based on numerical progressions. But there are two kinds of progressions: arithmetical ones, which alone involve zero (0, 1, 2, 3, 4 . . . or 0, 2, 4, 6, 8 . . .), and geometrical ones, obtained by multiplying each new term by the same number (for example, 2, 4, 8, 16 . . .) or, inversely, by dividing by the same number. In the latter case the progression will proceed by decreasing (8, 4, 2, 1, $\frac{1}{2}$, $\frac{1}{4}$ . . .). Smaller fractions will thus be generated, but never zero. While arithmetic progressions thus proceed from a zero to which units are added, geometric progressions proceed from any quantity whatever. However, in the latter case, since one starts with a magnitude, it is advantageous to choose the largest possible in order to be able to go in only one direction, always decreasing. In the case of an intermediate number, one would have to progress sometimes in one direction and sometimes in the other.

And this is exactly how Einstein proceeds. In all his calculations of velocities, he begins with the greatest possible velocity, which is that of light. We will see soon why the greatest velocity possible is that of light, and what great advantages Einstein derives by starting all calculations from it. For the moment we limit ourselves to showing this: by beginning with zero, we can have only arithmetical progressions; if, on the contrary, we begin with a real number, the geometric progression also becomes possible. If we now pass to practical applications, we would discover that in analytical geometry arithmetical progressions express straight lines, while geometric progressions express curves. And what

219

Einstein peremptorily demonstrates is that in the real world there can exist only curves. The straight line is that described by a body moved by a single natural force; as soon as you have to do with a combination of diverse forces, you have curves (the simplest of which is the circle, the resultant of the always equal action of centripetal and centrifugal forces).

Now in reality you always find yourself in the presence of diverse forces, hence of systems of curved motions. It is only by abstraction that you come to isolate one of these forces and to imagine an action which is rigorously rectilinear. It is not, as a simplistic geometry too often tends to make one believe, the curve which is a complication of a straight line, but the straight line which is the extreme limit of a curve. Pascal has already established this with great precision: the straight line is simply the arc of a circle whose radius is at infinity.

Again, this limiting case is never entirely realized. We can not even imagine it. Einstein shows that what we term a straight line is actually the line traced out by light. Light rays themselves curve because their velocity is constantly affected by all the countering forces of the lesser velocities of bodies. Since the speed of light represents the highest possible velocity, and therefore the *élan* least capable of being changed, the trajectory of the light ray is simply the minimal curvature which we can conceive. Everything demonstrates to us that the straight line is only a fiction of our mind. Nevertheless, it is with straight lines that we construct space; in order to measure space or determine directions we mentally apply it to the rectilinear scales, intersecting at right angles, which we call height, width, and depth. And our measurements and our concepts of direction—all of which are related to these rigid axes, which suffice for common practice—are found to be mathematically false when large magnitudes or velocities are involved because in determining them we have stretched out the whole concrete world upon a network of abstractions.

In the last analysis what Bergson combats is the importance accorded abstractions by philosophers, the attempt to make abstraction appear the essence of everything and to offer the simple as the original reality. It is not necessary to enter into Einstein's space-time geometry to see that he also insists that concrete complexity is not the complication of primordial regularity. Rather, for Einstein, regularity is a simplification (one, moreover, never completely realized) of the complexity of things.

An example, I believe, will help to illustrate these considerations. A painter, in order to facilitate the completion of his design, may trace construction lines on his canvas. These lines will perhaps be found in nature implicitly; but it will be absurd to believe (like our cubists) that nature begins with them and that they express the essence of things.

In the problems posed by Einstein, what is given is motion; the abstraction which is never realized is rest. It is therefore to motion that he will look for his starting point and, for reasons of convenience which we have noted, to the greatest motion possible, that is, that of light. This method, moreover, produces results. It is precisely the question of the speed of light which brought Michelson to an impasse. He was concerned with the trajectory of a light ray brought back to its point of departure by means of prisms. When a ray is thus reflected on itself, interference patterns are produced, *i.e.*, fringes of shadow resulting because the vibrations of the ray going and returning clash with each other. Now according to whether or not the ray is projected in the direction of the earth's rotation, the interference patterns would evidently be different since in one case the earth would accomplish a part of its trajectory which in the other case it would not. But, this difference is not produced. And this is what has thrown the scientific world into disorder. In reality, it is a matter of a very simple fact, but it is clear that only genius finds things simple. The objects— thus reasoned Einstein—appear to us as they do only through the effect of light; they absorb light rays or reflect them. If the objects were to move faster than the rays it is clear that they could neither intercept nor reflect light rays. This is why a velocity greater than that of light cannot be imagined.

Thus, objects whose speed is equal to that of light will not be apparent to us; their size will for us be zero. On the contrary, if they are motionless with respect to us, *i.e.*, animated with the same speed as we, they will appear to possess what is called their normal dimension. If, finally, they have a velocity intermediate between the limiting speed of light and our own velocity, they will appear to possess an intermediate dimension. The dimensions of bodies change, therefore, precisely according to the relation of their speed to the speed of light and that of the observer. This is what we expressed above in stating that measurements change according to the reference system adopted, that is, according to whether the observer's system is moving at a velocity more or less remote from that of the object in question. If it was not till recently that these differences became apparent, it is because the disproportion between the speed of light and that of other velocities is so great that the variations are imperceptible.

In all this, what is constant is the speed of light; what changes is the speed, and hence the dimensions, of objects. You see now what happened in Michelson's experiment. It had been assumed that the dimensions of bodies are constant, and on this assumption an effort was made to detect a variation in [the speed] of light. But this is to reverse the real problem. And why does the experiment contradict our assumptions? Because it had been imagined that immobility, an absolute zero of motion which exists nowhere, was the normal state of objects, and because motion itself had been refused consideration, while, in fact, rest is never more than an incomplete degradation of motion.

There is no absolute rest, there are only differences of velocity. Whenever a higher velocity and a lesser one are juxtaposed, a nucleus of resistance termed a body is produced between them. Light alone, since it possesses the highest possible velocity, may have independent existence and not form bodies. Reciprocally, it can be said that everything that exists is produced only by more or less pronounced decelerations in the speed of light.

It can be seen, therefore, without going into metaphysics, that Einstein proposes an entirely new concept of matter. Universal gravitation, which expresses the fundamental property of bodies, reduces to a difference in velocities, rejoining some to others or distancing them as if there were present some attraction or repulsion.[1] Over and over again we heard: nothing is created, nothing is lost, everything is transformed. Here it becomes: everything combines. There are only different mixtures of velocities, hence proportions, multiplications and divisions, the basis for geometrical progressions. Arithmetic progressions, on the contrary, proceeding by additions and subtractions, would have been simply the principle of a world where something is created and something destroyed.

And this is where we rejoin Bergson. If there exist only combinations, beings will be differentiated through their diverse ways of taking part in the universal combination, according to the proportion in which they enter into it. Until now the common opinion has been that objects *produce* perceptions in beings, or, put differently, that perceptions are superimposed on the reality that exists outside of the perceivers—a superimposition which is inexplicable, Bergson states, and which amounts to a perpetual miracle (see his book *Matter and Memory*). Perceptions cannot be a kind of felt, conscious double of the extended world, something other than the world which exists in us. We are part of that world, and what comprises our individuality, our special way of perceiving it, is the selection effected by us on the totality of its motions for the realization of our own personal ends. Through our perception we do not add anything to the external world. Quite the contrary. If we were inert beings, each change in the physical world would impress its trace on us. This is what takes place in brute matter. The motion of a flea jumping on the earth, it has been said, has repercussions even on the sun. But if we were this brute matter, we would be incapable of acting. The

1 [EDITOR'S NOTE: Reference is made here to Einstein's general theory of relativity, which deals, as the special theory of relativity does not, with gravitation. More particularly, Professor Berteval has in mind the principle of equivalence of gravity and inertia, which is basic to the general theory of relativity and which involves treating accelerated motions and gravitational attractions as if they were indistinguishable.]

totality of opposing forces in the world would exist within us in a perpetual equilibrium, rendering change impossible. It is precisely because we act that we limit ourselves to a certain number of perceptions; every living being submits to this voluntary diminution, termed choice.

Thus the individual life appears to us as a sort of cutting-out practiced on the universal fabric. Not being able to perceive everything, we grasp only the outlines of things, in each group of objects one or two common and characteristic qualities. These qualities, which we call on to replace the real objects, are the abstract ideas which we make of them. But, as we have noted, whoever says abstraction says diminution of reality, insists Bergson. How does it happen that from these very abstractions, which seem to represent an arbitrary cutting-up of the world, we come to erect real categories and, above these categories, laws which we consider absolutely universal?

Indeed, Bergson is not entirely clear on this point. He mistrusts laws; whoever says laws says regularity, and regularity is entirely mechanical. Spirit, according to him, is characterized precisely by its unpredictability. There is nevertheless in the spirit also an incontestable regularity, certainly not the regularity of inert matter, which is in fact mechanical, but that agreement of the spirit with itself which we describe as harmony. Is our presentiment of an agreement between the regularity of matter and the harmony of the spirit mistaken?

The regularity of matter is entirely passive, entirely negative, we will say. The water which flows in a determined path has no real reason to pursue this path; it only has motives for not taking others. The man who acts, on the contrary, always has a positive goal. And the more personality this man has, *i.e.*, the more spiritual value, the more constant he will be in his resolutions. There is therefore also something immutable in him. And it can be said, I believe, that the uniformity of the laws of matter would be useless and would not even have been noticed if it were not precisely at the service of the immutability of the human will. But between

224

human volition, which obeys certain reasons, and mechanical motion, which submits to certain necessities, there is a world full of other wills applied toward different ends, of other material objects subjected to different pressures, which may thwart the projected action. This world is what is termed the domain of chance. Man attempts to bypass the world of chance and to recover beyond it the simple necessity which corresponds to his single will. This relation which he seeks out between the one and the other, this relationship which eliminates chance, is precisely what he terms law.

There is, if one wishes, above things a complex unity which is the will, which is one by its very complexity, through the interpenetration of all its elements; and there is beneath this a unity which is such only through its almost absolute simplicity, through a lack of parts whose actions might conflict. And since the one is grounded in the other, there is an obvious relationship between them. It is the complexity of the first which has necessitated the simplicity of the second. Consider a living being. It must realize certain vital goals. In order to do this it must constitute for itself a certain matter wherein all its cells will resemble each other. The unity of the end explains the uniformity of matter; but to explain life through the constitution of the cell, as a certain materialistic biology attempted to do, is clearly an impossibility and a contradiction. And when Bergson cautions against the uniformity of laws, he evidently is protesting against those who see in the lower uniformity, that of the laws of physics, the prototype of the higher unity, which results from the constancy of wills and the harmony of the universe.

Bergson's point of view is actually always the same: one will never be able to explain the moving through the immobile; it is, on the contrary, rest which is a particular and extreme case of motion. Only, here the philosopher collides with an opposite point of view: it is nevertheless through fixed laws that one determines motion. We have seen that in pushing the doctrine a little further one arrives at a reconciliation. In Einstein one encounters the same antinomy. But with him equally, in the ultimate consequences of the theory, one will find an analogous reconciliation. In Einstein's relativism as well, one must be able to find something fixed, for if not, all the figures will be up in the air; it will not even be possible to make calculations.

Einstein discovers only motion. And, as soon as we advance a little further in his system, we see that it is a matter not of simple motion, such as would be produced by a single force, a case practically unrealizable and conceivable only by abstraction, but always and everywhere of accelerated motion.

It is known that by virtue of inertia, a body projected at a given velocity persists in its motion. But at each instant the force which sets the body in motion adds its initial velocity to the velocity acquired. Thus the velocity increases indefinitely and multiplies itself like compound interest on a capital investment. This is *acceleration*, proportional, according to a well-known formula, to the square of distances, developing itself consequently in a geometric progression.

In reality, all motions are accelerated. There are no simple motions save in relation to other motions: the relation between one motion and another may be simple, but each of them, taken in itself, is accelerated. And all these accelerations are constant; the velocity in the world always increases and tends consequently toward an infinite velocity. This appears fantastic only if we compare this perpetual acceleration to an original supposed immobility which, I repeat, is a pure chimera.

But this acceleration is material reality, and, we have seen, this reality is simply a combination of retardations of a primordial velocity. The greatest perceptible velocity is that of light, but this is not a definitive velocity taken in itself, since it accelerates also. The primordial velocity will be always greater than any real velocity, than any finite velocity. It must be considered an infinite velocity. Now, suppose the world to be animated by this infinite velocity. At each instant of time the world will pass through each fragment of space; the universe in its totality will be able to be considered as immobile in each of its points.

All real motion will be simply a degradation of this primitive motion, or, if we wish, of this primitive immobility. That is how it is possible to say nonetheless that motion derives from immobility. The error will be to make it derive from the other immobility, from the lower immobility, from that which is nothing but the privation of all motion. As we have seen, there are for man two immutabilities—above, the constancy of the will, below, the inertia of matter; and change is simply what participates imperfectly in the one and the other. Likewise, in physics we know two immobilities, both, however, outside of reality and at its extremes: that which does not find outside of itself any reason to change since it contains everything, and that which has no reason to vary since it contains nothing. The second is only the symbol of the first, as the inertia of matter is only the image of the constancy of the will. Bergson's entire effort is directed to preventing our taking the symbol for the thing signified, the image for the model, mechanical regularity for the harmony of the universe.

OLIVIER COSTA DE BEAUREGARD
The Principle of Relativity and the Spatialization of Time

Remarks by the Editor. Physics ultimately possesses two contrary ways of viewing time. The first, which might be termed Aristotelian, involves the persistent attempt to represent time in terms of space. The second, which finds its support in thermodynamics, involves the denial that time is space-like. The most explicit proponent of the latter view is Bergson. In this essay Professor Olivier Costa de Beauregard traces the development of the first tendency from its incomplete fruition in classical Newtonian physics to its culmination in Einstein's relativity, while concluding that physics may still have much to learn from the study of the second.

In classical Newtonian physics the concepts of absolute space and absolute time stood implicitly in contradiction. Absolute time (the same for all reference systems) implied the relativity of motion, while absolute space, which involved the concept of an absolute frame of reference, implied that some motions must be absolute. In Einstein's relativity theory the former conception "betrays" the latter, and the complete equivalence of all physical systems is thereby established. But the correct translation of the relativity inherent in the concept of an absolute time had to await a satisfactory interpretation of the status of the speed of light. That is, relativity was not possible until it was realized that the speed of light is a *universal constant* or, more particularly, a *coefficient of equivalence between space and time*. But, in turn, this realization was not possible until the relations between optics and kinetics were clarified.

In pre-relativistic optics it was assumed that uniform motions were "absolute" (that is, detectable as moving relative to the ether), while in pre-relativistic kinetics uniform motions were conceived of as "relative" (that is, not discernible as moving relative to absolute space). This contradiction became particularly acute when the ether and absolute space came, in the nineteenth century, to be virtually identified. In retrospect, it is clear that nineteenth-century electromagnetic theory actually supplied a means of resolving this contradiction since it implied that the speed of light must be the same for all systems, whether at rest or in uniform motion. To take this step and thereby unite optics and kinetics and thoroughly relativize all uniform motions seemed impossible to the physicists of the time, even though experiments by François Arago (1818), Augustin Fresnel, and Armand Fizeau (1851) and theoretical reasonings by Weltman (1873), Potier (1874), Lorentz, Mascart and others seemed to call for it. The famous Michelson-Morley experiment (1887), which proved conclusively that absolute motions cannot be detected in optics, made explicit a fact which might have been obvious from the beginning. Einstein's great contribution was to put optics and dynamics on the same footing by finally declaring the speed of light to be a universal constant. But this was precisely to treat c as a "coefficient of reciprocal transformation between space and time."

For relativity physics, Costa de Beauregard concludes, time defined as a function of the speed of light is the only time there is. Such a "relativistic" time, moreover, since it is measured by means of the trajectory of light rays through space, is the most thoroughly "spatialized" time imaginable. Bergson's arguments in *Duration and Simultaneity* against relativity's conception of a plurality of time-series are clearly erroneous. Yet in one respect his criticisms of relativity's thoroughly spatialized time continue to appear valid. Any purely geometrical time-concept would seem to ignore the "irreducible originality of time" and therefore be partial or one-sided. The verdict of incompetence with which Bergson has been charged ought not to be thoughtlessly accepted, therefore, and physicists ought to study Bergson's concept of time as a challenge. *Professor Costa de Beauregard's essay was originally published in* REVUE DES QUESTIONS SCIENTIFIQUES, Ve *Série, T. VII (1949). It appears here in translation with the permission of the author and the* REVUE DES QUESTIONS SCIENTIFIQUES.

S PACE AND TIME: in philosophy, since the age of the Greeks, it has been traditional to open all cosmologies with an analysis of these notions, which are taken to be closely related. Physics, further, has never ceased to consider the parameters x, y, z, and t to be basic and to locate phenomena in space and time by means of them, as well as relate to these four parameters all the quantities which it studies.

The two concepts of space and time, when associated among themselves with the idea of a physical content, engender the concept of motion. In physics the science of kinetics is thereby created, a science which, by fact and by right, constitutes the essential foundation of all physics. Recent scientific developments have made it evident that to limit kinetics to the study of "material points" is to thoroughly misconstrue the manner in which its problems are posed. The kinetics of waves is no less important that the kinetics of material points.

Since motion forms an intermediary between time and space, it is possible to express time-lengths as functions of space. This is what Aristotle meant when he said that "time is the number of motion, and motion the number of time." Kinetics states the same assumption in its equation:

(1) $dx = K v \, dt.$

K is indispensible if x, v, t (space, velocity, time) are to be independently chosen.

There is in physics, therefore, a current of thought, which may be termed Aristotelian, which attempts to represent time in terms of space. This tendency is found, at the level of technical science, in the problem of the measurement of time, a problem which physics resolves by relating the measure of time to the measure of space in a more and more direct and universal fashion.[1] The purpose of this essay will to be follow, throughout the history of modern physical theories, marked, in what concerns us, by the great names of Galileo, Newton, Fresnel, Maxwell, Einstein, and Minkowski, the unceasing development of this Aristotelian tendency, which (as we believe we are in a position to demonstrate) reaches its fulfillment in the special theory of relativity and the four-dimensional universe of Einstein and Minkowski.

But there exists, alongside this Aristotelian tendency, another current of thought that is just as vigorous but less fully aware of itself. This is the current that in philosophy finally found its herald in Bergson; but we believe that it had already begun to manifest itself previously in physics.

It is quite characteristic that the science of thermodynamics, based on the work of Carnot and Clausius, makes no explicit appeal to the notion of space; it speaks not of motions but of transformations and makes an essential appeal to the notion of time.

[1] We understand the adjective *universal* in the technical sense which it has in physics, a point to which we will return later.

Its discovery of the impossibility of an "isothermal" generation of energy makes thermodynamics the first science to discover the irreversibility in time of a whole class of physical phenomena. The second law of thermodynamics has re-established a concept of heat which the first law of thermodynamics, quite paradoxically in one sense, had identified with energy. According to the first law, heat and energy are two quantities of the same physical nature, while according to the second law they are not. There was something obscure in this which the statistical mechanics of Clerk Maxwell, Ludwig Boltzmann, and Josiah Gibbs was able to clarify.

This article does not discuss the paradox, first pointed out by Loschmidt, that the same theory should unite under one roof both the rigorous determinism of theoretical mechanics and the uncertainty required by all applications of probability and then conclude that phenomena are irreversible while maintaining that time is reversible.

Statistical mechanics has had the virtue of making concrete the abstract affirmations contained in the first and second laws of thermodynamics and making clear what distinguishes the two notions of energy and heat. As the first law proclaims, heat really is an energy—a *kinetic energy*. But in a state of maximum disorder. In an isothermal state it is completely neutralized through the effect of the law of large numbers. The distinction between heat and energy is therefore statistical.

Quantum and wave mechanics intends to supplant rational mechanics entirely; it generalizes this mechanics through its mathematical formalism and goes beyond it by extending its jurisdiction to the movements of both waves and bodies. This theory is a new form of statistical mechanics, one in which the notion of probability is introduced at the level of the individual. We do not intend here to discuss the imperfectly elucidated problem of the relations between classical statistical mechanics and quantum theory; we wish simply to point out that, like all statistical doctrines, quantum mechanics theoretically rediscovers the concept of irreversibility (Johan von Neumann) and that among the innumerable questions which arise from its explication, the manifestly irreversible phenomenon of radioactive disintegration figures.

Hence there is alongside of Aristotelianism (which can be traced through rational mechanics, electromagnetism, and relativity theory) another current of thought in which the primacy belonging to the concept of time is affirmed more and more precisely. To differing schemata involving mechanical and kinetic clocks which measure time by relating it to space through motion (schemata which will comprise the object of this study) there stand opposed other schemata involving statistical clocks, schemata into which the concept of space does not enter explicitly and which possess the great advantage of producing an irreversible time.[2]

There is one remark we must make concerning statistical clocks before proceeding. In classical physics the notion of chance contained a subjective element. The paradox of the older statistical mechanics lay in the desire to explain objective effects (increase in entropy) through a purely subjective cause (chance as a result of ignorance). Quantum mechanics, however, takes our ignorance to be *invincible*, or, in other words, takes phenomena to be objectively indeterminate. Further, and simultaneously, it forbids by its very mathematics treating phenomena as if they existed *en soi*, independent of the presence and the operations of the subject who perceives them; it takes account essentially of the reaction (by nature unknowable) of the measuring instrument and the object measured through the finite value of its constant h. It is not sufficient to say therefore that the new quantum indeterminism is invincible or objective; it should be added that what is henceforth not allowed is the concept of a physical object isolated from the mind which perceives or knows it.[3]

---

[2] Cf. on this subject Ilya Prigogine, *Thermodynamique des phénomènes irréversibles* (in press at Liège); J. L. Destouches, *Corpuscles et systèmes de corpuscles* (Paris, 1941), I, 51–53, and *Principes fondamentaux de physique théorique* (Paris, 1943), II, 354–55 and 366–69; Robert Lennuier, "L'idée de temps dans la physique moderne," *Travaux et Documents du C.C.I.F.*, May, 1946.

[3] All of the theoreticians of quantum physics have insisted, in diverse ways, on

We think that the very Bergsonian sound of especially these last two conclusions cannot fail to be noted, and from this fact we will draw two more conclusions. First, the theoretical physicist will have no difficulty in subscribing to the essential features of Bergson's notion of time; second, he will consider quite unjust the verdict of incompetence on this subject with which Bergson charges him. But there is more: however decidedly one may wish to go deeply into the vast and complex question which we have just discussed, he nevertheless should neither assume he has gained nothing from the attitude of the opposing position, nor renounce some of the most valid traditions of his art. The physicist will never agree that an entity—time—whose symbol figures in his calculations, ought not to be considered and treated as a physical extent; he will not be able to abandon the search for definitions of this extent which make it measurable, that is, juxtaposable with itself in its own domain, duration. He will refuse to believe, finally, that an extent which, from Aristotle to Einstein, allows itself to be more and more "spatialized" with ease and with profit does not really possess an extremely close affinity with space. Even if he postpones the elucidation of the antinomy which can be symbolized by the great names of Aristotle and Bergson, the physicist does not feel he has the right to sacrifice either of the two veridical sides of the question to the other.

Now, after this too-long introduction, we will leave the examination of time's Bergsonian aspect and look at its "spatializable" or Aristotelian properties.

The essential elements of our argument will be 1) the universal constant and 2) the physical equivalence of two lengths. The constants in a physical relation merit the name "universals" because they do not depend on the particular nature of the matter studied. For example, the fundamental formula of the Galilean-Newtonian dynamics is "universal" because it applies to all "material points." If two lengths, mutually heterogeneous as regards

the very novel characteristics of quantum physics. See especially J. von Neumann, *Mathematische Grundlagen der Quantenmechanik* (Berlin, 1932).

their mode of perception, figure in a mathematically homogeneous manner in a universal physical relation, one has the right to term them equivalent. One can then, in modifying, if necessary, the choice of fundamental units, act in such a way as to attribute to multiplied constants the dimension zero and the numerical value 1; the lengths considered are thus rendered measurable with the same unit. It may be said, in a sense, that these lengths have in some way the same nature, which is concealed by the heterogeneity of the modes of perception through which they are revealed. For example, following the fundamental relations of dynamics, a force and the derivative with respect to time of an impulsion are two equivalent quantities; and this is what the ordinary inertial or Coriolis forces prove experimentally. It can happen that two universal constants, expressed as a function of the same fundamental units, are not independent, in which case it is not possible to dispose simultaneously of their dimensions and their values. For example, in the system of classical M.L.T. units, the expression e^2/hc, termed the fine structure constant, is a pure number; [4] e designates electron charge, h Planck's constant, and c the velocity of light *in vacuo*, and all three are universal constants. The quantum of electrical charge e will in fact be found to be the same for particles as diverse as the electrons (electron and positron), the nucleons (proton and neutron), and the various mesons; at most, therefore, it is possible to dispose of two of the three constants, e, h, c, and reduce the number of fundamental units to 1.

Perhaps the reader will permit one or two digressions intended to illustrate these considerations through examples. In the experiments of Joseph Gay-Lussac the two coefficients of expansion of a perfect gas are equal among themselves, and their common value is independent of the chemical nature of the gas. This coefficient $1/\theta$ is nevertheless not a universal constant because its value depends on the zero temperature t_0 chosen. Introducing the *absolute zero* $t_0\text{-}\theta$ and the *absolute temperature* $T = t\text{-}t_0 + \theta$, the

---

[4] It is well known that A. S. Eddington sought a theoretical evaluation of the number e^2/hc.

well-known formula $pv = RT$ appears, in which the constant R $= p_o\, v_o/\theta$ only appears to depend on the relative zero of temperature. Nevertheless R is still not an authentic universal constant because it is found to contain an extensive coefficient[5] corresponding to v. But thanks to the notion of the molecule, and to the inspired hypothesis of Amedeo Avogadro and André Ampère, the amount pv/T finds itself in principle quantified; and kinetic theory, after having furnished the interpretation of this quantum, surrenders the value to Jean Perrin. Finally, Boltzmann's constant k, independent of the chemical nature of gas (as Gay-Lussac's coefficient already was) but free of the double arbitrariness of the zero of temperature and the quantity of gas, is seen plainly to merit the name universal constant. Nothing forbids our attributing to this constant the dimension zero and a numerical value a priori, and this is to state again that temperature is physically homogeneous with an energy, but with an intensive energy. Temperature *is*, precisely, according to the kinetic theory, the median value of the kinetic energy of the translation of molecules; to take $k = 2/3$, is to measure temperature in units of energy.[6]

It is known that the coefficients of capacity and influence of a system of conductors placed in a void are homogeneous with lengths and, further, that they depend only on the geometrical disposition of these bodies. It is reasonable to say, therefore, that they *are* in a sense, lengths. If the void is replaced by a dielectric, the values of these purely geometric coefficients will be found to be multiples of the specific inductive capacity.

We consider finally the constant which is the measure of the speed of light *in vacuo*, one that is so important for our subject. The speed of light in any material medium, even supposing that it were definite, could not be a universal constant for the simple

[5] We use, it must be understood, this adjective in the technical sense in which it is employed in thermodynamics.

[6] Cf. on this subject Jean Villey, "On the Dimensions of Temperature," *Comptes Rendus des Séances de l'Académie des Sciences*, CCXVIII (1944), 583–84. Since R is 13.7 × 10^{-17} C.G.S., the "degree" theoretically proposed in the text would be 0.229 × 10^{-15} K.

reason that this speed depends on the milieu. Classical physicists, it can be said, had done the impossible by representing the void in optics through the image of a material medium, and this prejudice prevented them from recognizing the character of c as a universal constant. Nevertheless, the void is not an optical medium like the others, if only because of the nearly perfect absence of dispersion that it displays in astronomy. With Lorentz, the theory of the velocity of the transmission of light through material mediums was given as a function of the coefficient of velocity relative to a vacuum, on the one hand, and of the intervention of the material oscillators forming the medium under consideration, on the other hand. Thus, before its final demise, the ether was elevated and singularized on a last pedestal; and in the same stroke a characteristic absolutely transcending the notion of a propagational velocity in any medium whatever was attributed to the constant c. Our formal conclusion is therefore that even in pre-relativistic physics, the constant c appeared as authentically universal; and we recall that Maxwell's electromagnetism had imposed on it this status even before Lorentz engaged in his research.

It is clear, after what we have said, that a velocity which is a universal constant is nothing more or less than a coefficient of equivalence between space and time; it was Einstein's task to show the role this equivalence played in the facts. But before we turn to relativity theory, we ought to follow the progress of the Aristotelian current of thought.

It was customary in the nineteenth century to present kinetics, as well as the problem of the change of spatial reference which is one of its essential parts, as a branch of theoretical mechanics; this was to misconstrue the fundamental character of kinetics for all branches of physics, and particularly to sacrifice the kinetics of waves to that of the "material point." In 1924 Louis de Broglie's wave mechanics showed how close a tie binds the concepts of wave and point and with what equity both these notions must be treated.

As to the problem of the change of reference system, classical kinetics was always curiously divided between two extreme and opposed views which, quite paradoxically, directly engendered each other. The concept of universal time (the same for all reference sytsems) and the idea of an absolute reference point (most succinctly termed absolute space) immediately occur to a mind informed by current experiment; Newton initially explained these postulates clearly in order to found his entire mechanics on them. These postulates, combined with those of the Euclidean character of space and the concept of velocity, make it possible to write in the most general case the formulas for changes of reference system; and it is at this point that the paradox arises. *All modes of spatial reference prove strictly equivalent for the kinetic description of phenomena, in particular in the case of two solids accelerating or uniformly rotating with respect to each other.* If we may be allowed an imaginative form of expression, we will state that the postulate of universal time betrays the postulate of absolute space, and that in the end it imposes on kinetics the idea of a complete equivalence of all the referential solids in space. Following a terminology well-known in dynamics, Newton's kinetics, having in its foundations formulated a principle of relativity so absolutely strict that there is no relativity in it, soon moved to another principle of relativity so absolutely extensive that everything was relative, even accelerations. Einstein produced the solution to this paradox in 1905 by establishing the unique principle of the relativity of kinetics at the same intermediate level as that of dynamics.

In the particular case of two referential solids in space in relative uniform translation, the formulas of Galilean-Newtonian physics take the form,

$$(2) \qquad x' = x - vt, \quad y' = y, \quad z' = z, \quad t' = t.$$

These are, it must be understood, the formulas which Einstein's kinetics must rediscover as a first approximation for the change of Galilean reference.

We now consider the well-known equations for the propagation of a plane monochromatic wave with the speed c:

$$(3) \qquad \vec{A} = \vec{A_o} \, e^{2\,\pi l \phi} , \phi = \frac{\vec{\alpha}\,.\,\vec{r}}{L} - \frac{t}{T} ; L = c\,T.$$

The Galilean-Newtonian formulas transform this plane wave into another plane wave, altering not only its direction but also its velocity of propagation. If, by hypothesis, this wave is assimilated to an elastic wave propagating itself in a certain "homogeneous medium," the speed c is evidently isotropic in the spatial reference points bound to this medium; this we term c_o. With the classical concepts the speed of these same waves can no longer be isotropic in a referential solid in uniform translation $\vec{v}$ with respect to the preceding; it will have values varying, according to the direction, between $c_o \pm v$. We thus see optics (or still more, the idea classical physicists had of it) coming to conspire with one of its kinetic conceptions of things; the ether, a hypothetical medium for the propagation of light waves, was quite naturally identified with Newton's absolute space. If it is observed that, abstracting from questions of intensity, optics is an essentially kinetic science which speaks only of space (wave lengths), time (periods), and pure numbers (phases), it can certainly be considered that the paradox discussed above is thus reborn in a new form. Under that form also, the paradox was resolved by Einstein, thanks to an authentic identification of optics and kinetics, of the science of the void and that of space. That this almost magical solution of an old latent conflict is really inscribed in the authentic axis of the entire physical tradition can be proved in the classical case of the two notions of the ether and absolute space.

All wave or point motion in principle furnishes a means of relating temporal intervals through the measurement of units of space, and it is this fact that our clocks and chronometers take advantage of. It follows from this that if no physical argument comes to justify the definition of velocity used as a natural constant, time is thereby not defined as a measurable length.

Now, since the mechanism invented by Huygens permits us to make use of the law of the independence of the period of the

238

pendulum's swing in relation to its length, our clocks actually define time as a measurable length: two identical clocks, examined at different stages of the unwinding of their spring motors, will give the same time value.

The justification of this law of pendulums follows from the fundamental formula of point dynamics:

$$(4) \qquad \vec{f} = \mathrm{Im}\vec{\gamma}, \text{ or } \quad \vec{\gamma} = \frac{d^2}{dt^2} \vec{r}.$$

This formula interrelates the four quantities, force, mass, space, and time; and the coefficient in this formula may be made equal to 1 by a coherent choice of units. The Galilean-Newtonian dynamics makes it possible, therefore, to relate the temporal to the spatial dimensions, to force, and to mass; and the relation thereby established is guaranteed by a universal law, the resulting time-definition itself being universal in the physical sense of that term. Only, it is not given as a function of a single spatial dimension, so that, to speak like Bergson, time is not thereby totally spatialized, but two-thirds dynamized.

This law (4) is formulated essentially with a frame of reference identified with space. As is well known, the only changes of reference which leave the law invariant are uniform translations; in systems in accelerated transformation with respect to these last, well-known inertial forces appear, and in revolving reference systems inertial forces which Gaspard Coriolis discovered and calculated. As is known, the theory agreed perfectly with experiment at all points, and astronomy recognized that fixed directions in Galileo's sense are directions established relative to the fixed stars. Contrary to classical kinetics, dynamics therefore considers accelerations and rotations as absolute, but, contrary to the optics associated with that kinetics, it considers uniform translations to be relative. In 1905 Einstein's relativity theory universally established the principle of the relativity of physics at the middle level that dynamics had discovered.

Starting from the Galilean-Newtonian formula (4), it is possible to imagine innumerable dynamic standards of time: the isochronous pendulum is one, but the material point directed in a straight line or the solid in uniform rotation are others, theoretically simpler. Thus the Earth is in principle the standard of measurement of siderial time, and certain anomalies in the motion of the moon and planets make it possible to prove a systematic retardation of the Earth due to energy dissipated by the tides, as well as various irregularities of motion still incompletely explained.[7]

Formula (4), in which force, mass, and the differences of spatial interval are transformed by invariance, defines in principle, in a universal way, within all Galilean reference systems, and as a function of the three standards of mass, force, and space, a single universal time; it also makes it possible thereby, in taking account of calculable inertial forces, to extend that definition to accelerated and rotating spaces. Relativity theory changes all this: while it deprives the parameter t of its universal signification, it radically simplifies the universal standard of time. We must, before explicating this apparent paradox, complete our inventory of classical physics.

We ask, in order to terminate our discussion of theoretical mechanics, what the Newtonian theory of gravity adds to our subject in the way of new elements. Pierre Laplace's Newtonian potential, assumed to be transmitted instantaneously, does not furnish a new time-standard. Only (and this is a point classical treatises have generally omitted to point out) by taking simultaneously Newton's formula

$$(5) \qquad\qquad f = G \frac{mm'}{r^2}$$

and Galileo's formula (4) is it possible to reduce the number of independent standards by one: if we eliminate the constant G, we can express the unit of force, for example, as a function of the units of space and mass, and if we then eliminate the constant I, we can express the unit of time in the same terms.[8]

---

[7] On this subject—and on many other subjects which we treat—cf. the interesting article by Henri Mineur, "La notion de temps," *La Nature* (1934), nos. 2933, 2934, 2935, and 2937.

[8] We argue, for example, in units C.G.S. in which G $= 6.7 \times 10^{-8}$ and

We now enter the terrain of electromagnetism: it is known that the relation of the constants K_1 and K_2, of the electric and magnetic permeability of the void, which has the dimensions of a velocity, is numerically equal to the speed of light, as Maxwell's theory had already predicted. This being the case, classical physicists have defined their coherent systems of units within the system M.L.T. in taking either $K_1 = 1$ or $K_2 = 1$; thus they had to choose between two equally recommendable systems, that of E.S.U. and that of E.M.U. In order to resolve this dilemma it should have sufficed, for them, to posit $c = 1$ by definition, which amounts to choosing the standard of time as a function of length; [9] but because of a scruple which Einstein's and Minkowski's intervention has rendered surprising for us, no one dared to dispose of the time standard in order to simplify the equations, as would have been done with any other physical unit. Nevertheless, these three nonindependent constants, K_1, K_2, and c, were equally attached to the void; and so long as the first two were considered, theoretically and practically, to be universals, it would have been wrong, in all logic, to do otherwise with the third. It was Einstein's new solution of the problem of change of reference systems in kinetics and in optics which was definitely to impose this view.

The simplest optical phenomena caused by the motion of sources or receptors are aberration (1728) and the Doppler effect (1842). Both can easily be explained quantitatively within the Galilean-Newtonian physics, and through the ether hypothesis, in such a way that they do not initially support relativity theory. But a more careful analysis changes this impression: if the mathematical consequences are developed as a function of the successive powers of velocities, it is seen that in the first order absolute velocities are eliminated, to leave only the relative veloc-

---

suppose that one wishes to retain the gram as a unit of mass and the centimeter as a unit of length; G will be made equal to 1 by taking $G^{-1} = 0.149 \times 10^8$ dynes as a new unit of force, and I will be retained equal to 1 in Galileo's formula by taking $G^{1/2} = 2.59 \times 10^{-4}$ seconds as a new time unit.

[9] For example, the time unit thus associated with the centimeter would be 0.33×10^{-10} seconds.

ity of the source and of the receptor. The first order $\beta = v/c$ being the only one accessible to experiment, it appears that neither the one nor the other makes it possible to attain the hypothetical absolute reference system, if it exists. The direct measurement of the speed of light does not permit it either. Actually, in order to synchronize the clocks at the far limits of the base, it is necessary to exchange optical signals; this amounts to measuring the speed of light in a double trajectory, and in practice that is what is done. Here further, the hypothetical ether wind (as it was expressed in Michelson's time) occurs only through a term in β^2, which is experimentally inaccessible.

In 1818 François Arago studied the refraction of starlight by a prism; contrary to his expectations, he found things to be the same as if the source were bound to the Earth. In spite of both the imperfect operational techniques of the time and theoretical interpretations like the one given by Augustin Fresnel (the Doppler effect was not discovered until twenty-four years later), Arago's experiment marks an important date in the history of physics; it is really the first experiment in which the ether wind refused to manifest itself, and, as we will recall, it was bound up with Michelson's crucial experiment by a continous chain of long-considered theoretical-experimental thinking. In a direct experiment, later repeated by others, Armand Fizeau showed in 1851 that Fresnel's formula is actually correct; supporting themselves on this fact Weltmann, in 1873, and Potier, in 1874, showed that an ether wind can under no circumstances manifest itself optically except by an effect of the second order in β; Heinrich Hertz and Lorentz extended this result to electromagnetism. Now, if one disregards the hypothetical ether wind, the Fresnel-Fizeau formula

$$(6) \qquad c' = \frac{c}{n} \pm v \left(1 - \frac{1}{n^2} \right)$$

is reduced to a special law of the composition of wave velocities with that of their propagational medium; Einstein's entire revolutionary kinetics is virtually contained in this law, but at the time

242

of Weltmann and Potier, no one knew how to view this explosive enigma.

Nevertheless, the problem was perfectly posed: in order to prove the existence of the ether wind, it was necessary to conceive, and realize, an experiment which reached the second order in β. Now, prior to Poincaré, Lorentz, and Einstein, some physicists believed that the ether wind would not show itself. They had the feeling that the mechanical formulation of the principle of relativity ought to be valid for optics as well, and for the rest of physics; Eleuthère Mascart was the most explicit of these premature relativists.

The doors, it is clear, were open; when Michelson and Morley, in their still celebrated experiment in 1887, compared the speed of light in two trajectories at right angles to each other and bound to the earth with the precision of the second order in β, the paradoxical conclusion that there is no ether wind fell into a prepared climate. Nevertheless, the mathematical explication of Mascart's views again had to wait twenty years. The Michelson-Morley experiment was repeated innumerable times by different investigators at all times of year, always with a negative result; other experiments of the second order, optical or electromagnetic, later came to confirm it: Lord Rayleigh (1902) and Brace (1904), Trouton and Andrew Noble (1903), Trouton and William Rankine (1908). It also turned out, to complete the analogy with mechanics, that rotations instead of nonaccelerated translations manifested themselves in optics, and this in the same way as if the ether of the classical physicists were not carried along (Harress, 1912; Sagnac, 1913). Michelson's and Gale's experiment, in which the Earth at rest is taken to be a turning solid, is the veritable optical analogue of Jean Foucault's mechanical experiment with the pendulum.

Following the Michelson-Morley results, Lorentz and Poincaré, the former as a theoretician of electromagnetism, the latter as a philosopher of science and a mathematician, began to establish a

243

doctrine of the privileged equivalence of Galilean frames extended from dynamics to optics and electromagnetism.

All the philsophical and mathematical materials of Einstein's and Minkowski's future monument were present without exception in the storehouse they opened. In order to get hold of the seamless whole and create *the* theory of relativity, nothing was lacking but the precise identification of the mathematical and philosophical principles on which to build. Following the pure Poincaréian epistemology which, working here as an explorer Poincaré himself had not pushed to its final conclusions, they found it necessary to affirm that the symbols employed as the most useful thoretically *are* the adequate expression of physical reality.

The Lorentz-Poincaré formulas,

$$(7) \quad x' = \frac{x\text{-}vt}{\sqrt{1\text{-}\beta^2}}, t' = \frac{t\text{-}vx/c^2}{\sqrt{1\text{-}\beta^2}}, \beta = \frac{v}{c},$$

which Einstein took as his foundation, define as many local times and spatial standards as there are Galilean frames. They are, by means of their construction, such that the measurement of the speed of light describes the same value c in all Galilean frames moving in any direction. They constitute a group, finally, and are in particular reversible in the same form through the substitution of v for $\text{-}v$. Thus, the contraction Lorentz postulated in 1887 in order to account for Michelson's result appeared to be reciprocal.

It seems surprising today that the author of *Science and Method* after having initially provided the philosophical, then the mathematical, bases of the theory of the principle of relativity did not complete the cycle of his work by insisting that the local space and time x' and t' of the same Galilean frame *are* the space and time perceived and experienced in that frame, and that he continued, like Lorentz, to refer in thought to the ideal frame, termed absolute, in which the ether was supposed motionless and in which space and time were considered authentic. There was no mathematical reason obligating one to think elsewhere what is expressed equivalently here, nor to retain the notion of an ether since in each Galilean frame everything takes place as if the frame were at rest. The unconscious scruple which caused Maxwell and his successors to posit $c = 1$ in their equations we find in Poincaré in another form: the refusal to discern in c an authentic coefficient of equivalence between space and time, while his formulas transform the one into the other. Maxwell had not dared, for electromagnetic reasons, to dispose of the temporal standard; and for reasons of the same order Poincaré did not dream for an instant of *in fact* denying universal time, that ancient belief which Newton had given its explicit form.

The revolution was to be the work of Einstein. Forty years after the event, both the current theories and the most recent experiments continue to justify his audacity. For Einstein as for Mascart and for Poincaré, the lesson of all experimentation undertaken in optics since Arago is that the principle of relativity formulated by classical dynamics also holds for electromagnetism, and for all physics; Einstein was to make systematic concrete applications of that principle to the different chapters of physics. First, as concerns the optics of a vacuum, he assumed that the Michelson experiment showed that the speed of light not only seems to be but *is* isotropic in all Galilean frames; and this makes it possible to take validly a further step. Through a convention, which again mutually relates the units of time and length universally among themselves, he posited that this isotropic velocity had the same value in all Galilean frames. It follows from these postulates that the local variables x' and t' of Lorentz and Poincaré *are* the space and time physically perceived and experienced in each Galilean frame (promoted reference system not only of space but also of time), and that the constant c, for the first time invested with a purely kinetic role, plays the part of a coefficient of reciprocal transformation of space into time. In the material expression of the formulas nothing of the Lorentz-Poincaré theory is changed; yet in fact, everything has taken on a new meaning and finds itself transfigured.

245

In 1908, and with Einstein's acknowledgment, Minkowski made a decisive step for the progress of relativity. Positing

(8) $\qquad x_1 = x, \quad x_2 = y, \quad x_3 = z, \quad x_4 = ict,$

he ideally juxtaposed these four Galilean coordinates along the length of four orthogonal Cartesian axes, thus structuring all events in a four-dimensional universe; he made the essential remark that the Lorentz-Poincaré formulas for the change of Galilean frames correspond to a rotation of the quadrirectangle of the universe. For the first time, and in this form, the law of the privileged equivalence of Galilean frames received a purely kinetic, or geometric, perfectly clear interpretation: these frames were identified with the well-known privileged equivalence of systems of Cartesian coordinates in Euclidean space.[10] In this epoch it did not seem less paradoxical to see Einstein and Minkowski limit the principle of relativity to kinetics than to extend it into electromagnetism; it is difficult to understand, notably, that relativity considers accelerations and rotations to be kinetically absolute. The a priori arguments which Bergson himself opposed to Einstein in *Duration and Simultaneity* do not apply at this point.

Given two events $\vec{r}$, t and $\vec{r}'$, t', perceived in the same Galilean frames, the Lorentz-Poincaré formulas leave the formulas,

(9) $\qquad\qquad \Delta s^2 = \Delta r^2 - c^2 \Delta t^2,$

invariant, although, as he stated, they make the two terms of the second member vary, and they are relative. When Minkowski, having in mind the vision of the universe which he defined, wrote forcefully that "space and time considered separately must disappear into shadows, and their union alone retain any individuality," it must be recognized that this was really the essence of relativity theory: an equivalence of space and time, fusing geometrically to constitute the universe, as previously work and heat were fused algebraically to constitute energy. It is really impossible to push the "spatialization of time" any further than Einstein and Minkowski did; the ancient tendency stemming

[10] Or, speaking more rigorously here, *pseudo-Euclidean* (due to the imaginary character of the fourth coordinate).

246

from Aristotle here actually attains its final development—a point on which Bergson was not mistaken.

Let us note a striking example, made famous by Paul Langevin,[11] which actually shows the reality of the equivalence of space and time established by relativity. Let (1) and (2), supposed for purposes of simplicity to be points, be two beings subjected to change and having the same nature: for example, two radioactive nuclei of the same chemical isotope, or two microbes of the same species. If these two beings initially coincide in space and time, and if they are initially the same age, they will continue indefinitely to be the same age[12] if they describe the same world-line. Suppose now that at point I, (1) is immobilized at the origin of a certain Galilean frame $\mathcal{G}$, and that, with respect to $\mathcal{G}$, (2) proceeds to describe with uniform velocity v a circle which periodically passes through (1); at the end of a certain number of periods, terminating in a point F, (1) and (2) definitively coincide and describe the same world-line. As, in the pseudo-Euclidean universe, the spiral arc I (2) F is shorter than the cord I (1) F between I and F, (2) has aged less than (1), proportionally as the relation $\beta = v/c$ is greater. Here, contrary to the problem of the change of Galilean frames, there is an initial and final coincidence of the two "observers," so that they are mutually in accord to discover that (2) has aged less than (1); the phenomenon thus should be termed absolute, and it is a consequence of the absolute kinetic character of accelerations in relativity. It can be said that, between I and F, (2) gained over (1) in duration by transforming space $v\triangle t$, which it has traversed in G, into time. The fact that between I and F, (1) and (2) have traced different diagrams through the universe is translated by an inequality of corresponding internal durations. Now, either relativity theory does not hold, or the phenomenon in question is really produced and can be observed if $\beta = v/c$ is sufficiently large. In fact, everything converges to force the ac-

[11] The problem of Langevin's projectile has been exposed by its author within general relativity; here we remain, by choice, within the limits of special relativity.

[12] Statistical age, on the hypothesis of radioactive nuclei.

ceptance of the physical validity of relativity; for example, the phenomenon of "clock retardation" through change of Galilean frames, from which the former is necessarily derived, seems to be directly verified today in the case of the duration of cosmic ray mesons.

For Einstein, we believe we have shown that "time defined as a function of the speed of light is the only time that exists." [13] Even today a similar view of things seems to some entirely arbitrary, and the abandoning of universal time, which accepting this view entails, scarcely seems founded *de jure*. This is so, it is thought, because since Einstein's theory defines simultaneity through an exchange of optical signals, and lengths by numbers of stationary waves, it ends in conclusions which seem paradoxical. Nevertheless, it remains true that all metrics and all high-precision chronometry are today tributaries, the one of the luminous spatial dimension, the other of the Herzian temporal dimension; if Poincaré may be believed, in science the fact creates the right, and definitions ought to be cut out according to the measure of experimental techniques.

But it is not simply through its unequaled precision that the science of waves was predestined to dominate geometry and kinetics. Really, it *is* the most geometric and the most kinetic of physical sciences, that in which the essential quantities are spaces, times, and pure numbers. If, as Poincaré also wished, geometry and kinetics are physical sciences, it is not surprising to see Einstein identify them with optics: the science of space and that of the void ought to be, simply, one.

To the camp followers of theoretical mechanics, finally, from whom the reproach is most often heard that relativity subjects kinetics and all physics to optics, it must be noted that dynamics,

---

[13] A. Sesmat, II, 54. The two volumes *Le système absolu classique et les mouvements réels* (Paris, 1936) and *Les systèmes privilégiés de la physique relativiste* (Paris, 1936) contain a remarkable exposition of the entire historical problem of relativity, and of the essence of its solution. It is surprising that such excellent views are not convincing to the author, who is anti-relativistic, and we do not see that these two factors can be reconciled.

with de Broglie, has become undulatory and that it has required the services of the constant c; the formula

$$(10) \qquad vw = c^2$$

of de Broglie universally binds the speed of corpuscles to that of their periodic waves [*ondes de phase*]. Nonetheless, the mechanist's argument remains sound in one respect: it is because optics is a mechanics employing evanescent material points, photons, that the fundamental constant of velocities appears. Actually, Einstein's constant c, like Planck's constant h, is a property common to all physics; it enters into each of its branches and is there a criterion of universality.

Really, no fissure appears in the application of Poincaré's epistemological criteria to Einstein's theory. Initially drawing as near to experiment as possible through its "convenient" definitions, rigorously developing its deduction following a formalism cut to the exact measure of its definitions, it ends by being in agreement with observation. Today, some of the most direct consequences of these principles are coming into the field of experiment; for example the law of the retardation of clocks seems well verified, although in a qualitative way, in the lifetime of the cosmic ray meson.

Now, it is by continuity that the transition is made from current experience to scientific experiment; or, if it is wished, there is a single order of phenomena. It seems really difficult to disagree with the Einsteinians that the space and time they define are not those which appear to us, that is, those which, for us, exist. If this is so, the universal expression Einstein gives to the principle of relativity, and its mathematical exploitation, comprise the discovery and exposition of one of those grand views which have marked each important advance of theory in physics.

Thus, at the end of a long examination of the history and philosophy of science, we must formally conclude, against Bergson, that the entire current of thought proceeding from Aristotle to Einstein and Minkowski, passing through the great "legislators" of classical mechanics, optics, and electromagnetism, corresponds to an incontestable physical reality. The technical arguments produced by Bergson in *Duration and Simultaneity* are absolutely erroneous and do not apply.

Nevertheless, the paradox denounced by Bergson remains, and it must be insisted, in a way, that a theory which completely "spatializes" time fails absolutely to realize the irreducible originality of time; is it not this apparent contradiction which de Broglie notes with humor when, himself the illustrious creator of an essentially relativistic theory, his wave mechanics, he considers that "the theory of relativity pushes to the end, and to the absurd, the ideas of rational mechanics"?

But let us go back in thought to the epoch when James Joule demonstrated the equivalence of the notions of heat and work; that verification simply sharpened the necessity of legally recognizing an entire order of facts which Meyer's principle seemed, paradoxically, to ignore. This equilibrium was not established until Rudolf Clausius, exploiting Carnot's profound ideas, defined entropy and accorded the concept of heat its essential originality. Statistical mechanics has come on the one hand to confirm the identity of the nature of work and heat and on the other to interpret what essentially distinguishes them.

It therefore seems to us that Einstein's great discovery and Bergson's just claims may be much less incompatible than they appear at first glance. It is not stated that the path Einstein opened cannot lead further, and that the study of light, of its absorption and emission, does not have a great deal more to tell us about the physical secrets of time. We consider here, notably, M. R. Lennuier's fine study in which, concerning the interaction of matter and rays, he made such penetrating remarks on quantum time.[14] We think that, far from accepting the verdict of incompetence with which Bergson charges it, physics on the contrary ought to accept it as a challenge. If it is true that Einstein's and Minkowski's physics have finally expressed the first principle of the still faltering science of time, perhaps it remains for them to discover the second, and perhaps to attach its expression to the statistical formalism of quantum theory.

[14] *Annales de Physique*, 11° Série, 20 (1945), 91.

BERGSON AND ZENO'S PARADOXES

The Continuity and Discontinuity of Time

VERE C. CHAPPELL

Time and Zeno's Arrow

Remarks by the Editor. "Zeno's arguments, in some form," Bertrand Russell once asserted, "have afforded ground for almost all the theories of space and time and infinity which have been constructed from his day to our own." [1] Professor Vere C. Chappell, in his carefully reasoned article "Time and Zeno's Arrow," submits Zeno's paradox to a thoroughgoing analysis and arrives at a surprising conclusion. Though many philosophers, including Bergson, Russell, Whitehead, and Paul Weiss, have sought to establish their own views of the nature of time and motion by refuting Zeno, no attempt to establish a view about time on the basis of Zeno's argument, Chappell insists, could succeed.

Zeno's arguments have generally been taken as attempts to prove that motion is impossible. Beginning with Aristotle's discussion of Zeno, Chappell analyzes the paradox of the Flying Arrow as follows:

1. Nothing occupying a space[2] is in motion.
2. The flying arrow is always "at some moment."
3. Whatever is at some moment occupies a space.
4. Therefore the flying arrow occupies a space.
5. And so (by 1) it is not in motion.

Thus, if there is motion, *then there is no motion*. Philosophers have often felt that because this conclusion renders space, time, and motion radically unintelligible, it also makes the achievement of a consistent philosophy of nature impossible. For this reason they have believed it necessary to prove Zeno wrong. But they

[1] Bertrand Russell, *Our Knowledge of the External World* (New York: New American Library, 1960), 140.
[2] More precisely "occupying a space equal to itself." Sentence 3 is, for purposes of exposition, similarly simplified.

have also attempted to show that by refuting Zeno they have established their own theories. This latter use of Zeno's paradox is invalid.

The metaphysical impotence of any *reductio ad absurdum* argument directed against Zeno rests on the fact that, once Zeno's arguments against the reality of "time" or "motion" are refuted, it is always possible to suggest other meanings of the words "time" or "motion" not considered in the original refutation. Thus Bergson, in attempting to prove his own theory that time and motion are "radically continuous," merely shows that Zeno's paradox of the arrow is invalid because it fails to account for time and motion in Bergson's special sense. Similarly, Russell, in attempting to demonstrate the invalidity of Zeno's argument, only shows that Zeno's argument is fallacious *if* Russell's own theory of motion, based on the concept of *mathematical* continuity, is presupposed. Russell's theory that motion consists "merely in the occupation of different times," if true, would invalidate both Bergson's theory that motion consists in radically continuous, qualitative change and Zeno's opinion that "motion" is impossible. But it is necessary to prove first that Russell's (or Bergson's or Whitehead's or Weiss's) view is correct. And this cannot be accomplished simply through the "refutation" of Zeno. *Professor Chappell's essay, originally published in the* JOURNAL OF PHILOSOPHY, *LIX (April 12, 1962), is reprinted here with the permission of the author and the* JOURNAL OF PHILOSOPHY.

PHILOSOPHERS HAVE REACTED to Zeno's celebrated arguments on motion in very different ways. For the most part they have sought to destroy them, to show that they are invalid. And this is reasonable, for if the arguments are valid it seems to follow that such things as motion, time, and space are radically unintelligible; yet it is just such things, among others, that philosophers try to understand. Philosophers of nature, at any rate, have had to refute Zeno in order to guarantee the feasibility of their own enterprise, or so they have generally thought. A number of recent philosophers, however, have taken a quite different view of Zeno's arguments. Far from attacking Zeno, they have embraced him as an ally. Among others, James, Bergson, Whitehead, Russell, and Weiss have made use of arguments of Zeno, one or more of them, to help establish crucial tenets in their own philosophies of nature, to help support particular positive views of motion, space, and time. The Zenonian argument is typically employed by these philosophers as a *reductio ad absurdum* of some (in their eyes) false view of time or space or motion. Supposing that their own view is the only possible alternative to the false view in question, they then regard the Zenonian argument as a demonstration of the truth of their view. In any case the argument is taken to be valid, and its conclusion is held really to follow from its premises.

I want in this paper to examine such use by such philosophers of one of Zeno's four motion arguments, the so-called Flying Arrow. My main purpose will be to throw light on some of the views of motion and time that have been proposed in recent times and to offer some considerations relevant to their assessment.

It is first necessary to get clear what Zeno's argument is. Unfortunately we have only Aristotle's statement of the argument to go on, and there is some uncertainty even about Aristotle's text in the relevant passage.[1] I shall adopt the version given by H. D. P. Lee in his book on Zeno: "[Zeno says that] if . . . everything is either at rest or in motion, but nothing is in motion when it occupies a space equal to itself [ὅταν ἦ κατὰ τὸ ἴσον], and what is in flight is always at any given moment [ἐν τῷ νῦν] occupying a space equal to itself, then the flying arrow is motionless [ἀκίνητον]."[2] In his only other reference to the argument, Aristotle says Zeno's conclusion is "that the flying arrow stands still [ἔστηκεν]."[3]

---

[1] *Phys.* Z, 9, 239b5-7.

[2] H. D. P. Lee, *Zeno of Elea* (Cambridge, 1936), 52–53 (I have substituted "moment" for Lee's "instant" in the translation). Lee follows the standard text of Bekker but adds to it at two points. The additions are: (1) "nothing is in motion [οὐδὲν δὲ κινεῖται]" in l. 6, and (2) "occupying a space equal to itself [κατὰ τὸ ἴσον]" in l. 7. Lee's case for making these additions, which I find altogether convincing, is presented on pp. 78–82 of his book.

[3] *Phys.* Z, 9, 239b30. Both Lee and the Oxford translators translate "ἔστηκεν" as "is at rest," thus taking it as a synonym for "ἠρεμεῖ," and there is no doubt that these terms are sometimes used interchangeably in the *Physics*—see, e.g.,

255

Lee (p. 81) analyzes the argument contained in these statements of Aristotle into the following seven steps:

(1) Everything must be either at rest or in motion.
(2) Nothing κατὰ τὸ ἴσον . . . is in motion.
(3) The flying arrow is always ἐν τῷ νῦν.
(4) Whatever is ἐν τῷ νῦν is κατὰ τὸ ἴσον.
(5) Therefore, the flying arrow is [always] κατὰ τὸ ἴσον.
(6) And so (by 2) not in motion.
(7) Therefore (by 1) the flying arrow is at rest.

Actually, steps 2 to 6 are the only ones needed to derive the conclusion, "If there is motion, then there is no motion," which is what I take Zeno to be trying to show in this argument. Furthermore, the disjunction asserted in step 1 is false (see pp. 260–62 below), so that the conclusion in 7 cannot be inferred in any case; indeed the argument for 6 can, under certain conditions, be used to establish the contradictory of 7, as we shall see. We may therefore restrict our attention to that part of Zeno's argument which is contained in steps 2 to 6 of the above analysis.

Aristotle says that the Flying Arrow argument is based on the assumption that time is composed of indivisible moments, or "nows." This assumption he himself rejects, though he concedes that the argument is valid if it is granted. But there is an ambiguity in saying that time is composed of indivisibles, and the argument may take different forms accordingly. For the indivisibles in question may be taken to be either (a) extended and (in any stretch of finite length) finite in number, or (b) unextended and infinite

---

230a4 (ἔστηκεν and ἠρέμησις), 230b21–26 (ἴστασθαι and ἠρεμία), and 238b24–26 (ἴσταται and ἠρεμίζεσθαι)—although the standard term for "is at rest" in the technical sense of "can move but doesn't" (cf. 226b14–16) is "ἠρεμεῖ." But if we could suppose that Aristotle distinguished these two terms on occasion, we should not have to say that he took "being motionless" and "being at rest" to be equivalent, which otherwise, on the basis of the two passages referring to Zeno just cited, seems unavoidable. For it is a mistake to identify "motionless" and "at rest," as we shall see below and as Aristotle himself insisted in other passages (e.g., *Phys.* △, 12, 221b12–13); even the Oxford translators acknowledge, in a note *ad* 239b7, that "Zeno's argument apparently does not prove that the arrow is at rest because it is not in motion." At any rate, I have given Aristotle the benefit of the doubt and translated "ἔστηκεν" here as "stands still" rather than "is at rest" (cf. n. 16 below).

in number. We might also list as a third possibility that the indivisibles be unextended and finite in number, except that the view that time is composed of indivisibles is then so obviously false as to make it pointless to consider how the Arrow argument would look when constructed on its basis; the argument then is obviously unsound. For there is no way in which a finite number of unextended elements can combine to form an extended interval, of time or of anything else. Aristotle held that version *b* of the view that time is composed of indivisibles is false for a similar reason, for he thought that an infinite number of unextended elements could no more constitute an extension than could a finite number. Thus in discussing whether a magnitude consists of (unextended) points he says, "even if all the points [sc. into which a body has been dissolved by "through and through" division, *i.e.*, division actually carried out *ad infinitum*] be put together, they will not make any magnitude." [4] Of course Aristotle was wrong in this, as we now know. The mathematical methods developed by Cantor have made it possible to show both that and how, under certain conditions, an infinitely numerous collection of unextended points does form an extended interval, although it does not follow that such points can be reached by *dividing* the interval.[5] And indeed it is in just this way that time is composed, according to modern (relativity) physics. Modern physicists also hold that time is continuous and hence infinitely divisible, but for them there is no inconsistency in saying that something is infinitely divisible and yet is composed of indivisibles, as there was for Aristotle.[6] At any rate, so long as we adopt version *b* of the doctrine that time is composed of indivisibles, we cannot suppose, as Aristotle did, that Zeno's Arrow argument is founded upon a false premise. It remains to be determined whether the argument is valid on this premise, as not only Aristotle but also Bergson and perhaps Russell have held it to be.

[4] *De gen. et cor.* A, 2, 316a15 ff. (Here I use, and henceforth shall use, the Oxford translation in quoting Artistotle.)
[5] See Adolph Grünbaum, "A Consistent Conception of the Extended Linear Continuum as an Aggregate of Unextended Elements," *Philosophy of Science*, XIX (1952), 228–306.
[6] See *Phys.* Z, 1, 231a18 ff.

257

Against version *a* of the view that time is composed of indivisibles, *i.e.*, against the view that time is composed of a finite number of extended elements, Aristotle offers an argument to prove
that time is continuous. For if time is continuous it is "divisible
into divisibles that are infinitely divisible," [7] and this does rule out
the possibility that time is composed of extended indivisibles
finite in number (though not, as noted above, the possibility that
time is composed of unextended indivisibles infinite in number).
Aristotle's argument runs as follows. Taking two moving bodies,
A and B, he writes,

> . . . suppose that A is quicker and B slower, and that the slower
> has traversed the magnitude CD in the time EF. Now it is clear
> that the quicker will traverse the same magnitude in less time than
> this: let us say in the time EG. Again, since the quicker has passed
> over the whole CD in the time EG, the slower will in the same
> time pass over CH, say, which is less than CD. And since B, the
> slower, has passed over CH in the time EG, the quicker will pass
> over it in less time: so that the time EG will again be divided. And
> if this is divided the magnitude CH will also be divided just as CD
> was: and again, if the magnitude is divided, the time will also be
> divided. And we can carry on this process forever, taking the
> slower after the quicker and the quicker after the slower alter-
> nately, and using what has been demonstrated at each stage as a
> new point of departure: for the quicker will divide the time and
> the slower will divide the length. If, then, this alternation always
> holds good, and at every turn involves a division, it is evident
> that all time must be continuous.[8]

The difficulty with this argument, of course, is that it begs the
very question at issue. For we are trying to determine *whether*
time can be divided in *infinitum*; and to assume, as Aristotle does,
that "we can carry on this process forever" and that "this alter-
nation always holds good, and at every turn involves a division"
is to assume the very thing to be established. Besides, it may just
be the case that time is composed of extended indivisibles which
are, in any stretch of finite length, finite in number. Whitehead

[7] *Phys.* Z, 2, 232, 324–25.
[8] *Ibid.*, 232ff.

and Weiss have both argued that this is the case; indeed both do so on the basis of an argument of Zeno's, though not of course the Flying Arrow: Whitehead employs the Dichotomy and Weiss the Achilles for this purpose.[9] These arguments show, according to these philosophers, that becoming and motion and change and temporal process generally are discontinuous, which is to say, occur in discrete atomic stages; and if becoming and the rest are discontinuous, so too is time. In Weiss's words, "Motion is not a progression through the conceivable subdivisions of a space, but a series of episodic occupations of some of those subdivisions."[10] And in answer to the argument of Aristotle just quoted, Weiss writes:

It is, of course, true that if time is divided without end, a faster body will always take less time to cover the same distance than a slower, but it does not follow that if one body is faster than another there is always a common distance for them to traverse and that therefore time is divisible without end. Aristotle makes his point only by assuming that all motion involves the successive occupancy of points of space, for only then will it be necessary for there to be an earlier time at which the faster body is at the position to be reached by the slower. But one body is faster than another, not because it takes less time than the slower to cover the distance, but because it covers a greater distance than the slower in the same interval of time. In a single instant [sc. extended subdivision] of time a slower and a faster body cover different distances, the faster covering the distance traversed by the slower only in the sense that an analytic part of itself covers the lesser distance while it, as a unit, covers a greater distance. A faster body will travel the same distance as a slower in a shorter interval of time only if the slower body takes at least two instants to traverse that distance. There is no half of an instant in which A can cover the same distance that B does in an instant. Both A and B, in an instant, attain to new

---

9 See A. N. Whitehead, *Process and Reality* (New York, 1929), 105–107 (on p. 106 Whitehead unaccountably refers to the Zenonian argument that he employs as "The Arrow in Its Flight," but it is clearly the Dichotomy that he has in mind). Paul Weiss, *Reality* (Princeton, 1938), 239–41.
10 Weiss, *Reality*, 238.

positions, not by progressively occupying each point of the new positions but by engaging in single, discrete, and equally enduring acts of making contiguous spatial regions, no greater than the magnitude of the smallest possible body, integral to themselves.[11]

I do not wish to decide on the truth of the Weiss-Whitehead view of motion and time or on the validity of the Zenonian arguments whereby it is supported;[12] I want simply to point out that there is reason to question Aristotle's claim that it is false and, hence, also to question Aristotle's rejection of Zeno's Arrow argument on the grounds that it is founded on a false premise. For the Weiss-Whitehead view is the same as version a of the doctrine that time is composed of indivisibles. Of course even if it is established that this version of the doctrine is true, the question whether Zeno's argument is valid when based on it as a premise remains open. Again, as is the case when the argument is taken as resting on version b of the doctrine that time is composed of indivisibles, not only Aristotle but also Bergson and Russell have held that the argument is valid on this premise.

We have now to see in more detail what Zeno's argument comes to and to determine whether it is valid when it is based on each of versions a and b of the view that time is composed of indivisibles. Let us first examine the argument based on version a, whereby the indivisibles that compose time are extended and, in any stretch of finite length, finite in number.

We may begin by recapitulating the steps into which the argument, or that portion of it with which we are concerned, is analyzed by Lee. These are (re-numbered so as to begin with 1):

(1) Nothing κατὰ τὸ ἴσον . . . is in motion.

(2) The flying arrow is always ἐν τῷ νῦν.

(3) Whatever is ἐν τῷ νῦν is κατὰ τὸ ἴσον.

(4) Therefore the flying arrow is [always] κατὰ τὸ ἴσον.

(5) And so (by 1) not in motion.

11 *Ibid.*
12 In fact, I think they are invalid; I have tried to show that they are in my paper, "Whitehead's Theory of Becoming," *Journal of Philosophy*, LVIII (1961), 516–28.

Step 1 states that nothing can be said to move if it is in one place only. Literally, "κατὰ τὸ ἴσον" means "over against the equal," [13] but what "the equal" refers to, clearly, is the region of space in which, we say, a physical body is located. To say that a thing is over against an equal space is to say that it is located in a region exactly coincident in size and shape with its own spatial boundaries. But there is, in such a region, only one position which the thing in question can occupy, only one place in which it can be. And since a thing is said to move only if it is in two places at least, what is κατὰ τὸ ἴσον is motionless.

It must be noticed that no reference is made in step 1 to time, and that to say that something is κατὰ τὸ ἴσον is ambiguous without such a reference. For a thing can be κατὰ τὸ ἴσον either for a (period of) time or for no time, either at two or more times (moments) or at one time only. The thing is motionless in either case, but is not properly at *rest* unless it *remains* κατὰ τὸ ἴσον for some period of time, *i.e.*, unless it is κατὰ τὸ ἴσον at more than one moment of time.[14] For this reason it is wrong to say, as Lee does,[15] that "being κατὰ τὸ ἴσον" is a definition of "being at rest"; and for the same reason too it is a mistake to suppose that the disjunction expressed in Lee's original step 1, "Everything must be either at rest or in motion," is true.[16] What is at rest is motionless, but we

---

[13] Cf. W. D. Ross (ed.), *Aristotle's Physics* (Oxford, 1936), 416.

[14] Cf. Aristotle, *Phys.* Z, 3, 234a31-34; 234b5-7; 8, 239a14-18; 239a35-b2. It is clear, incidentally, that a period of time cannot, on the view that the moments of time are extended, be defined as any extended interval, since moments too are extended intervals. Hence to preserve the distinction between moment and period we must define the latter as an aggregate of two or more moments. This might seem odd, but the alternative is to make rest the contradictory rather than the contrary of motion (since a thing could then rest but could not move in a single moment; indeed everything would rest at every moment), which would be odder still.

[15] Lee, *Zeno of Elea*, 79.

[16] Neither of these points, however, need affect our acceptance of Lee's emendation of Aristotle's text at 239b6 (see n. 2 above). For the added phrase, "but nothing is in motion [οὐδὲν δὲ κινεῖται]," is needed to establish the conclusion that the arrow is motionless in any case, whether or not the question of its being at rest arises as well. No doubt Zeno himself took the disjunction, "Everything is either at rest or in motion," to be true and made the inference from the arrow's being motionless to its being at rest accordingly. Aristotle, however, held this disjunction to be false, and thus could not consistently have made the inference just mentioned, although he does seem to do so at 239b30. For he says there

cannot infer that what is motionless is at rest without the added premise that it is motionless through a period of time, or at more than one moment, for at a single moment there is neither motion nor rest.

Step 2 of Zeno's argument says that the flying arrow is always "in the present." "The present" is a term used to refer to a particular moment of time, and "always" here means simply "at any (or at every) moment." Hence what step 2 asserts is the tautology: The flying arrow is, at any moment (during its flight), at some moment, viz., that at which it is.

Step 3 then lays down the general principle that a thing cannot be in more than one place "in the present," which is to say at, or during, a moment of time. According to version *a* of the view that time is composed of indivisibles, which we are now assuming to be the premise on which Zeno's argument is based, the moments of time are extended; it follows that the present is extended too, *i.e.*, that what we use the term "the present" to refer to are extended moments of time. But these moments are also indivisible, and it is for this reason that a thing can be in only one place per moment. For if it could be in two places, we could distinguish that portion of the moment at or during which it was in the first place from that at or during which it was in the second, and the moment would not, as stipulated, be indivisible after all.

Step 4 draws the conclusion from steps 2 and 3, viz., that the flying arrow is always in one and only one place.[17] Step 5 then draws the conclusion from 1 and 4: The flying arrow is motionless. We must be careful not to misinterpret these conclusions, however. In the first place, to say that the flying arrow is always

---

that Zeno's argument establishes that the arrow ἕστηκεν and that this argument is valid on the premise that time is composed of indivisibles. But what is established on this premise, if anything is, is that the arrow does not move, not that it is at rest; indeed Aristotle himself gave this as Zeno's conclusion at 239b7. If, however, as I have already suggested (n. 3 above), we can suppose that Aristotle distinguished "ἕστηκεν" from "ἠρεμεῖ" on occasion, taking the former more in the sense of "ἀκίνητον" than as a synonym for the technical term "ἠρεμεῖ," we can avoid saying that Aristotle is guilty of inconsistency on this point.

17 The "always" is unaccountably omitted from step 4 in Lee's analysis of the argument, although it both appears in his step 2 and is essential for the proper interpretation of the argument (see just below).

in one and only one place is not to say that it remains forever in the *same* place. In commenting on step 2 I noted that "always" means simply "at any moment"; step 4 ought then to read: "The flying arrow is, at any moment, in one and only one place, *i.e.*, occupies no more than one position per moment of its flight." The arrow may be in the same place at two successive moments, or it may not—presumably the latter, if it is flying. All that step 4 establishes is that the arrow is not in two or more places at a single moment. And from this it follows, in the second place, that one can hold the flying arrow to be motionless, as in step 5, and yet maintain that it occupies a number of different positions during the time of its flight, one position, in fact, for each different moment of time. The sense of saying, under such circumstances, that the arrow is motionless may well be questioned, but this can be justified as follows. The arrow does not move during the span of any single moment; to do so it would have to be capable of being in more than one place per moment. Also, the moments into which the time taken by the arrow's flight is divided jointly exhaust this time; there is no time in addition to that contained in these moments, no time, in particular, "between" the moments. Hence there is no time at or during which the arrow is moving, even though it is in a number of different places in succession. The arrow can be said to be *at* one position in space and then *at* another, but it cannot be said to move *from* the one *to* the other. Nor will it do to say that the arrow moves from position to position "instantaneously," *i.e.*, in no time. For the phrase "instantaneous movement" is a contradiction in terms.[18]

The argument is then this. If there is motion, then whatever moves must move from the place where it starts to the place where it finishes its movement, and from each place along the way to the place next in order. But a moving thing is, at each moment of the time of its movement, at one and only one place, and the whole

---

[18] Cf. Bertrand Russell, *Our Knowledge of the External World* (London, 1914), p. 179; Andrew Ushenko, "Zeno's Paradoxes," *Mind*, LV (1946), 158; and H. R. King, "Aristotle and the Paradoxes of Zeno," *Journal of Philosophy*, XLVI (1949), 659. Ushenko attributes the distinction between "at-at" and "from-to" descriptions of motion to W. P. Montague, but gives no specific reference.

time of its movement is exhausted by moments. Thus, there is no time during which a thing can move from any place to any other. Hence there is no motion, even if a number of different positions are occupied in succession. Thus if there is motion, then there is no motion.

The same argument shows that no thing can be at rest, either, if by being at rest we understand not merely *being* in the same place at each of a succession of moments but *remaining* in the same place from one moment to another. The distinction between being twice *at* a position and *remaining* there through a period of time comprising two moments at least is perhaps harder to maintain than the corresponding distinction between being *at* two different positions at two different times and moving *from* one *to* the other. But rest is the contrary of motion, and we must, in all strictness, treat the two in analogous ways. The argument, furthermore, can be made to apply to temporal processes of all sorts, in addition to motion through space. Given the doctrine that time is composed of extended, indivisible moments, then qualitative change and growth and coming-into-being as well as motion will have to occur in discrete stages, no one of which is itself a change or growth or coming-into-being, and "between" which there is no time for any further change or growth or coming-into-being to occur. And the same can be shown to hold for the contraries of these temporal processes too, and hence that no thing can persist unchanged or remain for any time the same size, and so on. Hence what is established in the end by Zeno's argument, on the premise that time is composed of extended indivisibles and if the argument is valid, is not simply that motion and rest are impossible, but that nothing can, in Whitehead's phrase, "survive the lapse of time" at all.

I want now to raise the question whether Zeno's argument is valid on the premise that time is composed of extended moments, *i.e.*, on version *a* of the doctrine that time is composed of indivisibles. And I propose to do this by examining the views of those recent philosophers who have held the argument to be valid on this premise, viz., Bergson and Russell. It is worth noting at the outset, however, that two other recent philosophers, Whitehead and Weiss, must deny that the argument is valid on this premise; at least it seems that they must do so. For the premise in question is just the view of time—what Whitehead calls "the epochal theory of time" [19]—that these philosophers adopt. And the conclusion of Zeno's argument is a self-contradiction. If the argument is valid, this can only mean that one or more of the premises is false; the most likely offender is this premise about the nature of time. Hence it appears that Whitehead and Weiss must find some way of showing that the argument is invalid on this premise. But I shall return to this question later on.

The flying arrow "is motionless during all the time that it is moving," according to Bergson,

> if we suppose that the arrow can ever be in a point of its course . . . [and also] if the arrow, which is moving, ever coincides with a position, which is motionless. But the arrow never *is* in any point of its course. The most we can say is that it might be there, in this sense, that it passes there and might stop there. It is true that if it did stop there, it would be at rest there, and at this point it is no longer movement that we have to do with. . . . At bottom, [Zeno's] illusion arises from this, that the movement, *once effected*, has laid along its course a motionless trajectory on which we can count as many immobilities as we will. From this we conclude that the movement, *whilst being effected*, lays at each instant beneath it a position with which it coincides. We do not see that the trajectory is created in one stroke, although a certain time is required for it; and that though we can divide at will the trajectory once created, we cannot divide its creation, which is an act in progress and not a thing. To suppose that the moving body *is* at a point of its course . . . is to attribute to the course itself of the arrow everything that can be said of the interval that the arrow has traversed, that is to say, to admit *a priori* the absurdity that movement coincides with immobility (CE 308–10; EC 309–309).

The Zenonian "illusion" to which Bergson refers in this passage

[19] Whitehead, *Process and Reality*, 105; cf. Whitehead, *Science and the Modern World* (New York, 1925), 183 ff.

is the supposition that motion occurs in discrete stages, no one of which is itself a motion. This supposition is required, we have seen, by the epochal theory of time, the view that time is an aggregate of extended, indivisible moments. Because he thinks that Zeno's argument is valid when it is founded on this view as a premise, Bergson finds it necessary to reject this view of time. Furthermore, he takes the (alleged) fact that the argument, with its absurd conclusion, is valid to be a *reason* for rejecting the epochal theory of time and for adopting his own, alternative theory, whereby time is radically continuous, a whole in which there is "succession without distinction . . . a mutual penetration, an interconnexion and organization of elements, each one of which represents the whole, and cannot be distinguished or isolated from it except by abstract thought"; the elements of time therefore form "a continuous or qualitative multiplicity with no resemblance to number," *i.e.*, with no resemblance to the sort of multiplicity whose constituents can be numbered (TFW 101, 105; *Essai* 75, 78). Here, then, is one instance of the use of Zeno's argument by a philosopher to establish a positive view of time and motion, and a use wherein the validity of Zeno's argument is presupposed.

Russell is another recent philosopher who has used Zeno's Arrow argument in this way and who takes the argument, on the premise that time is composed of extended indivisible moments, to be valid. What Zeno's argument shows on this premise, according to Russell, is that the arrow "is never moving [and that] in some miraculous way the change of positions has to occur *between* the instants, that is to say, not at any time whatever." [20] For Russell, as for Bergson, this is a real difficulty, and "the more [it] is meditated, the more real it becomes." The difficulty is to be removed, Russell holds, again with Bergson, by denying the premise about time on which the conclusion to Zeno's argument is based. But Russell disagrees with Bergson on the positive view about time with which the premise is to be replaced. We escape

[20] Russell, *Our Knowledge of the External World,* 179; cf. pp. 140, 174, 183.

Zeno's conclusion not by holding time to be without distinct parts altogether, Russell says, but "by maintaining that, though space and time do consist of points and instants, the number of them in any finite interval is infinite." [21] Hence Russell does not reject the doctrine that time is composed of indivisibles, as Bergson does; he only rejects one version of that doctrine, version *a*, whereby the indivisibles composing time are extended and, in infinite stretches, finite in number. The other version of this doctrine, version *b*, Russell accepts; on his view time is composed of indivisibles, but the indivisibles are unextended and, in any stretch of finite length, infinite in number. Zeno's problem is solved by adopting this view of time (and of space), Russell says, because the arrow is not then required to change position in no time, or to "jump suddenly from one [position] to the other," on pain of not changing position at all; this view provides a possibility which was closed on the rejected view of time. Indeed, Russell goes on, motion is *continuous* on this view of space and time, just as space and time themselves are. For since between any two positions occupied by a moving body at any two instants, "there are an infinite number of positions still nearer together, which are occupied at instants that are also still nearer together," the body "never jumps from one position to another, but always passes by a gradual transition through an infinite number of intermediaries." [22] "At a given instant," Russell says, a moving body "is where it is, like Zeno's arrow." Nonetheless, although "we find it hard to avoid supposing that, when the arrow is in flight, there is a *next* position occupied at the *next* moment, . . . in fact there is no next position and no next moment, and once this is imaginatively realized, the difficulty [sc. brought to light by Zeno's argument] is seen to disappear." [23]

Are Bergson and Russell correct in their supposition that Zeno's Arrow argument is valid on the premise that time is composed of extended indivisibles? Before answering this question I want to

[21] *Ibid.*, 183.
[22] *Ibid.*, 140, 142.
[23] *Ibid.*, 142, 179-80.

note briefly how the argument appears when it is based upon the other version, version *b*, of the view that time is composed of indivisibles. And the best way to do this is to look further at the difference between the responses of Bergson and Russell to the argument when it is based upon version *a* of this view. For Bergson would object to Russell's response by saying that it provides no escape from the difficulty posed by Zeno. The proposition that "movement is made of immobilities," Bergson would say, is no less absurd when the "immobilities" are infinite in number than it is when they are finite (CM 213; PM 203). In other words, Bergson holds that Zeno's Arrow argument is valid on the premise that time is composed of unextended moments as well as on the premise that it is composed of moments that are extended. But this is just our version *b* of the view that time is composed of indivisibles, and it is the version which, as we have seen, Russell adopts in order to escape the conclusion which, he thought, Zeno showed does follow from version *a* of that view. According to Bergson, time and motion are not really continuous at all on Russell's view, since their elements remain distinct and external to one another. The moving arrow still *is* at each of the positions along the course it traverses; the entire course is exhausted by the positions at which the arrow is in turn, and the entire time of its flight is exhausted by the moments at which it is at each of the positions along the course; the arrow does not move insofar as it is at a position; yet to move does take time; hence, since there is no time at or during which the arrow is not at some position, there is no time at or during which it moves; hence the arrow does not move. The conclusion is the same, Bergson claims, whether the positions along the arrow's course and the moments of its flight are finite or infinite in number, and it is only by adopting his own view, that time and motion are radically continuous, that time is not composed of moments at all, and that moving bodies do not occupy positions, that Zeno's conclusion is avoided. Here, it may be noted, is still another instance of the use of Zeno's argument to establish a positive view of the nature of time, and a use which presupposes that the argument is valid; only now it is the argument based on version *b* of the view that time is composed of indivisibles, the version whereby the indivisibles are unextended and infinite in number.

But again, is Zeno's argument valid on this premise, as Bergson maintains that it is? This, we have seen, is equivalent to the question whether Bergson's objection to Russell's view, the view whereby Russell sought to escape Zeno's conclusion from the alternative premise about time, is just or not. And I think it is clear that it is not. For the objection is founded on what is, quite plainly, a confusion on Bergson's part, viz., the confusion of being *at* or *occupying* a spatial position with being at *rest* or *remaining* there. The confusion is shown, e.g., in the passage from *Creative Evolution* already quoted (p. 265 above), where it is denied that Zeno's arrow ever *is* at any point of its course. For if it were, Bergson says, it would *stop* there and hence be at *rest* there. But surely, as I noted earlier, the notions of *being* at a point and being at *rest* there are distinct. This is so even when time and space are thought of as composed of extended elements; it is all the more obvious on the Russellian view whereby the components of space and time are unextended. For in this case, as Russell notes, although it is true that "at a given instant [a moving body] is where it is, . . . we cannot say that it is at rest at the instant, since the instant does not last for a finite time, and there is not a beginning and end of the instant with an interval between them. Rest consists in being in the same position at all the instants throughout a certain infinite period, however short; it does not consist simply in a body's being where it is at a given instant." [24] Furthermore, it is not the case, as Bergson seems to suppose, that on Russell's view a moving body must, in the end, get from position to position on its course in no time whatsoever. For the number of positions is infinite on Russell's view, as is the number of moments. Hence between any two positions occupied by a moving body there are always intervening positions, and, correspondingly, there are always intervening

[24] Russell, *Our Knowledge of the External World*, 142.

moments between those at which any two positions are occupied; thus there is always time for the movement from any position to any other to occur.

I think we must conclude, therefore, that Bergson's objection to Russell's view of time and motion is unfounded. And this is equivalent to saying that Bergson's use of Zeno's Arrow argument in this connection is illegitimate. It seems clear that the argument is not a valid argument when it is founded on the Russellian view of time, our version *b* of the doctrine that time is composed of indivisibles. On this view, whereby the indivisibles composing time are unextended and, in any interval, infinite in number, the conclusion that the arrow does not move does not follow. For motion on this view simply consists in the occupation of different spatial positions at different times, and this, as we say, is in no way ruled out by Zeno's argument.

But there is a curious feature of this conclusion which must be noted. In an earlier discussion of Zeno's Arrow argument, Russell confessed that to him the argument "seems a very plain statement of a very elementary fact," the fact "that we live in an unchanging world, and that the arrow, at every moment of its flight, is truly at rest. The only point where Zeno probably erred was in inferring (if he did infer) that because there is no change, therefore the world must be in the same state at one time as at another. This consequence by no means follows. . . ." Russell is not quite serious when he says in this passage that there is no change, and hence no motion either; presumably he is overstating his point here for emphasis. What he means is expressed in a later passage: we must, he says, "entirely reject the notion of a *state* of motion. Motion consists *merely* in the occupation of different places at different times. . . ." [25] What is disquieting about these statements is that in them Russell seems to be granting that Zeno's argument is valid, given his own view of time as a premise. He seems to be saying that Zeno's argument, on this premise (which is our version *b* of the doctrine that time is composed of indivisibles) does show something. But if so, he cannot be granting that what the

[25] Russell, *The Principles of Mathematics* (Cambridge, 1903), 350, 347, 473.

argument shows is that his view of time is false. What, then, does he think the argument shows? I think this: that a certain *view* of motion is *false* and that his own view of motion is therefore *true*. Zeno's argument is valid, Russell seems to be saying; its conclusion is a contradiction; this shows that one or more of its premises must be false. But the offending premise is not, as Bergson (and Aristotle) thought, the doctrine that time is composed of indivisible "nows," but rather a premise to the effect that motion is such and such, or that the word "motion" has such and such a meaning, the meaning, whatever it is, that is ruled out by Russell's apparent redefinition: "Motion consists *merely* in the occupation of different places at different times." Russell must be supposing that some such premise is included in the argument, and that it is this premise which is to be rejected on the appearance of the paradoxical conclusion. But what exactly is this premise, what is the view or conception of motion that Russell is (or seems to be) rejecting? Russell says that we must reject "the notion of a *state* of motion," and he also says or implies that this is the (or a) common, prephilosophical notion of motion, and that it is this notion which is defended by Bergson. This does not tell us what motion is according to this notion—indeed, Bergson held that one could not *say* what motion (as he conceived it) is at all—but it gives us an idea of the sort of thing that Russell takes himself to be rejecting, viz., a view of unreflective or deliberately irrational men, held on the basis of immediate experience unilluminated by philosophical analysis. And this of course is not the only instance (if it is an instance) in which Russell did reject a view (allegedly) of this sort.

In any case it seems that our question whether Zeno's Arrow argument is valid on Russell's view of time, that is, on version *b* of the doctrine that time is composed of indivisibles, cannot after all be answered in the simple way we earlier supposed. We said before that Bergson was wrong to claim that the argument was valid against Russell's view of time, since it does not follow from the argument that the arrow does not move. But we can now see that what precisely does not follow is the conclusion that the arrow does not move *in any sense of "move."* It is this precise conclusion

271

that Bergson appears to be arguing for, and it is because there is a sense of "move" in which the arrow does move—the very sense, indeed, that is required if Russell's view of time is true—that this conclusion does not follow. But suppose Bergson had argued not for this conclusion but for a different one, viz., that the arrow does not move *in his* (Bergson's) *sense of "move."* Would not his argument have then been valid? Is it not the case that this latter conclusion does follow from the argument's premises? This is the very conclusion that Russell did draw from Zeno's argument, at least in the passages cited just above, and Russell evidently did think the argument valid when construed in this way, as we have seen. And Bergson *could* have argued for this conclusion, too, had he included, as Russell did, a statement of his (Bergson's) view of motion among the argument's premises. The difference between Bergson and Russell would then have come to this: that the one chose one premise of the argument to reject and the other another. For there would have been agreement between Bergson and Russell that, given Russell's view of time and Bergson's conception of motion, among other things, the conclusion that the arrow does not move in Bergson's sense of "move" does follow. But Bergson would have drawn the further conclusion that Russell's view of time is to be rejected, whereas Russell did conclude that it is Bergson's conception of motion that is faulty. We should not be troubled by the fact that Bergson *did* not argue in this way, for it is plain that Zeno's argument can be so interpreted, and this is all that is important here.

Nor need we be surprised at this result, considering the form of Zeno's argument. For the situation that emerges is characteristic of *reductio ad absurdum* arguments generally. *Something* is wrong if a self-contradictory conclusion can be deduced from a set of premises, but the mere fact that the deduction is legitimate, that the argument is valid, does not tell us *what* is wrong; it does not tell us which premise or combination of premises is the offender, as it were. Hence the question, "Is such and such argument valid on such and such premise?" is never the simple question that it sometimes seems to be when the argument is one of the *reductio ad absurdum* form.

I have talked so far about the validity of Zeno's argument when it is founded upon version *b* of the doctrine that time is composed of indivisibles, the version whereby the components of time are unextended and infinite in number. But I think that similar points can be made in answer to the question, before postponed, about the validity of Zeno's argument on the alternative version of this doctrine, version *a*, whereby the components of time are extended and, in a finite stretch, finite in number. For if the Russellian view of motion, required by version *b* of the doctrine that time is composed of indivisibles, is different from some common, pre-philosophical view of motion, then *a fortiori*, the Whitehead-Weiss view of motion which is required by version *a* is different too; indeed both Whitehead and Weiss take specific note of the fact that the conception of motion that their views of time require is somewhat at variance with the common conception. Furthermore, if we can say that Zeno's argument is valid on version *b* of the doctrine that time is composed of indivisibles, although it is valid not against this but against some premise stating this common conception of motion, so too we can say this when the argument is based on version *a*. We can, in other words, admit that Zeno's argument is valid with the Weiss-Whitehead view of time as a premise without drawing the conclusion, drawn by Russell and Bergson, that this view of time is false; the validity of Zeno's argument need not be taken as a reason for rejecting the Weiss-Whitehead view. And there seems to be no reason for denying that the argument is valid when taken in this way. Both on version *b* (the Russellian view) and on version *a* (the view of Whitehead and Weiss), we may say, Zeno's Flying Arrow argument is valid. But this fact need not have the consequence that might naturally be supposed to ensue, viz., that these respective views of time are false. Only Russell, of the three philosophers now being discussed, tried to establish the falsity of a view of time (that of Weiss and Whitehead) on the basis of Zeno's Flying Arrow argument; and

273

this attempt, we may now conclude, is a failure. But more generally, I think we could say that *no* attempt to establish a view about time on the basis of Zeno's argument could succeed. For it would always be open to a proponent of the view in question to change the meaning of "motion" or to claim that the meaning had been changed as a consequence of his view of time, so that Zeno's conclusion would not apply to motion in his new, changed sense, but only in the old, rejected sense. He could further claim that Zeno's argument indeed provides a reason for making just this change.

And now a new question arises: Which view of motion or of time is *correct*; which is the *true* or *right* view, among these various alternatives? Or if it is not a matter of the correct or true view, which view is the most successful or defensible or adequate? It seems clear that an appeal to arguments such as that of Zeno, valid though they may be, can never settle this question decisively. What does "motion" mean, or what ought it to mean? What *is* motion, really? Should reference to that root and common notion of motion which Bergson claims to defend and from which Russell and Whitehead and Weiss seem in their different ways to depart play any part in answering these questions? Does what we now think, how we now conceive motion, the rules whereby the words "move" and "motion" are used in our everyday dealings with one another, have anything to do with philosophical inquiries into the nature of motion? *Are* there even rules for the use of "motion" in ordinary affairs, or rules that can be stated with any precision? I do not know the answers to these questions, but I would suggest that some answer to them is needed if we are to hope to settle the philosophical questions that the use of Zeno's arguments, among others, ultimately raises—if, *i.e.*, we are to settle those questions about the nature of motion and time and the rest with which philosophers, at least since the time of Zeno, have seen fit to occupy themselves.

DAVID A. SIPFLE

Henri Bergson and the Epochal Theory of Time

Remarks by the Editor. In his discussion of the paradox of the
Flying Arrow, Professor Chappell describes Bergson as holding
the view that time is "radically continuous" and as, therefore,
specifically rejecting the thesis that time is composed of distinct
"epochs." This interpretation of Bergson's viewpoint is challenged
by Professor David A. Sipfle in his essay "Henri Bergson and the
Epochal Theory of Time." Bergson, Professor Sipfle argues, does
hold that time consists in a "mutual interpenetration of elements";
but—and this is of greatest importance—he also depicts this interpenetration as a "qualitative multiplicity," a "heterogeneity" involving a real "difference between *same* and *other*." In order for
time to exhibit qualitative multiplicity, however, it must contain
distinguishable elements or parts. Yet such distinguishable elements or parts are precisely what is assumed in the "epochal"
theory of time.

That Bergson's theory of time should have been wrongly construed as a rejection of epochal theories is, Professor Sipfle holds,
understandable. In his zeal to effect a complete separation between
temporal and spatial categories, Bergson exaggerated the incommensurability of the temporal and the discrete. The distinction
between the qualitative interpenetration characteristic of duration
and the simple juxtaposition of spatial point, is, however, attenuated in Bergson's later works, where the relative "discreteness"
of temporal elements is stressed. Another cause of misunderstanding lies in the misinterpretation of what is involved in epochal
theories of time. If a theory which allows a "mutual penetration,
an interconnexion and organization of elements" is disqualified as
an epochal theory of time, then not only Bergson but Whitehead himself (whom Professor Chappell represents as holding an
"epochal" view) must be characterized as denying the epochal
theory of time.

In reality, just as Whitehead allows for both the "separative" and the "prehensive" aspects of time, so Bergson insists on the reality of both distinguishable temporal epochs and their profound interrelatedness. Moreover, this view of the nature of time includes not only psychological but physical duration. Once Bergson's account of the duration of matter is clarified, it is clear that, for Bergson, real time, whether endured by mind or by matter, is epochal. In arriving at this conclusion, it should be noted, Professor Sipfle contradicts a very widely held view of Bergson's concept of duration. In this volume not only Professor Chappell, but Professor Blanché as well, propose the opposite interpretation. *Professor Sipfle's essay is published here for the first time.*

I N AN EXCELLENT DISCUSSION of "Time and Zeno's Arrow" [1] Vere Chappell points out that "there is an ambiguity in saying that time is composed of indivisibles. . . . For the indivisibles in question may be taken to be either (*a*) extended and (in any stretch of finite length) finite in number, or (*b*) unextended and infinite in number (Chappell 256–57). He quite properly identifies the first alternative with "what Whitehead calls "the epocal theory of time' " (Chappell 265), and argues that "because he thinks that Zeno's argument is valid when it is founded on this view as a premise, Bergson finds it necessary to reject this view of time" (Chappell 266).

Is it in fact this view of time which Bergson rejects? The passage from *Creative Evolution* which Chappell quotes specifically states that: "At bottom, [Zeno's] illusion arises from this, that the movement, *once effected,* has laid along its course a motionless trajectory *on which we can count as many immobilities as we will.* From this we conclude that the movement, *whilst being effected,* lays at each instant beneath it a position with which it

---

[1] This essay was originally published in the *Journal of Philosophy*, LIX (April 12, 1962), 197–213. It is included in this volume on pp. 254–74, and the page numbers cited will refer to the article as it appears here.

coincides" (CE 309; EC 309).[2] "The Zenonian 'illusion' to which Bergson refers in this passage is the supposition that motion occurs in discrete stages, no one of which is itself a motion," Chappell explains. "This supposition is required, we have seen, by the epochal theory of time, the view that time is an aggregate of extended, indivisible moments" (Chappell 266). But the text does not bear him out. Bergson is characteristically objecting to treating time and motion in spatial terms. The difficulty in all four of Zeno's paradoxes of motion, he explains, is "that they all consist in applying the movement to the line traversed, and supposing that what is true of the line is true of the movement. The line, for example, may be divided into *as many parts as we wish, of any length* that we wish, and it is always the same line" (CE 310; EC 309; italics added). He is denying that motion can be arbitrarily and *indefinitely* divided, as can a line segment. He is not concerned with a finite number of discrete, extended indivisibles here; he explicitly rejects only alternative *b*, not *a*.

Chappell recognizes that Bergson means to reject alternative *b*, of course; "the proposition that 'movement is made of immobilities,' Bergson would say, is no less absurd when the 'immobilities' are infinite in number than it is when they are finite" (Chappell 268).[3] Chappell's position is that Bergson means to reject both *a* and *b;* but the passage to which he refers here can no more be extended to *a* than can the previously cited passage from *Creative Evolution.* Here, too, Bergson is clearly referring to unextended points, not extended indivisibles: "Consider, for example, the variability which is nearest to homogeneity, that of movement in space. Along the whole of this movement we can imagine possible stoppages; these are what we call the positions of the moving body, or the points by which it passes. But with these positions, even with an infinite number of them, we shall never make movement. They are not parts of the movement, they are so many snapshots of it; they are, one might say, only supposed stopping-places" (CM 213; PM 203).

[2] Quoted in Chappell on p. 265. The second italics are mine.
[3] Chappell is quoting CM 213; PM 203.

In this passage Bergson is not contrasting an infinite number of unextended instants (represented as points on a trajectory) with a finite number of extended units of time; the "stoppages," "positions," or "snapshots" he refers to have no temporal extension. He is rejecting the use of unextended points to represent time, *even if* they be infinite; it is the same unextended points he refers to if they happen to be finite. Chappell points out that "we might also list as a third possibility [in addition to *a* and *b*] that the indivisibles be unextended and finite in number, except that the view that time is composed of indivisibles is then so obviously false as to make it pointless to consider how the Arrow argument would look when constructed on its basis" (Chappell 257). It is this third possibility, not *a*, which Bergson is rejecting here. He agrees that it is obviously false. His purpose is to show that *b* is no more plausible than this obviously implausible third alternative; *a* is irrelevant to his argument.

These three alternatives do not yet exhaust the views of time with which Chappell is concerned.

[Bergson] takes the (alleged) fact that [Zeno's] argument, with its absurd conclusion, is valid to be a *reason* for rejecting the epochal theory of time and for adopting his own, alternative theory, whereby time is radically continuous, a whole in which there is "succession without distinction . . . a mutual penetration, an interconnexion and organization of elements, each one of which represents the whole, and cannot be distinguished or isolated from it except by abstract thought"; the elements of time therefore form "a continuous or qualitative multiplicity with no resemblance to number", *i.e.*, with no resemblance to the sort of multiplicity whose constituents can be numbered (Chappell 266).[4]

We have denied that Bergson explicitly rejects the epochal theory of time in his discussion of Zeno's paradoxes. Even if this is granted, however, the description of time as "radically contin-

---

[4] The quotations are from TFW 101, 105; *Essai* 75, 78.

uous" seems to preclude such a view.[5] Can we accept this description of Bergson's view of time? If so, does it follow that Bergson must deny the epochal theory of time?

Chappell appeals here to *Time and Free Will*. In this work, Bergson begins his discussion of "the immediate data of consciousness" by insisting upon the complete exclusion of any quantitative distinctions within or between qualities. He argues that measurement depends upon number, that number depends upon homogeneous units, and that only space can provide the homogeneous medium required for these units (TFW 75–85; *Essai* 56–63). Duration, on the other hand, he describes as "a wholly qualitative multiplicity, an absolute heterogeneity of elements which pass over into one another" (TFW 229; *Essai* 172). This dualism between the quantitative, homogeneous, and spatial characteristics of the external world versus the qualitative, heterogeneous, and temporal properties of consciousness is characterized as absolute. "The fact is that there is no point of contact between the unextended and the extended, between quality and quantity" (TFW 70; *Essai* 52). While "the moments of inner duration are not external to one another" (TFW 226; *Essai* 170), "we must not say that external things *endure*" (TFW 227; *Essai* 171). "In consciousness we find states which succeed, without being distinguished from one another; and in space simultaneities which, without succeeding, are distinguished from one another, in the sense that one has ceased to exist when the other appears.[6] Out-

[5] In reading Bergson one must take care not to confuse the continuity characteristic of temporal phenomena with the mathematical continuity characteristic of alternative *b*. The former is indivisible; it cannot be divided without being radically changed or destroyed in the process. The infinite divisibility which characterizes "mathematical continuity" is, in these terms, radically discontinuous (cf. CE 162; EC 162–63). It follows, of course, that Bergsonian continuity precludes *b*, whatever its implications with respect to *a*.

[6] Cf. Chappell, p. 270, where he quotes Russell, *The Principles of Mathematics* (Cambridge, 1903), 350, 347, 473. Or cf. Russell's "Mathematics and the Metaphysicians," in *Mysticism and Logic* (London: Penguin, 1953), 80. The external world of *Time and Free Will* is very much like Russell's—a world in which Zeno's arrow does not move. No wonder Bergson is so concerned to isolate all temporal phenomena from it!

side us, mutual externality without succession; within us, succession without mutual externality" (TFW 227; *Essai* 171).

Nevertheless, to suggest that Bergson cannot hold an epochal theory of time while insisting that states of consciousness are not external to one another or distinguished from one another is to ignore half of what he is saying. Though he denies that they are distinguishable, he does speak of states; and moments which are not external to one another are, nevertheless, moments. While, as Chappell points out (266), time is "a continuous or qualitative multiplicity with no resemblance to number" (TFW 105; *Essai* 78), it *is* a multiplicity. Bergson denies that time is measurable *because* he denies that it is homogeneous. It is a radical heterogeneity which distinguishes the temporal from the spatial, and there can hardly be heterogeneity without multiplicity *of some sort*.

> In short, we must admit two kinds of multiplicity, two possible senses of the word "distinguish," two conceptions, the one qualitative and the other quantitative, of the difference between *same* and *other*. Sometimes this multiplicity, this distinctness, this heterogeneity contains number only potentially, as Aristotle would have said. Consciousness, then, makes a qualitative discrimination without any further thought of counting the qualities or even of distinguishing them as *several*. In such a case we have multiplicity without quantity. Sometimes, on the other hand, it is a question of a multiplicity of terms which are counted or which are conceived as capable of being counted; but we think then of the possibility of externalizing them in relation to one another; we set them out in space. Unfortunately, we are so accustomed to illustrate one of these two meanings of the same word by the other, and even to perceive the one in the other, that we find it extraordinarily difficult to distinguish between them or at least to express this distinction in words (TFW 121–22; *Essai* 90–91).

Bergson is not concerned to deny a multiplicity of temporal elements, but only to deny that they can be counted. Although time is conceived as "a duration whose heterogeneous moments permeate one another . . . , a qualitative multiplicity . . . in which *succeeding each other* means *melting into one another*" (TFW 128; *Essai* 95) in a very non-atomic way, we must note also that there *is* a "multiplicity," a "distinctness," a "heterogeneity," a "difference between *same* and *other*," which entails some sort of real distinctions between the qualitatively multiple states within duration. Chappell cites the denial of a *quantitative* multiplicity as evidence that Bergson rejects an epochal theory of time. On the contrary, Bergson's insistence on a *qualitative* multiplicity is evidence in its favor.

If it seems premature to suggest at this point that Bergson holds something very much like an epochal theory of time, there are probably two reasons. First of all, in his zeal to effect a complete separation between spatial and temporal categories, Bergson has overstated the incommensurability of the temporal and the discrete. In later works, the radical dualism of *Time and Free Will* is attenuated and, as we shall see, the case for an epochal theory is easier to defend. Secondly, Chappell has exaggerated the mutual exclusiveness of temporal "epochs." If a theory is disqualified because it allows a "mutual penetration, an interconnexion and organization of elements, each one of which represents the whole" (Chappell 266; TFW 101; *Essai* 75), then Whitehead, as well as Bergson, fails to qualify. Bergsonian duration is more discrete and Whiteheadian temporal epochs are less discontinuous than Chappell suggests.

Alternative *a*, which Chappell identifies as the epochal theory (Chappell 265), states only that time is composed of extended indivisibles (Chappell 256); Chappell assumes that these elements, presumably because they are extended and indivisible, must be external to one another in every respect. But to assert that there are indivisible extended units of time is one thing; to deny all continuity between them is yet another. If we are to identify *a* with Whitehead's epochal theory of time, we cannot interpret *a*

281

in such a way that it commits the fallacy of simple location[7] and violates the principle of relativity.[8]

While we cannot deny that for Whitehead "becoming and motion and change and temporal process generally are discontinuous, which is to say, occur in discrete atomic stages, and if becoming and rest are discontinuous, so too is time" (Chappell 259), this, again, is only half the story. Time for Whitehead has a *prehensive* as well as a *modal* (and separative) character. It is true that the indivisible temporal element, the actual occasion, like all events, is "in some sense . . . in this place and in no other," and "endures during a certain period, and through no other period." This is "the *modal* character of space-time"; but "it is evident that the modal character taken by itself gives rise to the idea of simple location," so "it must be conjoined with the separative and prehensive character." [9]

While Whitehead insists that "temporalisation is not another continuous process," [10] that "time is sheer succession of epochal durations," [11] he also insists that "this passage is not a mere linear procession of discrete entities," [12] that "each volume of space, or each lapse of time, includes in its essence aspects of all volumes of space, or of all lapses of time." [13] "Every volume mirrors in itself every other volume in space," and "each duration of time mirrors in itself all temporal durations." [14] "In a certain sense, everything is everywhere at all times." [15] Here we have an "interpenetration" of events which is surely as radical as Bergson's. Nor is this continuity between temporal epochs any less fundamental than the

---

[7] I have cited the 1925 edition of Whitehead's *Science and the Modern World* (New York: Macmillan), 69 ff. The reader must be warned, however, that the pagination of later "reprintings" of the Macmillan edition does not correspond to the 1925 printing (thus the discrepancy between my citations and Chappell's).

Note the explicit reference to Bergson on p. 72. Whitehead identifies his protest against simple location, "so far as it concerns time," with Bergson's protest against "spatialization." He disagrees with Bergson that this spatialization is inevitable, but it is the same example of "misplaced concreteness" which both writers are concerned to expose.

[8] Whitehead, *Process and Reality* (New York: Macmillan, 1929).

[9] Whitehead, *Science and the Modern World*, 90.

[10] *Ibid.*, 179.
[11] *Ibid.*, 177.
[12] *Ibid.*, 130.
[13] *Ibid.*, 100.
[14] *Ibid.*, 92.
[15] *Ibid.*, 128.

discreteness of the epochs; "the first analysis of an actual entity, into its most concrete elements, discloses it to be a concrescence of prehensions," [16] and "the vector character of prehension is fundamental." [17] Though simply located when considered only in its modal character, "an actual entity has a perfectly definite bond with each item in the universe. This determinate bond is its prehension of that item." [18]

In Whiteheadian terms, Bergson's *Time and Free Will* exaggerates the prehensive unity of time and neglects its modal, or epochal character. His dualistic stance assigns modal distinctions (in Whitehead's sense) exclusively to space, which is characterized as qualitatively homogeneous and radically discontinuous.[19] Time is described as a qualitatively heterogeneous continuum; excluding all spatial categories, it cannot tolerate any discontinuity which might be effected by discrete temporal elements. *Matter and Memory*, too, is "frankly dualistic" (MM vii; MMf 1), but now Bergson suggests that "just because we have pushed dualism to an extreme, our analysis has perhaps dissociated its contradictory elements" (MM 236; MMf 202). He believes that his analysis of perception and memory "may thus prepare the way for a reconciliation between the unextended and the extended, between quality and quantity" (MM 236–37; MMf 202).

In *Matter and Memory*, the external world becomes less homogeneous and takes upon itself qualitative distinctions. Time becomes more discrete (see MM 35–36 and 271–72; MMf 39 and 230, both quoted on p. 289 below). We find Bergson speaking not only of "a duration wherein our states melt into each other" (MM 243–44; MMf 207) and the indivisibility of all movement and of the time in which it takes place (MM 246ff; MMf 209), but also of "the real, concrete, live present—that of which I speak when I speak of my present perception" (MM 176; MMf 152). This concrete present is what James, following E. R. Clay, calls

---

[16] Whitehead, *Process and Reality*, 35.
[17] *Ibid.*, 483.   [18] *Ibid.*, 66.
[19] *I.e.*, mathematically continuous; see note 5.

"the *specious* present"; [20] it occupies a finite temporal duration and is an irreducible element of our consciousness of time. Although he does not seem to realize the full implications of his argument himself until *Creative Evolution*, Bergson presents us with a view of time in *Matter and Memory* which requires that such concrete, extended, indivisible elements are characteristic not only of the time which we experience, but of physical time as well.

The reconciliation between the temporal and the measurable which makes it possible to speak of discrete temporal elements is effected by means of a theory of perception which identifies the lowest mental faculties, which remain fundamentally temporal, with material reality, hitherto exclusively spatial, and does so in a manner which anticipates the Whiteheadian theory of perception. I will use Whitehead's terminology freely in what follows in order to illustrate their fundamental agreement with respect to the issues which concern us here. I do not mean to suggest that the two theories of perception are similar in all respects, of course. There is much in Whitehead which Bergson would reject—specifically the appeal to "eternal objects."

For Bergson, our perception is prehensive. "External objects are perceived by me where they are, in themselves and not in me" (MM 59; MMf 58); "in pure perception we are actually placed outside ourselves; we touch the reality of the object in an immediate intuition" (MM 84; MMf 79). In fact, "pure perception, which is the lowest degree of mind—mind without memory—is really part of matter, as we understand matter" (MM 297; MMf 250). Below the threshold of conscious perception, there is a "pure perception," which "conforms" to matter, and "mere-

---

[20] William James, *The Principles of Psychology* (New York: Henry Holt, 1890), I, 609. "Specious present" is a misnomer for James, as it would be for Bergson, for James too takes only this extended psychological present to be given; the instantaneous mathematical present is "an altogether ideal abstraction" (I, 609). Though he allows here that "reflection leads us to the conclusion that it [the instantaneous present] *must* exist" (I, 608–609), though incapable of being experienced, James explicitly extends the epochal theory of all temporal duration in Chapters 10 and 11 of *Some Problems of Philosophy* (London: Longmans, Green, 1911).

ly transforms the objective content into subjective feelings." [21] "Pure perception" is less selective than our conscious perception; it is less than conscious precisely because it lacks the "abrupt- ness" [22] characteristic of consciousness. "In one sense we might say that the perception of any unconscious material point what- ever, in its instantaneousness, [23] is infinitely greater and more complete than ours, since this point gathers and transmits the in- fluences of all the points of the material universe, whereas our con- sciousness only attains to certain parts and to certain aspects of those parts" (MM 30–31; MMf 35). Using the word "image" in a technical sense, which denotes both physical objects and our perceptions of them, he asserts "that which distinguishes it ["a material object" (MM 27; MMf 32)] as a *present* image, as an objective reality, from a *represented* image is the necessity which obliges it to act through every one of its points upon all the points of all other images, to transmit the whole of what it receives, to oppose to every action an equal and contrary reaction, to be, in short, merely a road by which pass, in every direction, the modifi- cations propagated throughout the immensity of the universe" (MM 28; MMf 33).

Because the feelings which constitute consciousness are more selective than the merely conformal feelings of low grade physi- cal prehensions, "the coincidence of perception with the object perceived exists in theory rather than in fact" (MM 71; MMf 68). "An impersonal basis remains," however, "in which percep- tion coincides with the object perceived" (MM 71; MMf 69), so there is "merely a difference of degree, and not of kind, be- tween *being* and *being consciously perceived*" (MM 30; MMf 35). "The reality of matter consists in the totality of its elements and of their actions of every kind. Our representation of matter is the measure of our possible action upon bodies: it results from the discarding of what has no interest for our needs, or more generally for our functions" (MM 30; MMf 35).

---

21 Whitehead, *Process and Reality*, 250.
22 Whitehead, *Science and the Modern World*, 239.
23 We will have more to say about this phrase later (cf. note 6).

Not only does conscious perception discard part of what is immediately given; it revises and transmutes what it accepts to fit its own subjective aim.

> We assert, at the outset, that if there be memory, that is, the survival of past images, these images must constantly mingle with our perception of the present, and may even take its place. For if they have survived it is with a view to utility; at every moment they complete our present experience, enriching it with experience already acquired; and, as the latter is ever increasing, it must end by covering up and submerging the former. It is indisputable that the basis of real, and so to speak instantaneous, intuition, on which our perception of the external world is developed, is a small matter compared with all that memory adds to it (MM 70; MMf 68).

Just as, for Whitehead, consciousness arises only when there is sufficient contrast felt between reality and relevant possibility,[24] for Bergson it arises only when there is a sufficient feeling of the relevance of the past. The relevance of the immediate past and the relevance of the distant past manifest themselves in radically different ways, however; and the relevance of the former is such that it entails an epochal theory of time.

> However brief we suppose any perception to be, *it always occupies a certain duration,* and involves consequently an effort of memory which prolongs one into another a plurality of moments. As we shall endeavour to show, even the "subjectivity" of sensible qualities consists above all else in a kind of contraction of the real, effected by our memory. In short, memory in these two forms, covering as it does with a cloak of recollections a core of immediate perception, and also *contracting a number of external moments into a single internal moment,* constitutes the principal share of individual consciousness in perception, the subjective side of the knowledge of things (MM 25; MMf 30–31; italics added. Cf. CE 301; EC 301).

If "the qualitative heterogeneity of our successive perceptions

24 Whitehead, *Process and Reality,* 407.

of the universe results from the fact that *each*, in itself, *extends over a certain depth of duration*, and that memory condenses in each an enormous multiplicity of vibrations which appear to us all at once, although they are successive" (MM 76–77; MMf 73; italics added), then our experience of time is accurately described by Chappell's alternative *a*. Bergson describes our experience of time as a multiplicity of discrete extended moments; our thesis is established. If our experience of time is also radically continuous, it is because it is a prehensive unity of these discrete moments. We must insist on the unity, but on the multiplicity no less than the unity. Time, for Bergson, as for Whitehead, consists of radically continuous, but genuinely discrete, epochs. "If you try to imagine this doctrine in terms of our conventional views of space and time, which presuppose simple location, it is a great paradox. But if you think of it in terms of our naïve experience, it is a mere transcript of the obvious facts." [25] Our present experience is obviously distinct from our past experience, obviously endures, and is just as obviously continuous with our preceding conscious states.

"The duration lived by our consciousness is a duration with its own determined rhythm" (MM 272; MMf 230). A rhythmical duration must accommodate the discrete in order to have rhythm; and, since rhythms can be faster or slower, the description of time Bergson offers us here, unlike that of *Time and Free Will*, clearly accommodates the quantitative. This becomes even more obvious when he asserts that "in reality there is no one rhythm of duration; it is possible to imagine many different rhythms which, slower or faster, measure the degree of tension or relaxation of different kinds of consciousness, and thereby fix their respective places in the scale of being" (MM 275; MMf 232). [26]

I take it that we have established that for Bergson, in *Matter and Memory*, time, as "lived by our consciousness," is epochal. It re-

---

[25] Whitehead, *Science and the Modern World*, 128.
[26] Cf. Whitehead, *Science and the Modern World*, 191; James, *Principles of Psychology*, I, 639 ff; TFW 194–95; *Essai* 146.

mains to ask the status of material reality and of the elementary vibrations which, in radically different ways, play such an important part in both the Bergsonian and the orthodox scientific accounts of perception. This will be our concern in the remainder of this paper. If our perception of time involves a contraction of material vibrations, it can be argued that the fundamental nature of time must be sought in the medium of these vibrations, not in the phenomena of consciousness, however un-Bergsonian such a suggestion might appear.

Bergson's understanding of the relation of perceived qualities to material reality presents a striking analogy to Locke's. Locke would reduce the former to the latter by means of spatial magnification:

> Had we senses acute enough to discern the minute particles of bodies, and the real constitution on which their sensible qualities depend, I doubt not but they would produce quite different ideas in us, and that which is now the yellow colour of gold would then disappear, and instead of it we should see an admirable texture of parts of a certain size and figure. This microscopes plainly discover to us; for what to our naked eyes produces a certain colour is, by thus augmenting the acuteness of our senses, discovered to be quite a different thing; and the thus altering, as it were, the proportion of the bulk of the minute parts of a coloured object to our usual sight, produces different ideas from what it did before. Thus sand, or pounded glass, which is opaque and white to the naked eye, is pellucid in a microscope....[27]

To accomplish this reduction in Bergsonian terms, "we substitute a temporal for a spatial distinction" (MM 295; MMf 249).

> May we not conceive, for instance, that the irreducibility of two perceived colours is due mainly to the narrow duration into which are contracted the billions of vibrations which they execute in one of our moments? If we could stretch out this duration, that is to say, live it at a slower rhythm, should we not, as

[27] *An Essay Concerning Human Understanding*, II, 23, 11. I cannot refrain from quoting Pope's *Essay on Man*, as does A. S. Pringle-Pattison in his excellent abridged edition of Locke's *Essay* (Oxford: Oxford University Press, 1924), 162: "Why has not man a microscopic eye? / For this plain reason,—man is not a fly."

the rhythm slowed down, see these colours pale and lengthen into successive impressions, still coloured, no doubt, but nearer and nearer to coincidence with pure vibrations? In cases where the rhythm of the movement is slow enough to tally with the habits of our consciousness—as in the case of the deep notes of the musical scale, for instance—do we not feel that the quality perceived analyzes itself into repeated and successive vibrations, bound together by an inner continuity (MM 268–69; MMf 227–28)?

One would expect that matter, too, endures, manifesting this duration in a much quicker rhythm. If so, the epochal nature of time would be preserved on this level too, and, unless this rhythm were somehow to become infinite (cf. CE 338; EC 337), physical time, as well as our consciousness of it, would involve minimum extended elements.

In *Matter and Memory* Bergson often speaks in this spirit. In these passages it appears that the external and the temporal have been truly reconciled, that the dualism of *Time and Free Will* has been completely abandoned.

Take, for example, a luminous point P, of which the rays impinge on the different parts *a, b, c,* of the retina. At this point P science localizes vibrations of a certain amplitude and duration. At the same point P consciousness perceives light. We propose to show, in the course of this study, that both are right; and that there is no essential difference between the light and the movements, provided we restore to movement the unity, indivisibility, and qualitative heterogeneity denied to it by abstract mechanics; provided also that we see in sensible qualities *contractions* effected by our memory (MM 35–36; MMf 39).

. . . we cannot avoid placing those [material] movements *within* these [conscious] qualities, in the form of internal vibrations, and then considering the vibrations as less homogeneous, and the qualities as less heterogeneous, than they appear, and lastly attributing the difference of aspect in the two terms to the necessity which lies upon what may be called an endless multiplicity of contracting into a duration too narrow to permit of the separation of its moments (MM 271–72; MMf 230).

Unfortunately he sums up these remarks with the statement that "Science and consciousness would then meet in the instantaneous" (MM 36; MMf 39); and we have seen above (p. 286) that Bergson speaks of the "instantaneousness" of the "pure perception" which conforms to the rhythm of material existence.

Ironically, we seem to find Bergson presenting us with alternative *b* on the level of material reality in the very process of establishing alternative *a* on the level of our conscious experience of time. This is particularly embarrassing, for his theory of perception seems to build the former out of the latter, which leaves us with extended and indivisible units of time somehow built out of unextended points. Under the influence of his earlier, more radical dualism, the difference between consciousness and material existence, clearly identified in some passages as a difference only of degree, becomes a difference in kind.

Bergson is aware, however, that not only in *Time and Free Will*, but here as well, he has exaggerated the incommensurability of mind and matter. For Bergson, a finite rhythm of duration involves contingency, and only that which does not endure is necessary (e.g., see CE 336ff; EC 335ff). It is beyond the scope of this inquiry to investigate this profound claim, which is perhaps the key to his whole metaphysics, but it is in terms of this claim that the following passage from the final pages of *Matter and Memory* must be interpreted. "Can each moment be mathematically deduced from the preceding moment? We have throughout this work, and for the convenience of study, supposed that it was really so; and such is, in fact, the distance between the rhythm of our duration and that of the flow of things, that the contingency of the course of nature, so profoundly studied in recent philosophy, must, for us, be practically equivalent to necessity. So let us keep to our hypothesis, though it might have to be attenuated" (MM 331; MMf 279).

It does have to be attenuated, and, in *Creative Evolution*, it is. The "vital impetus" is introduced to account for any difference in kind between material and psychical existence (CE 87ff and 247ff; EC 88ff and 248ff). In temporal terms, there is only a difference of degree. Though "life is a movement, materiality is the inverse movement," and "of these two currents the second runs counter to the first"; still "each of these two movements is simple, the matter which forms a world being an undivided flux and undivided also the life that runs through it" (CE 249–50; EC 250).

This radical continuity of both life and matter precludes the instantaneous, and it does so as a prehensive unity of temporal epochs (cf. p. 287 above). "In the limit, we get a glimpse of an existence made of a present which recommences unceasingly— devoid of real duration, nothing but the instantaneous which dies and is born again endlessly. Is the existence of matter of this nature? Not altogether, for analysis resolves it into elementary vibrations, the shortest of which are of very slight duration, almost vanishing, but not nothing" (CE 200–201; EC 202).

The involvement of the immediate past in the present duration is necessary not only to consciousness (p. 286 above), but to duration itself, even on the material level. Just as we can speak of a "pure perception" below the level of human consciousness, we can speak of an "elementary memory." Bergson even extends his use of the term "consciousness" to the material level in order to emphasize the analogy between all levels of duration (cf. CE 237; EC 238) and to accommodate this elementary memory involved in all duration. He does not wish for these terms to be used in an anthropomorphic sense, however.[28]

> To imagine a thing that endures, there is no need to take one's own memory and transport it, even attenuated, into the interior of the thing. However much we may reduce the intensity of our memory, we risk leaving in it some degree of the variety and richness of our inner life; we are then preserving the personal, at all events, human character of memory. It is the opposite course we must follow. We shall have to consider a moment in the unfolding of the universe, that is, a snapshot that exists indepen-

---

[28] It was in order to avoid the anthropomorphic aspects of such usage that Whitehead coined the term "prehension" (*Science and the Modern World*, 97), though he is less circumspect later in his use of the term "feeling" (*Process and Reality*, 35). Though one chooses to extend the meaning of a traditional term and the other chooses to invent a new term, both writers are dealing with the same characteristics of material reality.

dently of any consciousness; then we shall try conjointly to summon another moment brought as close as possible to the first, and thus have a minimum of time enter into the world without allowing the faintest glimmer of memory to go with it. We shall see that this is impossible. Without an elementary memory that connects the two moments, there will be only one or the other, consequently a single instant, no before and after, no succession, no time. We can bestow upon this memory just what is needed to make the connection; it will be, if we like, this very connection, a mere continuing of the before into the immediate after with a perpetually renewed forgetfulness of what is not the immediately prior moment. We shall nonetheless have introduced memory. To tell the truth, it is impossible to distinguish between the duration, however short it may be, that separates two instants and a memory that connects them, because duration is essentially a continuation of what no longer exists into what does exist (DS 48–49; DSf 61–62).[29]

Matter, as well as life, endures. "Every duration is thick" (DS 52; DSf 68), for it must accommodate the continuation of the immediate past into the enduring present. "Real time cannot therefore supply the instant; the latter is born of the mathematical

[29] On first reading, an earlier passage seems to conflict with this position. Bergson asserts that "different durations, differently rhythmed, might co-exist," and notes that he "once advanced a theory" in which he "distinguished durations of higher and lower tension, characteristic of different levels of consciousness, ranging over the animal kingdom." But, in spite of the passages we have just quoted from both *Creative Evolution* and *Duration and Simultaneity*, he then goes on to say that "we did not perceive then, nor do we see even today any reason for extending this theory of a multiplicity of durations to the physical universe" (DS 46; DSf 57)! In the light of what follows, we find that we must interpret this passage not as a denial that matter endures but as a denial of a multiplicity of different rhythms of duration within the *material* universe. To avoid inconsistency, Bergson will have to admit some variation of rhythms within specific limits, e.g., in order to account for the physical basis of both high and low musical tones, or both red and blue light (cf. MM 268–69; MMF 225–26 quoted pp. 288–89 above). I see no reason why this need be embarrassing (though I see no reason for his insisting on it either). The duration of our unit of consciousness varies greatly (cf. James, *Principles of Psychology*, I, 613–14), but within upper and lower limits. In these terms, Bergson's claim would be that there are no discontinuities within the range of rhythms characteristic of physical things comparable to the gaps between different levels of consciousness.

The involvement of memory in duration, in both Whitehead and Bergson, is a topic worthy of separate treatment.

point" (DS 53; DSf 69) which is an intellectual abstraction, rather than a concrete fact. The rhythm of matter is less than infinite; it too survives time by means of epochs.[30]

The reason for Bergson's earlier suggestions to the contrary is not hard to find. If matter only inclines toward the instantaneous, it does so incline (CE 201; EC 202), and the minimum indivisible unit of physical duration is so much smaller than the smallest possible psychical duration as to suggest a difference in kind as well as in degree (MM 272ff, MMf 229ff).[31] The human intellect is quite open to this suggestion. At the end of his introduction to *Matter and Memory*, Bergson warns us that "we must never forget the utilitarian character of our mental functions, which are essentially turned toward action" for "the habits formed in action find their way to the sphere of speculation, where they create fictitious problems" (MM xvii; MMf 9). One of his primary aims in *Creative Evolution* is to preclude such fictitious problems by carefully distinguishing between the idealized concept of matter with which our intellect presents us and our immediate intuition of matter itself (e.g., see 206ff; EC 207ff). As he takes such great pains to show us in *An Introduction to Metaphysics*, "we do not aim generally at knowledge for the sake of knowledge, but in order to take sides, to draw profit" (IM 40–41; PM 198–99). The intellect is "far from being disinterested" (IM 40; PM 198); it is concerned to construct a useful concept of matter, not a true one (e.g., see CE 44ff; EC 44ff), and it finds matter easier to manipulate and its behavior easier to predict if it squeezes time and contingency out of it. We "spatialize" what we perceive (e.g., see CE 202ff; EC 203ff), substituting an abstract static configuration for immediately experienced concrete duration.

In *Time and Free Will*, Bergson presents us with a view of matter *as our intellect sees it*, creating the "fictitious problem" of the incommensurability of the mental and material. In *Matter and*

---

30 Cf. Whitehead, *Process and Reality*, 106: "The true difficulty is to understand how the arrow survives the lapse of time." Chappell discusses this on p. 265 Cf. Bergson, CE 312; EC 311: "Nothing would be easier, now, than to extend Zeno's argument to qualitative becoming and to evolutionary becoming."
31 Cf. James, *Principles of Psychology*, I, 611 ff; 639 ff.

Memory he is not as careful as he ought to be to distinguish between our intellectual concept of matter and matter itself—thus the ambiguity of the description of material reality in this work. In *Creative Evolution* he is careful to distinguish between our intellectual concept of matter, on the one hand, and matter itself, on the other. Though the former does not endure, the latter does. Once this distinction is clear, one can only conclude that, for Bergson, real time, whether endured by mind or by matter, is epochal.

CONCLUDING SUMMARY

MILIČ ČAPEK

Bergson's Theory of Matter and Modern Physics

Remarks by the Editor. Professor Milič Capek concludes this volume with a general survey of the relevance of Bergson's theory of matter to the basic concepts of twentieth-century physics, both quantum and relativistic. Professor Čapek's essay begins with an analysis of Bergson's concept of "psychological existence," which is basic to Bergson's theory of matter. According to Bergson: 1) Psychological existence consists in real duration, a dynamic and heterogeneous continuity in which "particles" or "states" have no real existence. 2) Real duration is by its very nature both creative and incomplete. 3) There is no basic difference between psychological duration and real time; hence there is *no homogeneous time* which contains events. 4) Real time is not composed of instants, nor is it infinitely divisible.

These four conclusions, which form the basis of Bergson's psychology, also form the basis for his theory of material existence. The following four propositions, therefore, are fundamental to Bergson's theory of matter: 1) Material particles are only more or less artificial entities, carved out of the totality of physical becoming. 2) There is no homogeneous absolute time, existing as a container of events. 3) The time of material events is not infinitely divisible. 4) The element of novelty, and therefore of indeterminacy, cannot be absent in the physical world. Common sense will doubtless protest against these assertions, which, if accepted, must involve a thoroughgoing revolution in our way of envisaging the physical world. But, Professor Čapek argues, both Bergson's insights and the discoveries of recent physics point in this direction, and suggest a transformation of the foundations of the physical sciences.

This transformation of the basic foundations of physics is termed by Professor Čapek "The End of the Laplacean Vision." If, Laplace held, one could know the precise positions and momenta of all the particles in the world, one could in principle calculate the entire future course of the universe. This characteristic mechanistic vision, however, rests on certain assumptions: that there exist permanent physical corpuscles, in a static, empty space, and a homogeneous time, controlled by a rigidly deterministic causality. When these assumptions are shaken, Laplace's vision perishes: a *dénouement* which Bergson had foreseen as early as 1896. For twentieth-century physics, the static absolute space of Newton no longer exists; instead space is fused with time in a new entity, time-space. In time-space, the instantaneous actions and attractions of the previous physics no longer exist; precise instants can no longer be ascribed to the entire physical universe. For quantum physics, similarly, physical sequences are no longer continuous but proceed by distinct pulsations, quanta of energy which are not infinitely divisible. Not only does quantum physics thus give up a mathematically continuous time; it rejects the concepts of the permanent particle and of deterministic causality as well. For twentieth-century physics as for Bergson, physical reality consists in "modifications, perturbations, changes of tension or of energy and nothing else." The end of the Laplacean vision marks the beginning of a physics of duration. *Professor Čapek's essay, which follows, was originally published in* REVUE PHILOSOPHIQUE, *LXXVII (1953). It appears here in translation with the permission of the author and the* REVUE PHILOSOPHIQUE.

When memory and anticipation are completely absent, there is complete conformity to the average influence of the immediate past. There is no conscious confrontation of memory with possibility. Such a situation produces the activity of mere matter. . . . Thus the universe is material in proportion to the restriction of memory and anticipation.

–A. N. WHITEHEAD, *Essays in Science and Philosophy.*

*Omne enim corpus est mens momentanea sive carens recordatione,
quia conatum simul suum et alienum contrarium non retinet ultra
momentum.*

–G. W. LEIBNIZ, *Theoria motus abstracti seu rationes motuum universales a sensu
et phaenomenis independentes.*

DURATION AND EXTENSION

V ERY FEW PHILOSOPHERS have seen so early and with such
clarity the insufficiency of the mechanical and visual models
invented to understand the intimate structure of matter as Henri
Bergson. As early as 1889, he realized the insurmountable difficulties inherent in purely kinetic explanations of nature and fore-
saw physics' increasing tendency toward mathematical formalism
(TFW 205–207; *Essai* 154–56). Seven years later he reaffirmed
his doubts: "Solidity and shock borrow their apparent clarity
from the habits and necessities of practical life—images of this
kind shed no light on the inner nature of things" (MM 195; MMf
222). At the same time, he affirmed the necessity of breaking, with
a vigorous and often painful effort, the habits which our imagination has contracted through its dealings with a relatively narrow
segment of reality, with that "world of the middle dimensions"
which alone is of practical importance to the human organism; by
creating new intellectual frames, more adequate and more flexible,
we will succeed perhaps in enlarging our imagination, which at
the present is too rigid and too narrow to comprehend reality in
all its extent and especially its microphysical strata [*couche*] (CE
198, 201; EC 199, 202; CM 79, 160, PM 85, 179). Bergson's theory
of matter is based precisely on this difficult effort to reorganize
our intellectual habits.

This effort is of the same kind as that which inspired Bergson's
first work, *Time and Free Will;* Bergson's physics is, so to speak,
an extension of Bergson's psychology. For even in psychology it
is necessary to break with the involuntary habits of spatialization
which our imagination, fashioned through prolonged contact with
the external world, retains and which vitiate the direct observa-

299

tion of our inner life. With the aid of an introspection thus puri-
fied, we arrive at the following conclusions:

1. The nature of the psychological existence is *real duration*,
that is, the dynamic and heterogeneous continuity whose successive phases, the past and the present, mutually interpenetrate in
spite of their qualitative heterogeneity, *or rather because of it.*[1]
The "ideas," "sensations," "states" of the associationist psychology
are conceived unconsciously in the image of physical particles,
whose solidity and permanence they share; they are nothing more
than artificial cuttings-out from the total psychological becoming, whose uninterrupted and living continuity they mask.

2. Psychological becoming is a *fact in the making* and not an
accomplished fact; it is created in proportion as it progresses; its
future is literally unreal, and the present, while prolonging the
past, surpasses it. It is precisely this trait of irreducible novelty
which is ignored by psychological atomism, for which all the
changes of the inner life are merely simply rearrangements of pre-
existing elements. Psychological duration is by its own nature
creative and *incomplete.*[2]

3. There is no difference between psychological becoming and
real time. Time and becoming are not related in the way that a
container is related to its content, as that which is filled to that
which fills; what we call empty and homogeneous time is merely
a *verbal time*, and is in all essential points equivalent to space.
There is no real temporal flux without the heterogeneity of successive phases; to suppress the qualitative difference between the
past and the present is to suppress their succession as well. Thus

---

[1] This is probably the most paradoxical trait of the "logic of duration," and
the most difficult to conceptualize: that the *novelty of the present* is constituted
by the *survival of the past;* for it is the retention of the immediately preceding
moment which makes the present richer with regard to the past. Bergson himself
had not made clearly evident this fundamental and "dialectical" identity of the
novelty of the present and the survival of the past before the publication of
Creative Evolution (pp. 19–20), *Evolution créatrice* (pp. 19–20) and *An Introduction to Metaphysics (The Creative Mind,* p. 237; also p. 95; *La pensée et le
mouvant,* p. 227; also p. 88).

[2] *Time and Free Will,* 180; *Essai,* 135. After Bergson, the unreality of the
future has been affirmed especially by C. D. Broad.

the notion of "homogeneous time" is merely a contradictory assemblage of words.

4. The *mathematical continuity* (infinite divisibility) of time
vanishes along with time's homogeneity. This alleged character
of time also stems from the confusion of duration with geometrical line ("axis of succession") on which an unlimited number of
points can be discerned.[3] Novelty, which is the very essence of
the present moment, is not a point-like instant, but a concrete
quality, and thus possesses a certain temporal thickness. Real
duration progresses only through pulsations (having thickness),
through indivisible increments of novelty, through droplets of
"elementary memory."

By these conclusions, the book *Time and Free Will*, conceived
initially as a purely psychological study, goes beyond pure psychology because it attempts to explore the nature of time in general. If we draw from it the conclusions concerning physical duration, we will understand the essentials of Bergson's theory of
matter. It is true that in his first book, Bergson, doubtless under
the influence of Laplacean physics, was inclined to deny the
reality of time in the material world (TFW 108; *Essai* 81). But
already in *Matter and Memory* he insisted on the real and effective character of "the duration of things." [4] This affirmation seems
banal because it is that of common sense and was accepted by all
the scientists who had not taken Laplace literally. Its revolutionary character will become apparent only when we realize that
time thus affirmed has essentially the same structure as the duration of *Time and Free Will*. Thus conclusions similar to those
which we have just enumerated are obtained:

[3] Clearly we must never confuse "the melodic continuity" of duration
with mathematical continuity, which, according to Bergson, is merely discontinuity infinitely repeated, "being, at bottom, only a refusal of our mind, before
any actually given system of decomposition, to regard it as the only possible one" (CE 154; EC 155). Bergson's opinion is basically the same as Poincaré's: "Of that celebrated formula, continuity is the unity in the multiplicity,
multiplicity alone subsists, unity has disappeared" (*La science et l'hypothèse*
[Paris: Flammarion, 1916], 30).

[4] It is difficult to believe that even so serious a thinker as Hans Driesch ignores
Bergson's affirmation of duration in the external world (*Metaphysik der Natur*
[München: R. Oldenbourg, 1927], 88).

301

1. Material particles, whatever name they are given, are only more or less artificial entities, carved out from the totality of physical becoming. Well before Whitehead, Bergson put us on guard against the "fallacy of simple location."

2. There is no absolute difference between real physical time and concrete becoming. Contrary to Newton's view, time is not an empty and homogeneous frame, filled *après coup* by concrete events. Physical time is identical with its content, that is, with physical events.

3. Physical time is no more infinitely divisible than psychological becoming. "*All duration has thickness; real time has no instants*" (DS 52; DSf 68). Mathematical continuity is *toto coelo* different from the dynamic continuity of duration.[5] Even in the material world, the concrete present is never equivalent to an infinitely short instant. Nonetheless, the elementary pulsations of physical duration are incomparably shorter than those of consciousness; while the minimum psychological time, William James's "specious present," is around .002 seconds, the minimum physical duration, the "chronon," is, according to Robert Lévi and others, of the order of 10^{-24} seconds.[6] We can say with Bergson that "the condensation of the past in the present" or "the degree of tension" is more intense in psychological time than in material duration. This is why what appears to our consciousness as the indivisible color red corresponds in the physical world to the vertiginous succession of 400 trillion electromagnetic vibrations.[7] Thus the illusion of homogeneous time and obstinacy

[5] This is why Whitehead himself avoids the ambiguous word continuity, by saying that there is a "becoming of continuity" rather than a "continuity of becoming" ("Time," *Proceedings of the Sixth International Congress of Philosophy*, 1927, p. 64).

[6] R. Lévi, "Théorie de l'action universelle et discontinue," *Journal de Physique et le Radium*, VIII (1927), 182. The same idea is found in H. Latzin, *Naturwissenschaften* (1927), 161; G. I. Pokrowski, (*Zeitschrift für Physik*, 1928, pp. 730, 737); G. Beck (*Ibid.*, 1929, p. 675). A. N. Whitehead, already, in 1920, introduced the word "quantum of time" (*Concept of Nature*, 162).

[7] According to René Berthelot, Bergson's assertion that the shortest sensation lasts .002 seconds implies the use of a certain unit of time-measurement which is the same for facts of consciousness as for physical phenomena and, consequently, the recourse to quantitative time (*Un romantisme utilitaire* [Paris: Alcan, 1913], II, 227). Does not this assertion contradict the principal thesis of *Time and Free*

with which it imposes itself on our mind is understandable; from the practical point of view, elementary physical events are *almost* without duration, that is, *almost* instantaneous. It is only in the interior of the atom that we are confronted with very short temporal intervals which cannot be divided further. The microcosmos is essentially the *microchronos*.

4. The element of novelty, which is an indispensable attribute of all duration, cannot be absent, not even in the material world. Beneath the apparently immobile and rigid surface of physical determinism, there are elementary indeterminations and real novelties.

Thus the material world conceived in this way is simply a less concentrated duration, or, as Bergson states, more "diluted," "scattered," "loosened," or "extended." But, if one thus understands that the illusion of homogeneous time is merely a practical approximation resulting from our macrochronic perspective, it is difficult to accept the view which reduces the extended world of matter to a simple temporal succession. It is quite natural that our common sense—and classical physics is simply, in E. LeRoy's words, "common sense refined"—violently protests against such elimination of motionless space and of the corporeal substances which are for it the prototypes of reality. This profound distrust of the "Bergsonian physics" is due to the resistance of our geometrical and Democritean subconscious. It was nearly completely overlooked that Bergson's negation of static and empty space, instead of eliminating concrete extension, reaffirms it. We now arrive at the most delicate, the most difficult, and the least known

---

Will, according to which duration is not measurable? But the contradiction is only apparent. According to Bergson, no duration, being heterogeneous, is measurable; physical duration consists in the succession of extremely short events, which are *almost* equivalent to dimensionless instants; hence this succession can *approximatively* be replaced by the *time-length* through which quantitative relations between intervals can be established. Then, if it is affirmed that the elementary sensation possesses a quantitatively determinate duration, it is simply established that it is *contemporaneous* (we do not forget that Bergson admits "the simultaneity of fluxes" [DS 52; DSf 67]) with a series of physical events which, being *almost* innumerable and, individually, *almost* without temporal thickness, are *almost* equivalent to a certain segment of homogeneous time and, consequently, measurable.

aspect of Bergsonism: its thesis that "extension appears simply as a tension which is interrupted" or, with greater strictness, that *static space is only an ideal limit of extensive duration.*[8]

There is no place here for a detailed analysis which I have attempted elsewhere. We limit ourselves to showing how, according to the author of *Creative Evolution,* extension arises through the loosening of temporal tension, that is, through the acceleration of the rhythm of duration. Because of the shrinking of the present moment, the immediate past, initially merging with "the specious present" in the intensive duration, detaches itself from it; the immediate past thus becomes "the distant past" which is *outside of the present* rather than within it, though a diminished link between them always remains. For, even in the most "diluted" duration, the exteriority of successive phases, even the most distant ones, is far from being as complete as that of arithmetic units or geometric points; their very succession prevents their complete separation. But the *tendency toward exteriorization* is there; and it is precisely this tendency which, according to Bergson, constitutes materiality, that is, concrete extension.

To what limit can temporal distension be pushed? Its theoretical limit would be *the suspension of time,* or, more accurately, its complete transformation into static and homogeneous space. For the successive phases, in being mutually separated more and more, will in the end be entirely external to each other; their mutual exclusion would amount *to the juxtaposition* which can only be simultaneous. The present will be reduced to a simple, dimensionless point which, bringing with it nothing new, will be qualitatively equivalent to the past. The past, not being differentiated from the present, would be merely the *verbal past,* whose anteriority will thus be irremediably destroyed; in other words, *it would not precede* the present, since the essence of succession is the qualitative difference between the anterior moment and the following moment, the difference which, as we have seen, depends on the

[8] "Introduction to Metaphysics" (in *The Creative Mind,* 127); "Introduction à la métaphysique" (in *La pensée et le mouvant,* 137); *Matter and Memory,* 272–76; *Matière et mémoire,* 229–33; *Creative Evolution,* 245; also 208–10, 218; *L' Évolution créatrice,* 246; also 209–11, 219.

fact of elementary memory, of the at least "infinitesimal" survival of the past in the present. But there is no survival of the past in the point-instant; *"mens momentanea"* lacks *"recordatio."* Thus the succession of heterogeneous phases would be transformed in the limiting case to the juxtaposition of homogeneous instants— or, rather, points.[9] This would be precisely the timeless and geometrical world of Spinoza and Laplace in which the future would be not only necessary, but even *pre-existing alongside* the "present" and the supposed "past." This would simply be space, that is, the mathematical continuity of points which are identical as regards their quality, mutually external, and devoid of succession.

Is this limiting case realized in the physical world? Nineteenth-century physicists and Bergson himself, in his first book, believed so. But the revolutionary discoveries of the twentieth century have shaken the entire edifice of classical physics, and it is only in the light of new facts that the value of Bergson's conceptions can be fully estimated. Thus it remains to be shown to what extent the tendencies of the present physics confirm his fundamental thesis, according to which *pure extension* and static space are realized only approximatively; in other words, that instantaneous and geometrical space is only an *ideal and unreal limit* which the physical world approaches without ever attaining. Physical extension is also a *tension*, that is, a real process possessing the general structure of duration without losing its concrete extensive character.

The End of the Laplacean Vision

It can be said without exaggeration that Laplace's famous and frequently quoted passage contains virtually the whole of classical physics and above all its corpuscular, kinetic, and deterministic character.[10] In spite of the elimination of secondary qualities, this

[9] Already in *Time and Free Will* Bergson, in applying the *principle of indiscernibles*, asserted not only that space is a homogeneous medium, but also that all homogeneous mediums are space (TFW 98; *Essai* 73). But, during this period Bergson still believed in the physical existence of instantaneous space (TFW 108; *Essai* 81). This is explicitly denied in *Matter and Memory* through the distinction between static and abstract space and concrete extensity.

[10] Laplace, *Introduction à la théorie analytique des probabilités (Oeuvres complètes)* VII, (Paris, 1886), vi: "An intelligence which, at a given instant, will know

classical conception still retained a sensory, more specifically, a *visual* (though colorless) character: the homogeneous and Euclidean space is *visually* imagined in which minute solids are displaced without changing their shapes and their masses; at each instant the entire universe can be represented as an immense configuration of an enormous number of permanent corpuscles. These configurations vary (that is, the corpuscles are displaced), and these variations may be followed continuously in space and in time, from one point to another and from one instant to the next, in such a way that a particular instantaneous configuration necessarily determines all the others which will follow. The sum total of the atoms and their masses being constant, change exists only on the surface and concerns only their mutual relations (positions and relative distances); moreover, change seems to be illusory by virtue of the fact that the future state of the universe actually pre-exists in the present, while "what we term the flow of time is nothing but the continual gliding of the screen and the gradually obtained vision of what waits, globally, in eternity" (DS 61; DSf 82). Time had thus become—already with Le Rond d'Alembert—a sort of fourth dimension on which the future events actually pre-exist; physics was thus transformed, in Joseph Lagrange's terms, into a four-dimensional geometry.[11]

We thus obtain the classical conception of the four-dimensional spatio-temporal continuum which, as we shall see, has nothing in common with the space-time of relativity theory, provided that the latter is clearly understood and purged of everything that our "Euclidean unconscious" adds to it. In classical space-time, all the fundamental notions involved—matter and causality, as well as space and time—are related in a definite way, and these relations are graphically represented by a model which contains one dimen-

---

all the forces with which nature is animated and the respective situation of the beings which comprise it, if moreover it is vast enough to submit these data to analysis, will embrace in one formula the motions of the largest bodies as well as the lightest atom: nothing will be for it uncertain, and the future, like the past, will be present to its eyes."

[11] Emile Meyerson, *La déduction relativiste* (Paris: Payot, 1925), 107.

sion less.[12] In this three-dimensional model, Euclidean space is represented through an infinite, vertical, two-dimensional plane, while "the fourth dimension of becoming" is symbolized by a horizontal line perpendicular to the plane. In truth, there are an infinity of instantaneous successive spaces symbolized by parallel planes which are all perpendicular to the "temporal axis"; each of these spaces contains an instantaneous configuration of material elements which constitutes "the state of the world at a given instant" or, rather, an instantaneous section of temporal becoming—if one can still use this word to describe something virtually finished, a *fait accompli*.

It is evident from this that this model adequately represents all the classical concepts and their mutual relationships: 1) homogeneous and continuous time, that is, an infinitely dense succession of infinitely thin instants; 2) the Euclidean and homogeneous space whose infinite divisibility makes possible the point-like localization of material particles and their continuous trajectories; 3) spatio-temporal becoming represented through a continuous series of successive and instantaneous spaces along with the momentary configuration of particles in each of them, while these configurations are bound to each other by the rigid and timeless bond of necessity; 4) the permanence of corpuscles through space and time; only their positions and velocities vary, and these can be followed continuously through all the points and all the instants of their trajectories. From this latter the significance of the whole of this view can be derived: the rigorous determinism understood in the sense of the ultimate identity of supposedly successive states and in which the future, though hidden from our awareness, *actually coexists* with the present and the past. To suppress a single one of the traits just enumerated is to shake the entire edifice of classical physics. Without continuity it is impossible to make three-dimensional "instantaneous cuts" in the flux of becoming; consequently, it is impossible to speak of "the

[12] Hermann Weyl, *Die Philosophie der Mathematik und Naturwissenschaft* (München: R. Oldenbourg, 1966), 65.

state of the world at a given moment" which determines the states to come; without the continuity of space and time, it is impossible to localize corpuscles and to apply infinitesimal analyses to their trajectories; without continuous trajectories, it is impossible to speak of the identity of particles in the different points of their orbits, and the very concept of the corpuscle is dissolved. Thus the entire kinetic conception of the universe is put in question. In brief, the classical edifice of Laplacean physics depends on the cohesion and the solidity of its constituent parts; without these, it loses its meaning and its justification.

This is precisely what the new physics discovered. All the elements of the Laplacean vision have undergone a profound transformation. What appeared initially to be a transitory crisis, and, later, as the impossibility of giving a concrete and mechanical interpretation of the ether and of subatomic particles finally proved to be a revolutionary transformation which strikes at the most inveterate and tenacious mental habits, not only of common sense, but of the classical scientific imagination as well.

First, the notion of space. It had always been hoped that the absolute motion of the earth, that is, its motion with respect to the semi-material medium of the ether, through which electromagnetic vibrations are propagated, could be found. In spite of increasing difficulties in conceiving a satisfactory mechanical model of the ether, it had always been thought possible at least to attribute to it elementary kinematic properties. This meant that the ether, being supposedly immobile, would coincide with the absolute rest of Newtonian space, of which it would be, so to speak, the concrete physical realization. Unfortunately, this absolute rest proved to be more and more elusive to the physicist and finally vanished altogether. The special theory of relativity, inspired by the negative results of Michelson's experiment, decisively proved the impossibility of absolute frame of reference, that is, of an absolute space, which would make it possible to distinguish absolute or real motion from relative or apparent one and which would be the support of the objective simultaneity of events. There is no space in the sense of the simultaneous juxtaposition of points; to claim the contrary would be also to assert the absolute simultaneity which is precisely excluded by Einstein's theory. In other words, spatio-temporal becoming does not admit instantaneous three-dimensional sections, which would contain simultaneous events; these cuts, which made possible in classical mechanics the separation of time from space, have no objective meaning in the new mechanics, for which, in A. S. Eddington's words, there are no "world-wide instants." [13] Classical physics imagined a "stratified" structure of spatio-temporal becoming, the successive layers of which are the sets of simultaneous states; it is not so in the relativity physics. Clearly, we must not persist in the hereditary illusion "which presupposes a definite present instant for which all matter is simultaneously real." [14] Thus we understand Whitehead's conclusion rejecting the notion of such an instant simultaneous for the whole of nature and explicitly rejoining Bergson in the refusal to consider becoming as a succession of instantaneous configurations of matter or of the ether. This fundamental impossibility of isolating the totality of simultaneous instants or what is the same thing, of juxtaposed points from the whole becoming, indicates that for the new physics space and time are merged into a single indivisible reality.

It is quite clear that such fusion of these two notions takes place in favor of time, and this is why the term "time-space" or "chronotope" is much more adequate than "space-time." But the character of this fusion is almost entirely masked by Minkowski's four-dimensional scheme or at least by the popular explanations which have been accorded it. It is wrongly imagined that the significance of the four-dimensional continuum consists in a *spatialization* of time such that future events are situated on the fourth dimension of time and that, consequently, they do not

[13] A. S. Eddington, *The Nature of the Physical World* (New York: Macmillan, 1929), 47.

[14] *Ibid.*, 63. Whitehead, *Science and the Modern World* (New York: Macmillan, 1925), 159. On this point Whitehead explicitly affirms his agreement with Bergson: "This simple location of instantaneous material particles is what Bergson protests against, insofar as it concerns time and insofar as it is viewed as the fundamental state of concrete nature" (p. 73).

309

occur; "they are there, and we encounter them in following our world-line." [15] Hermann Weyl affirms that "the world simply exists, it does not develop"; succession is conceived by him in a wholly Laplacean fashion as an illusion of our "blinded consciousness." [16] He even sees in Minowski's conception a confirmation of the Kantian theory of the ideality of time. Silberstein has gone even further, since he sees a predecessor of relativity theory in H. G. Wells, whose "time traveller" moves along the "fourth dimension" as well as along the three spatial dimensions; this fictitious personage discovers the future in the same sense as Columbus discovered a continent which existed prior to his discovery.[17] Evidently, the profound significance of the relativistic fusion of space and time has been singularly distorted because of the involuntary habits of spatialization of physicists. This false interpretation has rightly been criticized especially by Émile Meyerson[18] and by Eddington,[19] who has shown that relativistic time, in spite of its connection with space, does not have the same nature as the three other spatial dimensions, a fact which is shown in the necessity to be expressed in imaginary coordinates. Furthermore, it has been shown that the dissymmetry of time with regard to space signifies its irreversibility, and the inaccessibility of the "absolute future" is retained so that, although "the absolute past and the absolute future are not separated by an infinitely thin present," they cannot be confused because of the finite value of the velocity of electromagnetic waves. This is no place for more detailed analyses; let us say only that it is the finite velocity of light which

---

[15] A. S. Eddington, *Space, Time, and Gravitation* (New York: Harper and Row, 1959), 51, 57. Meyerson, who cites this passage (*La déduction relativiste*, p. 100), compares it with Einstein's statement that "becoming in a three dimensional space is transformed into being in a four dimensional world." It must be added that the passage quoted by Meyerson does not represent Eddington's view, but the view that he rejects. Meyerson somehow overlooked the context.

[16] Hermann Weyl, *Was ist Materie?* (Berlin: Julius Springer, 1924), 82, 87.

[17] Cited by Bergson, *Duration and Simultaneity*, 148–49; *Durée et simultanéité*, 223.

[18] Meyerson, *La déduction relativiste*, Chap. VII, "Le temps."

[19] Eddington, *The Nature of the Physical World*, 57–58: "The limit to the velocity of signals is our bulwark against that topsy-turveydom of past and future of which Einstein's theory is sometimes wrongfully accused."

310

provides the key for the comprehension of the dynamic nature of time-space. If an infinite value is substituted for c in Lorentz' equations the relativistic mechanics rejoins the Newtonian mechanics.[20] The revolutionary significance of this seemingly purely formal difference has generally escaped the interpreters of the theory. It was not realized that the new mechanics, in eliminating the possibility of velocities greater than those of electromagnetic perturbations and in particular of infinite velocities, has virtually rejected the very notion of instantaneous space. For from this negation follows a conclusion exceedingly important for the philosophy of nature: *in nature there are no infinite velocities, that is, physical interactions all of whose phases would exist simultaneously, i.e., outside of time;* in the real world there are no timeless connections joining distant and simultaneous events (or rather points); there are only *the successive relations of concrete physical interactions,* and there is no need to stretch a static and passive space beneath these temporal continuities which alone are real in the true sense of the word. Clearly, such conception is entirely contrary to the tendencies of classical physics; in the latter, physical interaction was at first localized in space which according to Newton's definition, in virtue of its absolutely rigid structure, was independent of its physical content. For example, if we consider the light emitted by Neptune and arriving at the Earth, we first imagine Neptune and the Earth juxtaposed in a static and inert space; their enormous respective distance is of secondary importance, since it does not affect the *simultaneous* character of this distance. On that distance, that is, along the line which joins the *simultaneous* positions of Neptune and of the Earth, we imagine the luminous vibrations propagating themselves from one point to the other. In such a view the static and simultaneous continuity of space is gradually occupied by the *successive* continuity of physical interaction. Such duplication of the concrete causal rela-

---

[20] A. d'Abro, *Bergson ou Einstein* (Paris: Gaulon, 1927), 304–305, stresses the fact that the totality of events which are simultaneous in the absolute and classical sense of this word can be conceived as situated on the world-line of the universe of an observer *moving with an infinite or instantaneous velocity.*

tion by another underlying relation which is timeless and geometrical does not exist in the relativity theory. It is entirely inaccurate to represent Neptune and the Earth as two objects *co-existing* in instantaneous space; it is known that the present moment on the Earth corresponds to the interval of *nine hours* on Neptune, and *the only real continuity* which joins them is not a geometrical and instantaneous distance but the concrete and temporal continuity of light signals and gravitational attractions. From this point of view it is possible to understand Hans Reichenbach's attempt to reverse the habitual direction of our thought and to consider causality as a primary fact through which the notion of distance can be defined.[21] It is the same idea which inspired Whitehead to formulate the law of gravitation in a new manner, since Newton's classical law was founded on the tacit supposition that two distant particles of matter which attract each other are located in an instantaneous space, which would permit us to consider their simultaneity as absolute and their distance as having a unique significance.[22]

We see now the correctness of Bergson's anticipations; for as early as in 1896, he considered space as a mere conceptual scheme of infinite divisibility which applies only approximately to the becoming of the physical world. We can also understand why Bergson protested so much against the spatialization of time in Minkowski's scheme and how that protestation was justified. But it seems that his profound distrust of any assimilation of time to a fourth dimension of space obscured to him the real and basic significance of the theory of relativity. He did not take into account the fact that the fusion of these two notions does not necessarily operate in favor of space, that, on the contrary, Lorentz' formulae, properly interpreted, disclose the very opposite, and that the supposed spatialization of time is really a temporalization of space. There is a strange contradiction here. How could Bergson who, in *Matter and Memory*, considered space to be an instantaneous and, consequently, unreal cut in the becoming of the

21 Hans Reichenbach, *Philosophie der Raum-Zeit Lehre* (Berlin, 1928), 181.
22 Whitehead, *Science and the Modern World*, 178.

world, in 1923 defend the idea of "extension independent of becoming" (MM 179; MMf 150; DS 30; DSf 33)? Did he forget the results of his brilliant analysis in *Creative Evolution*, in which he analyzed "the cinematographic mechanisms of thought," of which the concept of instantaneous space is only one product? Did he forget his prior views, according to which matter never coincides with pure space? It is difficult to believe so, since even in *Duration and Simultaneity* he insisted on the fictitious character of the instant. In this work he even drew the entirely relativistic conclusion that in the real world there is only "the simultaneity of flows," never that of instants (DS 53; DSf 68–69). Evidently there is here a certain distraction of Bergson's thought, which is not without analogy with another one concerning the philosophy of history and of religion.[23] This distraction was doubtless natural, and can be traced to the fact that the form of Minkowski's scheme concealed to him its true significance.

This explains certain weaknesses of *Duration and Simultaneity*, though the attitude of its author was favorable to the new theories: in contrast with other critics of relativity theory, like, for example, Hans Driesch and Jacques Maritain, Bergson does not preach a disguised return to the obsolete Newtonian views.[24]

---

[23] I am thinking of the strange contrast between his criticism of the "closed society" and of "closed religion" in *The Two Sources of Morality and Religion* and his "moral adhesion" to Catholicism several years later. Since Roman Catholicism was founded on authority and unchanging tradition, does it really approach the ideal of the "open society" and "dynamic religion"? But it must not be forgotten that Bergson, in spite of the prolonged and subtle pressure of certain of his visitors, in the end gave to Catholicism only his "moral" adherence; (or) that all of his books in which the essence of Bergsonism can be found, and without which the significance and the originality of *The Two Sources of Morality and Religion* cannot be understood, have been on the *Index* since June 1, 1914.

[24] Bergson himself states: "In sum, nothing in the mathematical expression of relativity requires to be changed. But the physicist would render [a] service to philosophy by abandoning certain manners of speaking which lead the philosopher into error and risk misleading the physicist himself concerning the metaphysical portent of his views" (DS 185; DSf 278–79). Contrary to Hans Driesch, Jacques Maritain, and René Berthelot, Bergson accepts the fact of the invariant velocity of light, independent of the motion of the observer, which destroys the notion of the immobile privileged system. ("But there is no longer an ether, absolute fixity no longer exists anywhere" [DS 32–33; DSf 36].) But he believes that the relativization of motion, instead of destroying the absolute character of cosmic duration, affirms it; in other words, "that a reciprocity of displacement is

A more thorough study of the general theory of relativity would have afforded Bergson a further proof of the view that in Minkowski's scheme there is a dynamization and "temporaliza-

the manifestation in our eyes of an internal and absolute change, occurring some-where in space" (DS 34; DSf 38). It is for this reason alone that Bergson evoked More's protest against Descartes in *Matter and Memory* as well as in *Duration and Simultaneity* in stressing the absolute character of *mobility* or of *change* as opposed to the essential relativity of spatial displacements. D'Abro, misled prob-ably by the fact that Bergson used the expressions "change," "mobility," and "movement" indiscriminately, concluded indignantly that *Duration and Simul-taneity* defends the Newtonian concept of absolute space. An attentive reading of *Matter and Memory* or at least of chapter four of this book would probably have prevented such a misunderstanding. In fact, the affirmation of the absolute character of duration is for Bergson closely tied to the denial of the absolute character of space (MM 254–59; MMf 213–18; DS 32–40; DSf 35–48). The absolute character of change finds its expression in the invariance of local times or "proper times" whose equality cannot be denied even by D'Abro (*Bergson ou Einstein*, p. 138). The plurality of times, that is, their lengthening, as well as the dislocation of simultaneity and the contraction of lengths, are for Bergson an effect of changing perspective which he, using a very appropriate term, describes as "the perspective of velocity." On this point there is a remarkable coincidence between Bergson's and Whitehead's views. The latter also establishes a distinction between the "creative advance of nature" and the plurality of time series, which are mere spatio-temporal perspectives of the "passage of nature." It is not sur-prising that these two thinkers should stress the agreement of their views on this point (*The Concept of Nature*, 54, 178; DS 62; DSf 83).

Far more disputable is Bergson's opinion that the lengthening of duration and the dislocation of simultaneity between distant events are entirely ideal and result from the substitution of the imaginary observer for the real observer. D'Abro is correct to insist on the *real and physical* character of all the spatio-temporal per-spectives, which are integral parts of reality: the lengthening of durations and the dislocation of simultaneity between distant events are as real and, at least in principle, as observable and perceptible as the increase in mass of an electron which is an effect of the relative motion of the observer. He is correct to say that Fizeau's experiment confirms the dilatation of duration at least indirectly and that the discovery of the lengthened vibratory period of solar or stellar atoms would provide a direct verification. But D'Abro goes too far in putting the proper times of events on the same level as those of durations lengthened by the "perspective of velocity." Why do we *prefer* the proper time of the atomic vibration while admitting that it would appear dilated to an observer moving at great speed relative to it? Why do we believe that the mass of an electron measured by an observer associated with it represents something more essential than the effects of the same mass increased by the perspective of velocity? Even though this in-crease in mass is observable and real for a moving observer, it remains, so to speak, outside of the intrinsic nature of the phenomenon.

Doubtless the hyper-relativists, like D'Abro, will object (*Bergson ou Einstein*, p. 214) that distinctions of this kind are contrary to the spirit of Einstein's theory. If a "more real" character is attributed to the proper time of the phenomenon, a privileged system at rest with respect to the vibrating atom is accepted; this would imply a relapse into Newton's absolute mechanics. But this conclusion is tion" of space rather than a spatialization of time.[25] This theory, by identifying the gravitational field and, *eo ipso*, matter itself, with the local curvature of space (or rather of non-Euclidean time-space) has eliminated the classical and Democritean distinction between space and its material content. There is no space in the sense of a homogeneous container, empty and indifferent, and there is no matter in the sense of a superadded content; there is only space or, rather, heterogeneous *time-space* whose curvature varies from one point to another and from one instant to another, thus producing the gravitational field and its changes. Matter is, in Meyerson's suggestive expression, "resorbed" into space, that is, geometrized; but we must not forget that this geometrization is entirely different from that proposed by Descartes and that it is equally correct to assert with Eddington that it is a geometry which is "mechanized." [26] One thing is certain: the rigid structure of space, that is, of spatial structure independent of time, is explicitly abandoned by the general theory of relativity. The latter, on the contrary, stresses the *temporalization of space*, which, moreover, was virtually present already in the special theory. Though Weyl's attempt to extend this geometrization of matter to electromagnetic phenomena and to explain the existence of electrons by the discontinuous structure of the non-Euclidean continuum did not have the same success, it is impos-

---

entirely unjustified. Even a relativist does not doubt that he is *at rest with respect to himself*, without identifying this rest, which is relative but undoubtedly real, with the absolute immobility of Newton's fictitious space. This unique relationship "of being at rest with respect to oneself," which is a physical expression of the law of contradiction, was correctly recognized by Bergson as *an absolutist element of relativism;* the privileged character of proper time as well as of "mass at rest" follows naturally from it.

25 The lack of interest in the general theory of relativity is probably the most serious flaw of *Duration and Simultaneity*. Bergson's error was to fail to appreciate the close connection between the special and the general theory; to see in this latter only the continuation of the Cartesian tendencies to reduce matter to geometrical space, which was replaced by Einstein by the dynamic time-space; to fail to see that the retardation of durations in the gravitational field is not reciprocal; to fail to see that his refusal to recognize the diverse rhythms of duration demanded by Einstein's gravitational theory is contrary to the spirit of *Matter and Memory*.

26 Meyerson, *La déduction relativiste*, 135; Eddington, *The Nature of the Physical World*, 137.

sible to doubt now the tendency of the new physics to eliminate the distinction between time-space and its material content, between *becoming* and *substance*. The preponderance of time in its fusion with space is still more evident in Georges Lemaître's and Willem de Sitter's theories of "the expanding universe," in which it is assumed that the "radius of curvature" of finite non-Euclidean space varies. Can a more radical incorporation of space into becoming be imagined? What, then, remains of the ancient idea of space as a "simultaneous juxtaposition of points"? Nothing but the words.

But, on the other hand, by creating the new notion of time-space, we also significantly modify the classical concept of time. When the distinction between time-space and its contents is effaced, the precise dividing line between time and becoming disappears. Time as well as space loses its status as an empty and homogeneous container and is identified with its content, that is, with concrete events. Time even becomes heterogeneous, in that its measures depend on the intensity of the gravitational field; from this follows the possibility of temporal rhythms which, though contemporaneous, remain different. As early as 1896 Bergson showed in *Matter and Memory* that the difference of temporal rhythms is perfectly compatible with the irreversibility of becoming.[27] According to Whitehead, who stresses his agreement with Bergson on this point, the different temporal series are only different and complementary aspects of a single "creative advance of nature." [28] This is the only meaning which can correctly be given to Bergson's "real and universal Time," if it is to be purged of a serious error, that is, of the erroneous belief in absolute simultaneity. Such a belief, it goes without saying, is contrary not only to the spirit, but also to the letter, of Bergsonism.

Only one classical trait of space and time remains intact in the

[27] S. Zawirski justly remarked that Bergson's opposition in his book *Duration and Simultaneity* to the concept of the plurality of temporal rhythms postulated by Einstein's theory of gravitation is contrary to the spirit of *Matter and Memory* (*L'évolution de la notion du temps*, 305–306).

[28] *Science and the Modern World*, 181. "It is not necessary that the temporal process, in this sense, should be constituted by a single series of linear successions."

relativity theory: that of their *mathematical continuity*. Einstein's time-space is composed of point-instants; in other words, its infinite divisibility is not questioned. An attempt has even been made to make the idea of the *precise coincidence* of point-events into one of the indispensable notions of the theory. Moreover, this is entirely natural; relativity theory is a *macroscopic* theory, and among the facts which it has tried to explain, none have been found which would directly threaten the concept of mathematical continuity. Let us not forget, however, that on this point there was still a sort of virtual threat: if instantaneous cuts in space-time have no objective meaning, or if, speaking with Eddington, there is no "world-wide instant," or if, in Whitehead's words, the state of nature at a given instant is only an *unreal fiction*, then do not the concept of mathematical continuity and the concept of the instant (for the latter is only an expression of the former) become themselves doubtful? Doubts of this kind increase if we consider, within the atomic world, the quantum phenomena to which the concept of spatio-temporal continuity is manifestly inapplicable. It is useless to recall the well-known facts of the quantification of the planetarian orbits, of the quantification of radiant energy, and, finally, of the quantification of the internal energy of matter, through which the puzzling idea of the "vibratory" or undulatory character of the ultimate material particles has been obtained without the possibility, further, of giving a coherent image of this strange dualism. Since the time of Niels Bohr it became clear that it is impossible to trace continuously the movement of electrons from one orbit to another and even on the same orbit; eventually physics has conceded the radical impossibility of precise localization, expressed in the principle of indeterminacy. Thus the concept of "coincidence," so dear to relativists, has become blurred, and attempts to introduce a sort of "cellular" space and "atomic" time (the chronon) are in this respect highly significant. It is thus possible to understand Louis de Broglie's conclusion that the new theories have introduced "the discontinuity of becoming" and that, consequently, the idea of temporal continuity is an illusion, "continuous macroscopic time

317

being only the result of a sort of averaging of an immense number of essentially discontinuous elementary phenomena." [29]

It is clear that the profound transformation of our habitual ideas of space and time also affects the classical concept of matter, a fact which is all the more natural if we recall that, according to the relativity theory, the sharp distinction between matter and spatio-temporal becoming is no longer recognized. The dissolution of matter in the local non-Euclidean modification of time-space shows how the primordial stuff of Democritus and Lucretius, which possessed "primary qualities," is deconcretized in modern physics. The laws of the conservation of mass and energy cease to be valid as separate laws; only by identifying mass with energy can we save the traditional permanence of matter, which seemed so clear, so intuitive, and so evident in classical physics. But, by associating the notion of mass with that of energy, we attribute mass to all forms of energy, and thus deprive it of its primitive pictorial character. How it is possible to conceive *in an intuitive manner*, for example, the increase of mass with velocity, which is one of the experimentally verified consequences of the fundamental equation $E = mc^2$? How can we imagine the mass of the photon, that is, of a particle without precise position, which exists only in motion and disappears completely inside of the atom—though it modifies it energetically? In particular, how is it pos-

---

[29] Louis de Broglie, "L'espace et le temps dans la physique quantique," *Revue de métaphysique et de morale*, LIV (1949), 115, 117. Concerning the revision of the relativistic notion of spatio-temporal coincidence by quantum theory, see Zawirski, *L'évolution de la notion du temps*, 195ff. The same author writes (p. 331) that Bergson's denial of the mathematical continuity of time does not signify "the atomism of duration," conceived as a succession of segments instead of a succession of point-instants. The dynamic indivisibility of temporal process is entirely different from the indivisibility of the rigid atom; while the former is due to its unique and transitory character (temporal process can be divided only retrospectively), the second is a result of the static permanence of the corpuscle. It is possible, then, to employ the word temporal "atom" only if one is on guard against all visual and tactile associations which are bound up with it. This is certainly true of Whitehead, who speaks of "atomic temporalization" (*Science and the Modern World*, 170). On the other hand, A. O. Lovejoy, in rejecting the idea of purely objective and uniform time, was evidently misled by another spatial image in regarding time as a succession of contiguous and discrete moments ("The Problem of Time in Recent French Philosophy," *Philosophical Review*, XXI [1912], 533).

sible to reconcile its supposed corpuscular character with its vibratory character? For we would miss completely the meaning of the quantum theory if we regard it as a simple return to the corpuscular theory of Newton. We are thus witnessing a very strange phenomenon: while our intellect is able to identify abstractly mass with energy, our imagination obstinately refuses to follow.

The evolution of the concept of the corpuscle is of the same kind. This is hardly surprising since this concept is based on the distinction between the full and the void which is definitely abolished in Einstein's theory. Elementary corpuscles, electrons, and *a fortiori* photons are losing more and more their character of miniscule solids resembling macroscopic bodies. The mass of the electron has ceased to be constant and has become a function of velocity, a fact which has demonstrated its close connection with the surrounding electromagnetic environment. This fact was already anticipated by classical physics, in particular by Michael Faraday, who asserted that, speaking properly, the atom is everywhere where its physical influence reaches; or by William Thomson, who conceived the atom as a gyrostatic formation within the ether. Weyl expressed the same idea more abstractly and without naïve mechanical models when he attempted to explain the "impenetrability" of the electron by the presence of "holes" in the non-Euclidean continuum.[30] Accepting Faraday's and Thomson's views, but at the same time rejecting their mechanical and visual models, Bergson insisted as early as 1896 that "all division of matter into independent bodies with absolutely determined outlines is an artificial division" (MM 259; MMf 218), a division which is simply a result of the selective character of our perception. The distinction established by our spontaneous perception between the well-delimited *thing* and the *actions*, which come [*sortent*] from it and are propagated across space, is merely practical and utilitarian; nonetheless it is retained by classical physics which is, in Whitehead's words, "organized common sense." The substantiality of corpuscles is thus dissolved

[30] Weyl, *Was ist Materie?* 57 ff.

in the universal interaction: "(physicists) show us, moving across concrete extensity, *modifications, perturbations, changes of tension* or of *energy* and nothing else" (MM 266; MMf 224). This anti-corpuscular and even anti-substantialist character of physics is still more apparent today; in exhibiting both the corpuscular transformation of the electrons into radiant energy and vice versa, the facts of the dematerialization and materialization of electrons demonstrate still more graphically that we are no longer dealing with the rigid and permanent particles of classical physics.[31] It is no longer possible even to speak of their *precise positions* and their well-defined velocities because of Heisenberg's principle of indeterminacy which, it will be seen, instead of being a result of our purely human technical inability to isolate all the antecedents of the phenomenon is a manifestation of the *objective* indetermination of microphysical reality. Thus it can be understood why de Broglie concluded that "the physical hypothesis tends to reduce to this simple arithmetic affirmation: the number of elementary particles of a particular species, which can be variable, always is an integer." [32] But if this is true, why continue to use the word "corpuscle," which is so charged with inadequate associations? If, as de Broglie has at the same time suggested, the concept of the corpuscle has been formed by initially using the image of a grain of sand or a lead sphere, disregarding its secondary qualities,[33] is it not true that classical physics retained of that image only a wholly schematic residue termed *"the material point,"* that is, an association of velocity with a certain position? Finally, if we admit

[31] These phenomena, moreover, are less exceptional than had originally been supposed. According to Niels Bohr, it is impossible to conceive electrons in the atomic nucleus as having an independent existence. "The emission of positive and negative electrons in radioactive processes ought to be conceived as *a creation* of these particles at the time of the emission in a manner analogous to the emission of a photon by the atom." We also recall Bialobrzeski's idea according to which particles exist within the atom and especially in the nucleus not in act, but "potentially, in the Aristotelian sense of the word" (C. Bialobrzeski, "Sur l'interprétation concrète de la mécanique quantique," *Revue de métaphysique et de morale*, XLI [1934], 97–98).

[32] Louis de Broglie, *Continu et discontinu en physique moderne* (Paris: Michel, 1941), 106.

[33] De Broglie, *Continu et discontinu*, 67.

today with the majority of physicists "that the association of an exact position with an exact quantity of motion cannot be discovered, because such a thing does not exist in nature," [34] is not the reality of corpuscles radically denied? And will it not be possible to interpret the individuality of "particles" rather as an individuality of *events*, thus avoiding the contradictions of corpuscular, and hence macroscopic, language?

This is what is suggested by wave mechanics, which constituted a magnificent, but still incomplete synthesis of relativity theory and early quantum theory. We must add that Erwin Schrödinger's original hopes of conceiving the "matter waves" of the new theory as concrete vibrations of the semi-material milieu of a hypothetical "sub-ether" are now entirely given up. This is because the failure of hydrodynamic models of the ether was even more complete than that of the corpuscular models of the atom, and had occurred even earlier. Confirming Bergson's prophecy that change has no need of support, microphysics refuses to speak of vibrations of *something*, but speaks simply of "waves of probability," that is, of pure events, of changes which do not imply things which change. Thus it will now be possible to understand more fully Bachelard's conclusion that, insofar as concerns the nature of the electron, "there are events at the very foundation of its being." [35] Thus the last traces of the Lucretian concept of nature disappear: the identity of particles and the continuity of their trajectories, which are only illegitimate extensions of macroscopic concepts into the world of atoms and photons. Evidently what classical physics designated as a "particle" is nothing less than an often temporary local disturbance of the chronotopic milieu; hence the close connection of the "corpuscle" with its surrounding environment, as well as its capacity to be dissolved completely into its environment. There are no permanent elements, as Lucretius and Gassendi imagined; there is not even a subtle liquid, as with Descartes and Huygens, filling all space; furthermore, *there is no space*, at least not in the Newtonian

---

[34] Eddington, *The Nature of the Physical World*, 225.
[35] Gaston Bachelard, *Le nouvel esprit scientifique*, 85–86.

sense; there remains only one "thing," a moving and extended continuity of events which still possess a certain temporal thickness and for which Whitehead's expression "the ether of events" is relatively the most adequate.[36]

All the constituent elements of the Laplacean view are thus profoundly and radically transformed: the concepts of space, of time, of motion, and of matter. It is then hardly surprising that the basic significance of that view, absolute classical determinism, for which the future pre-exists and becoming is only an appearance, is today less certain. This doubt is precisely expressed in Heisenberg's principle, mentioned above. There are, it is true, authors (Léon Brunschvicg, Édouard LeRoy, René Berthelot, Georges Matisse, Dominique Parodi) who deny the "reification" of indeterminism and regard the supposed indeterminacy as a mere human impossibility of knowing all the conditions necessary for the exact prediction of the future. This impossibility, according to them, is merely technical, being at bottom the impossibility of avoiding the disturbance of the observed phenomena by the observation itself; this does not entail the denial of determinism because the *complete* determinism of the phenomenon, which includes the determinism of the observation, remains intact.[37] It is true that Heisenberg's mode of expression easily suggests this interpretation. But if we regard more carefully the other phenomena in which the intervention of the observer has no disturbing (*perturbateur*) effect, such as radioactive explosions and luminous emissions, we arrive at the conclusion that the ultimate ground of microphysical reality consists in spontaneous and con-

---

[36] *The Concept of Nature*, 78; *Matter and Memory*, 260; *Matière et mémoire*, 219: "*A moving continuity* is given to us in which everything changes and yet remains."

[37] Léon Brunschvicg, "La science et la prise de conscience," *Scientia*, Annus XXVII, vol. LV (1934), 334; E. LeRoy, *Revue de métaphysique et de morale*, XLII (1935), 345, 347; R. Berthelot, *Bulletin de la Société française de Philosophie*, 34ᵉ année, n° 5, pp. 172–83; G. Matisse, "Le mécanisme du déterminisme," *Rev. ph.*, LII (1937), 190; D. Parodi, *En quête d'une philosophie*, 36. What is surprising is that even the Bergsonian Édouard LeRoy considers " the reification" of quantum indetermination to be "indefensible" ("Ce que la microphysique apporte et suggère à la philosophie," *Revue de métaphysique et de morale*, XLII [1935], 345–47).

tingent events, of "elementary variations" in Boutroux's sense, whose mutual interaction produces the macroscopic epiphenomenon of classical causality.[38] In eliminating all the components of the Laplacean view of reality, we eliminate the essence of the view itself, which is only an illusion resulting from the natural, but epistemologically unjustifiable, extrapolation of our kinetic, macroscopic concepts. It is this close connection of rigid determinism with the macroscopic concepts of space, time, matter, and motion which, in the eyes of the most eminent physicists, makes its return so improbable. There is nothing surprising, moreover, in the fact that the abandoning of an illusion so inveterate and so dear to philosophers encounters almost emotional resistance even among minds whose intellectual honesty is indisputable; Destouches has clearly recognized the philosophical motives which the opposition to the idea of the objective indetermination of microscopic events conceals.[39] But it is necessary to take account of the fact that this philosophical opposition is ultimately a dis-

[38] P. Jordan, "Die Erfahrungsgrundlagen der Quanten theorie," *Naturwissenschaften*, XVII (1929), 504: "Der rein statistisch Charakter der radioaktiven Substanzen ist experimentell gesichert; mit der Schwergewicht einer empirischen Tatsache zwingt er uns zum Verzicht auf jede Hoffnung künftig einmal vorausbestimmende Ursachen für das Zerfallen eines Atoms gerade zu einer Zeit aufzufinden [The purely statistical character of radioactive substances is experimentally established; he concludes that radioactive disintegrations are basically statistical and indeterminate events ('grundsatlich statistische, undeterminierte Ereignisse')]." According to Reichenbach (*Atom und Kosmos*, [Berlin, 1930], 297), an objective limit is imposed on the prediction of the future in such a way that even Laplace's omniscient intelligence will be incapable of achieving it. "Nature is not entirely determined [Die Natur ist eben nicht restlos bestimmt]."

[39] L. Destouches, *La physique moderne et la philosophie* (Actualités scientifique et industrielles), 39–40, 45. The author shows the ultimate impossibility of conceiving the hypothesis "of an appearance of indeterminism due to uncertainty relations with underlying mechanics of points." L. de Broglie had previously shown the extreme improbability of an eventual return to rigid determinism because microphysical indetermination is an inevitable result of the existence of Planck's quantum of action *h*. This latter, in turn, is irremediably opposed to the idea of spatio-temporal continuity, which constitutes the necessary foundation of Laplace's kinetic determinism ("La crise du déterminisme," in *Matière et lumière* [Paris: Michel, 1937], 273–74; "Réflexion sur l'indéterminisme en physique quantique," in *Continu et discontinu en physique moderne*, 61–66). In a more recent article L. de Broglie has refuted the subjectivist interpretation of microphysical indetermination ("Léon Brunschvicg et l'évolution des sciences," *Revue de métaphysique et de morale*, L [1945], 73–77).

guised psychological resistance; not only all our individual experience, but also all our phylogenetic heritage is opposed to it. The influence of the macroscopic milieu acting during (whole) geological periods has put its almost ineffaceable imprint on the mind of man. Bachelard does not exaggerate when he states that such a radical transformation of habitual notions as that which the recent development of physics demands of us will be a true *intellectual mutation;*[40] it only needs to be added that such a transformation cannot occur without an enormous and often painful effort. But this effort can be facilitated by showing how the paradoxical world of atoms and photons naturally rejoins that macrophysical zone which our biological interest and the structure of our bodies have carved out of the universe in order to put it into contact with our perception.

It is easy to understand why spatio-temporal becoming should appear continuous in the mathematical sense of the word even to relativity physicists. The elementary pulsations of the microphysical world possess such a vanishingly short duration by comparison with the habitual intervals of our consciousness that, *practically*, they can be considered instantaneous. This is why space-time appears to us as infinitely divisible at the macroscopic and, we also add, *macrochronic* level. If a *practically* justified perspective is accepted, *i.e.*, that which is adequate for speeds which are small by comparison with the velocity of light and for short distances, it is possible to divide the totality of the chronotopic dynamism into a continuous space, independent of duration, and a continuous time, entirely distinct from extension. At the same time, elementary indetermination, which is too small from the macroscopic point of view, can be considered negligible; consequently, matter is fitted into the framework of rigid determinism with an imprecision which does not disturb our technical calculations. For, once we possess continuous space and continuous time, nothing prevents us from considering all physical processes as infinitely divisible, even though in reality they consist of *brief pulsations;* their mathematical continuity is only ap-

[40] Bachelard, *Le nouvel esprit scientifique*, 178–79.

parent and masks their individuality in the same way in which the apparent individuality of drops of water disappears in the specious continuity of their flow. With the notion of the spatio-temporal continuity of events we also introduce the possibility of applying differential equations through which future states are bound to past states. If by a similar approximation we form the concept of isolated body (in neglecting all the tenuous ties which join it to the rest of the universe), and, by a still more advanced idealization, the concept of the material point, we finally possess all the constituent parts of the Laplacean vision, along with its significance—that is, rigorous determinism and a virtual negation of becoming. This kinetic and deterministic conception of the universe is virtually present in the double work of division and solidification which characterizes our spontaneous perception; our sense organs and then our thought as well ignore all the delicate and complex relationships which join each material element to the rest of the physical world; one thus arrives at the concept of *void* which separates bodies. But at the same time the same sensory perception neglects the entire complexity of the supposed "element" and all the real processes which, so to speak, produce it; one thus forms the concept of the homogeneous *solid*, indifferent to duration, always identical, and without internal structure. But a more profound analysis dispels this illusion: "What is the 'moving thing' to which our eye adds motion, as to a vehicle? Simply a colored spot, which we know reduces, in itself, to a series of extremely rapid oscillations. This alleged movement of a thing is in reality simply a movement of movements" (CM 175; PM 187). This is what Bergson wrote in 1911; at that time the physicist would have been able to object that electromagnetic waves can be considered as periodical displacements of *something*, that is, of the particles of the ether. It scarcely needs to be pointed out that such a hypothesis is insupportable today; needless also to repeat what has already been said concerning the crisis of the corpuscular concept and its paradoxical fusion with the concept of wave. The apparent immutability of the atom is nothing, in fact, but an immobility of the sense quality of touch which persists, though in an attenuated fashion, even in the abstract conception of the "material point." But it is clear that the apparent immobility of all sensory qualities is a condensation of an extremely large number of successive events; for example, the simplest and most fleeting sensation of touch conceals a vertiginous succession of innumerable molecular shocks. "To perceive means to immobilize" (MM 276; MMf 232). Consequently it is possible to understand Bergson's conclusion, which Louis de Broglie quoted with justified admiration:

"As I suggest above, one might ask himself if it is not precisely in order to pour matter into this determinism, to obtain in the phenomena which surround us a regularity of succession, thus permitting us to act upon them, that our perception stops at a certain particular degree of condensation of elementary events. In a more general sense, the activity of the living being leans upon and is measured by the necessity supporting things, by a condensation of their duration." [41]

[41] Louis de Broglie, "Les conceptions de la physique contemporaine et les idées de Bergson sur le Temps et le mouvement," *Revue de métaphysique et de morale*, XLVIII (1941), 257. The passage cited is among the last written by Bergson, "De la position des problèmes" (PM 73n; CM 303). This essay was completed in 1922, but the pages relative to present physical theories were added later, certainly after the formation of the uncertainty principle. But it would be a great error to believe that Bergson arrived at the affirmation of microphysical indetermination only after recent theoretical discoveries. A passage almost identical to the one cited by de Broglie can be found in *Matter and Memory*, 296 (*Matière et mémoire*, 248), and *Mind-Energy*, 16 (*L'énergie spirituelle*, 17). The conclusion of the former book, moreover, leaves no doubt concerning Bergson's real opinion:
"Absolute necessity will be represented by the perfect equivalence of the successive moments of duration with each other. Is this true of the duration of the material universe? Can each of its moments be mathematically deduced from those that precede it? We have supposed in this work, for *ease of study*, that this was actually the case; and such, in fact, is the distance between the rhythm of our duration and the flow of things that the contingency of the course of nature, so profoundly studied by a recent philosopher, ought to be practically equivalent to necessity" (MM 330–31; MMf 277–78; the italics are mine). Moreover, the entire logic of duration definitely demands the emergence of real novelty wherever temporal processes exist.
One sees that this very precise résumé of the present position of quantum physics contains more than a "certain perfume of Bergsonism" whose presence L. de Broglie admits; here there is a *precise* and *specific* anticipation. It is true that this anticipation was neither isolated, nor the first: before Bergson, Peirce, Boutroux, Renouvier, and Cournot had also indicated it. Moreover, Bergson himself takes account of this when he refers to the "philosophy of contingence."

How can we fail to recall Eugène Guye's profound idea that it is the scale of magnitude which creates the phenomenon? Determinism is essentially an effect of a *macroscopic* and *macrochronic* perspective; its reign in the inorganic world of the middle dimensions is almost absolute. But, though it is *convenient* and *useful* to consider physical reality as rigorously determined, the practical approximation must never be confused with the intimate structure of reality; the indetermination of microscopic events remains a fundamental fact.

We thus return by a long detour to the biological theory of knowledge without which, evidently, a true and complete understanding of Bergsonism is impossible. But, if macroscopic determinism remains intact, is it not true that the modification of our ideas concerning the ultimate structure of matter is totally devoid of all practical significance for man? Since man is a macroscopic animal, all human and social reality will continue to be dominated by practically inescapable laws. But such a conclusion would be hasty, because it ignores the well-established fact of continuity and of the gradual passage from microphysical to macrophysical reality, which includes the organism and the human environment. Émile Boutroux already remarked that there are cases "in which variations which are insignificant and imperceptible in themselves suffice to determine, definitively, through a series of purely mechanical chain-events, quite considerable results." [42] Bergson adopted this view in his book *Creative Evolution*, in which psycho-physical action is conceived as an explosive rupture of the unstable equilibrium in complex organic tissues, triggered by an almost infinitesimal initiative. There is no space here for a more detailed analysis; we say only that the scale of the most fundamental processes of organic life, like those which occur in the interior of cells and in particular within the cell nucleus, approaches the microphysical scale, and that biology, in spite of some indignant protests, will not be able indefinitely to ignore the revision of physical determinism. One thing is certain: to assert that the material world of the twentieth-century physics is as im-

---

[42] *De la contigence des lois de la nature* (Paris: Baillière, 1874), 60–61.

permeable to real novelty as the rigid world of Spinoza and Laplace would be an extreme dogmatism. Microphysical novelties
exist at the foundations of all matter, organic as well as inorganic;
in the latter, these novelties all cancel each other statistically in a
macroscopic determinism. But are we certain that this is so within
the cerebral cells in which the macroscopic reactions of animal
bodies have their mysterious sources? Is it not in particular true
that between the duration of consciousness and that of things
there is "such a difference of tension that innumerable instants of
the material world could be held within one single instant of conscious life, so that the voluntary action, accomplished by consciousness in one of its moments, could be distributed over an
enormous number of the moments of matter and so sum up within
itself the indeterminations almost infinitesimal which each of
them admits"? [43] It is possible that the words of Leibniz, according to which the relation of the body to the mind should be conceived as a function of time, find a new significance in the light
of the recent facts of physics and psychology.[44] Moreover, *Matter
and Memory* represents the most serious effort in the direction
indicated by Leibniz.

CONCLUSION

"Thus the manner in which Bergson's ideas on physics are developed can help us understand the uncertainties of his thought
and the oddness of its results." [45] Such was the final judgment of
René Berthelot about Bergson in 1913. Bergson himself has indicated the reasons and the motives behind this judgment: ". . . my
views on the question, stated at a time when it was considered
evident that the ultimate elements of matter ought to be understood in the image of the whole, misled readers and were most

[43] *Mind-Energy*, 16-17; *L'énergie spirituelle*, 17.
[44] ". . . hic apertur porta prosecuturo ad veram corporis mentisque discrimina-
tionem hactenus a nemine explicatam. Omne enim corpus est mens momentanea
sive carens recordatione, quia conatum simul suum et alineum contrarium . . .
non retinet ultra momentum: ergo caret memoria, caret sensu actionum pas-
sionumque suarum, caret cogitatione" (*Theoria motis abstracti seu rationes
motuum universales, a sensu phaenomonis independentes*).
[45] Berthelot, *Un romantisme utilitaire*, II, 250.

often left aside as being the incomprehensible part of my work." [46] It is true that even today there are thinkers who believe "that the ultimate elements of matter ought to be conceived by macroscopic images." But this attitude is invariably associated with a negative attitude with regard to the new theories of relativity, of quanta, and of wave mechanics. Berthelot's statements are very instructive in this respect.[47] He was truly shocked by the Bergsonian negation of homogeneous and continuous time; today a physicist as eminent as Louis de Broglie speaks of "the discontinuity of becoming," while A. N. Whitehead asserts that certain paradoxes of wave mechanics disappear "if we agree to apply to the undifferentiated and apparently constant duration of matter the same principles as those accepted for sound and light. . . . If we explain the constant permanence of matter by the same principle, we conceive each primordial element as a flux and reflux of the subjacent energy or activity." [48] Evidently, Whitehead accepts *the vibratory theory of matter*, which is in all essential points identical to that of *Matter and Memory*. It is known that this latter defines materiality as "a succession of elementary events" possessing an almost vanishing duration, that is, of events which have no need of a static substantial support and which are not located in the homogeneous mediums of inert space and empty time. For Whitehead as for Bergson there is only *extensive becoming differentiated rather than divided into elementary pulsations or events*.

[46] Letter from Bergson to the author of this article, July 3, 1938.

[47] At the November 17, 1934, meeting of the *Société française de Philosophie*, René Berthelot made known his views on the present problems of physics. According to him, the impossibility of establishing the simultaneity of events is purely *technical*, as is that of discovering the precise velocity and position of the electron. What is not observable today can be observable tomorrow (*Bulletin de la Société française de Philosophie*, 34ᵉ année [octobre-décembre 1934], 172–83). Evidently, Berthelot believes in the existence of absolute simultaneity and *eo ipso* of absolute space; moreover, he does not question the purely corpuscular character of the electron possessing a precise location and well-defined velocity. This means that he remains on the ground of Newtonian physics. If twenty years of evolution in physics have not shaken his adhesion to the pictorial simplicity of classical physics, is there any wonder that he was so hostile to an isolated anticipation of the new tendencies?

[48] *Science and the Modern World*, 53.

329

Evidently, today, when all the fundamental notions of physics have been profoundly transformed, Bergson's ideas can be judged more justly and with less indignation than in 1913. Nonetheless, even today the essence of Bergson's philosophy—and this in particular is true of his philosophy of matter—will consist always in intellectual effort, in the "dynamic schema" transcending the habitual and lazy associations of the spontaneous imagination. This is why it will remain "painful for our mind" and "fatiguing for our imagination" (MM 275, 276; MMf 231, 232). *To philosophize consists in inverting the habitual direction of the work of thought* (CM 224; PM 214). It is this almost moral quality of intellectual effort that the school of neo-positivism attempted to eliminate in the name of the "principle of economy." But today's science demands it more strongly than ever.

BIBLIOGRAPHY

WORKS BY HENRI BERGSON RELATING
TO THE PHILOSOPHY OF PHYSICS

"Solution to the 'Problem of the Three Circles,' " in Adolphe Desboves. *Étude sur Pascal et les géomètres contemporains.* Paris: Delagrave, 1878.

"Solution proposée par Henri Bergson," *Les Nouvelles annales de mathématiques,* XVII (1878), 268–76. (Also in Henri Bergson, *Écrits et paroles,* Paris: Presses Universitaires de France, 1957, I, 3–9.)

Extraits de Lucrèce. Paris: Delagrave, 1883. (*The Philosophy of Poetry,* ed. Wade Baskin. New York: The Wisdom Library, 1959.)

Quid Aristoteles de loco senserit, Thèse complémentaire. Paris: Félix Alcan, 1889. (French translation by Robert Mossé-Bastide, introduction by Rose-Marie Mossé-Bastide, in *Les Études Bergsoniennes.* Paris: Albin Michel, 1949, II, 9–104.)

Time and Free Will, an Essay on the Immediate Data of Consciousness. London: George Allen & Unwin Ltd., 1950.

Essai sur les données immédiates de la conscience (1889). Paris: Presses Universitaires de France, 1958.

Matter and Memory. London: George Allen & Unwin Ltd., 1950.

Matière et mémoire (1896). Paris: Félix Alcan, 1934.

"Note sur les origines psychologiques de notre croyance à la causalité." Communication au Congrès international de Philosophie, Paris, 1900. (Bibliothèque du Congrès de Philosophie, 1900.) Also in *Écrits et paroles,* I, 129–37.

"Cours de M. Bergson sur l'idée de cause," par C.C.J. *Revue de philosophie,* April, 1901.

331

An Introduction to Metaphysics. New York: Bobbs-Merrill, 1949.

"Introduction à la métaphysique," *Revue de métaphysique et de morale,* 1903.

"Les radiations N," *Bulletin de l'Institute général de Psychologie,* January-February, 1904.

Creative Evolution. New York: Henry Holt and Co., 1911.

L'Évolution créatrice. Paris: Presses Universitaires de France, 1959.

"A propos de l'évolution de l'intelligence géométrique" (reply to an article by Émile Borel charging that Bergson had neglected the existence of non-Euclidean geometries), *Revue de métaphysique et de morale,* January, 1908.

"Review of Meyerson's *Identité et réalité,*" *Séances et travaux de l'Académie des Sciences morales et politiques,* CLXXI (January-June, 1909), 664.

"La perception du changement" (two lectures at Oxford University, May 26, 27, 1911), reprinted in *La pensée et le mouvant,* 1934. (*The Creative Mind,* 1946.)

L'énergie spirituelle. Paris: Alcan, 1919.

Mind-Energy, Lectures and Essays. Translated by H. Wildon Carr. London: Macmillan and Co. Ltd., 1920.

"Remarques sur la théorie de la relativité," *Bulletin de la société française de philosophie,* July, 1922, pp. 102–13. (Also in *Écrits et paroles,* III, 497–503.)

Duration and Simultaneity, with Reference to Einstein's Theory. Translated by Leon Jacobson. New York: Bobbs-Merrill, 1966.

Durée et simultanéité (1922; 2nd ed. with three appendices, 1923). Paris: Alcan, 1924.

"Letter concerning 'Les temps fictives et les temps réels' " (reply to an article by André Metz), *Revue de philosophie,* XXXI (1924), 241–60.

"Second letter in reply to note by André Metz," *Revue de philosophie,* XXXI (1924), 437–40.

The Two Sources of Morality and Religion. Garden City, N.Y.:

Doubleday and Co., Inc., 1954. (*Les deux sources de la morale et de la religion*. Paris: Alcan, 1932.)
The Creative Mind. New York: Philosophical Library, 1946.
La pensée et le mouvant (1934). Paris: Presses Universitaires de France, 1958.

PUBLICATIONS RELATING TO BERGSON'S PHILOSOPHY OF PHYSICS

Adolphe, Lydie. *L'Universe Bergsonien*. Paris: Edit. du Vieux Colombier, 1955.
Ambacher, Michel. "Intelligence physicienne de la matière et expérience philosophique de la matérialité dans la philosophie naturelle de Bergson," *Actes du X⁰ Congrès des Sociétés de Philosophie de Langue Française* (Congrès Bergson). Paris: Armand Colin, 1959, I, 13–16.
Becquerel, Jean. "Rezension de Durée et simultanéité," *Bulletin scientifique des étudiants de Paris*, X (March-April, 1923).
Becquerel, Jean. Préface to *La relativité, exposé sans formules des théories d'Einstein* by André Metz. Paris: E. Chiron, 1923.
Berteval, W. "Bergson et Einstein," *Revue philosophique*, CXXXII (January-March, 1942–43), 17–28.
Berthelot, René. "L'espace et le temps chez les physiciens," *Revue de métaphysique et de morale*, XVII (1919), 744–75.
———. *Un romantisme utilitaire*. Vols. I-III. Paris: Alcan, 1911–22.
Blanché, Robert. "Psychologie de la durée et physique du champ," *Journal de Psychologie Normale et Pathologique*, XLIV (July-September, 1951), 411–24.
Bruzio, F. "Scienza e filosofia bergsoniana," *Rassegna d'Italia*, 1947.
Busch, J. F. "Einstein et Bergson, Convergence et divergence de leurs idées," *Proceedings of the Tenth International Congress of Philosophy*, North-Holland Publishing Co., 1959, pp. 872–75.
Butty, Enrique. "La duración de Bergson y el tiempo de Einstein," Preliminar. Cap. I: Objetividad científica. Cap. II: Movimiento,

espacio y tiempo. *Cursos y Conferencias*, Año V, No. 5 (1936), 449–89.

————. "La duración de Bergson y el tiempo de Einstein," Cap. III. Duración y tiempo, *Cursos y Conferencias*, Año V, No. 8 (1936), 825–45.

————. "La duración de Bergson y el tiempo de Einstein," Cap. IV: El tiempo físico, *Cursos y Conferencias*, Año V, No. 8 (1936), 825–45.

————. "La duración de Bergson y el tiempo de Einstein," Cap. V: El tiempo de teoría de la relatividad. Cap. VI: Los tiempos múltiples de Einstein y el tiempo universal, *Cursos y Conferencias*, Año V, No. 10 (1937), 1021–52. (Continua en el número siguiente, pp. 1203–28.)

————. "La duración de Bergson y el tiempo de Einstein," Cap. VII: El universo de Minkowski y la duración universal, *Cursos y Conferencias*, Año. V, No. 12 (1937), 1327–62.

————. *La duración de Bergson y el tiempo de Einstein*. Buenos Aires, 1937.

Čapek, Milič. "Bergson et l'esprit de la physique contemporaine," *Actes du Xᵉ Congrès des Sociétés de Philosophie de Langue Française* (Congrès Bergson). Paris: Armand Colin, 1959, I, 53–56.

————. "Discussion of Bergson's Philosophy of Physics," *Actes du Xᵉ Congrès des Sociétés de Philosophie de Langue Française* (Congrès Bergson). Paris: Armand Colin, 1959, II, 65–87.

————. "La genèse idéal de la matière chez Bergson, la structure de la durée," *Revue de métaphysique et de morale*, July-September, 1952, pp. 325–48.

————. "La théorie bergsonienne de la matière et la physique moderne," *Revue Philosophique*, LXXVII (1953), 30–44.

————. *The Philosophical Impact of Contemporary Physics*. New York: D. Van Nostrand Co., Inc., 1961 (esp. pp. 13–15, 126–33, 160–61, 194–205, 207–209, 271–78).

————. "La théorie biologique de la connaissance chez Bergson," *Revue de métaphysique et de morale*, LXIV (1959), 194–211.

Cardone, C. A. "Tempo obiettivo e tempo unico nella filosofia di Henri Bergson," *Logos*, 1934.

Carr, H. Wildon. "The Problem of Simultaneity," *Aristotelian Society Supplementary Volume III*, Symposium: The Problem of Simultaneity (1923), 15–25.

Cesselin, Félix. *La philosophie organique de Whitehead*. Paris: Presses Universitaires de France, 1950.

Cory, Charles E. "Bergson's Intellect and Matter," *Philosophical Review*, XXII (1913), 512–19.

Costa de Beauregard, Olivier. "Essai sur la physique du temps. Son équivalence avec l'espace; son irréversibilité," *Actes du Xe Congrès des Sociétés de Philosophie de Langue Française* (Congrès Bergson). Paris: Armand Colin, 1959, I, 77–80.

———. "Discussion of Bergson's Philosophy of Physics," *Actes du Xe Congrès des Sociétés de Philosophie de Langue Française* (Congrès Bergson). Paris: Armand Colin, 1959, II, 65–87.

———. "Quelques aspects de l'irréversibilité du temps dans la physique classique et quantique," *Revue des questions scientifiques*, Ve Série (April 20, 1952), 171–99.

———. "La part de la convention dans la définition physique et la mesure de temps," *Revue des questions scientifiques*, Ve Série, IX (October 20, 1948), 481–95.

———. "Le principe de relativité et la spatialisation de temps," *Revue des questions scientifiques*, Ve Série, VII (1949), 38–65.

Costa de Beauregard, Olivier, with B. d'Espagnat. "Quelques remarques sur les paradoxes de la mécanique statistique classique," *Revue des questions scientifiques*, Ve Série (January 20, 1947), 351–70.

D'Abro, Arthur. *Bergson ou Einstein*. Paris: Gaulon, 1927.

———. *The Evolution of Scientific Thought*. New York: Dover Publications, Inc., 1950, 2nd edition, pp. 214–27, pp. 345–46.

Dambska, Izydora. "Discussion of Bergson's Philosophy of Physics," *Actes du Xe Congrès des Sociétés de Philosophie de*

Langue Française (Congrès Bergson). Paris: Armand Colin, 1959, II, 65–87.

―――. "Sur quelques idées communes à Bergson, Poincaré et Eddington," *Actes du X° Congrès des Sociétés de Philosophie de Langue Française* (Congrès Bergson). Paris: Armand Colin, 1959, I, 85–89.

DeBroglie, Louis. "Les conceptions de la physique contemporaine et les idées de Bergson sur le temps et le mouvement," in *Physique et Microphysique*. Paris: Albin Michel, 1947, pp. 191–211. (English translation by Martin Davidson, *Physics and Microphysics*, New York: Grosset & Dunlap, 1966, pp. 186–94).

De Spengler, Boris. "Discussion of Bergson's Philosophy of Physics," *Actes du X° Congrès des Sociétés de Philosophie de Langue Française* (Congrès Bergson). Paris: Armand Colin, 1959, II, 65–87.

De Stefano, R. "Metafisica e scienza positiva in Bergson," *Ricerche Filosofiche*, V (1951), 16–30.

Dingle, Herbert. Introduction to *Duration and Simultaneity*. Indianapolis: Bobbs-Merrill Co., Inc., 1965.

Dunan, Renée. "Bergson contre Einstein," *Le vie des lettres*, January, 1923.

Einstein, Albert. "Remarques sur la théorie de la relativité," *Bulletin de la Société Française de philosophie*, July, 1922, pp. 102–13. (Also in *Les Études Bergsoniennes*, III, 497–503.)

―――. Letter to André Metz in "Un dernier mot d'André Metz," *Revue de philosophie*, XXXI (1924), 440.

Fleury, René Albert. *Bergson et la quantité*. Paris: Copy-Odéon, 1941.

Gardner, Martin. *Relativity for the Million*. New York: Macmillan Co., 1962.

Gillaum, Edouard. "La question du temps d'après Bergson," *Revue générale des sciences*, XXXIII (1922), 573–82.

Heidsieck, François. *Henri Bergson et la notion d'espace*. Paris: Le Cercle du Livre, 1957 (esp. pp. 147–70).

―――. "Discussion of Bergson's Philosophy of Physics," *Actes* *du Xe Congrès des Sociétés de Philosophie de Langue Française* (Congrès Bergson). Paris: Armand Colin, 1959, II, 65–87.

Jacobson, Leon. Translator's introduction to *Duration and Simultaneity*. Indianapolis: Bobbs-Merrill Co., Inc., 1965.

Langevin, Paul. "L'Évolution de l'espace et temps," *Revue de métaphysique et de morale*, XIX (1911), 455–66.

————. "Le temps, l'espace et la causalité dans la physique moderne," *Bulletin de la Société Française de philosophie*, XII (October 19, 1911), 21–38.

Matchinski, Matthias. "Discussion of Bergson's Philosophy of Physics," *Actes du Xe Congrès des Sociétés de Philosophie de Langue Française* (Congrès Bergson). Paris: Armand Colin, 1959, II, 65–87.

————. "Image scientifique du monde. Son caractère cinématographique d'après Bergson et principe de causalité," *Actes du Xe Congrès des Sociétés de Philosophie de Langue Française* (Congrès Bergson). Paris: Armand Colin, 1959, I, 225–28.

Mathieu, V. "Il tempo ritrovato: Bergson e Einstein," *Philosophia*, IV (1953), 625–56.

Mercier, André. "Discussion of Bergson's Philosophy of Physics," *Actes du Xe Congrès des Sociétés de Philosophie de Langue Française* (Congrès Bergson). Paris: Armand Colin, 1959, II, 65–87.

Merleau-Ponty, Maurice. *The Bergsonian Heritage*, Thomas Hanna, ed. New York: Columbia University Press, 1962, pp. 133–49.

Metz, André. "Bergson, Einstein et les relativistes," *Archives de philosophie*, XXXVII (1959), 369–84.

————. *Bergson et le bergsonisme*. Paris: Vrin, 1933.

————. "Bergson et Meyerson," *Actes du Xe Congrès des Sociétés de Philosophie de Langue Française* (Congrès Bergson). Paris: Armand Colin, 1959, I, 235–37.

————. "Discussion of Bergson's Philosophy of Physics," *Actes du Xe Congrès des Sociétés de Langue Française* (Congrès Bergson). Paris: Armand Colin, 1959, II, 65–87.

———. "Relativité et relativisme," *Revue philosophique*, V 1926), 63–87.

———. *La relativité, exposé sans formules des théories d'Einstein et réfutation des erreurs contenues dans les ouvrages les plus notoires (Durée et simultanéité).* Paris: E. Chiron, 1923. Preface by Jean Becquerel.

———. "Le Temps d'Einstein et la philosophie: à propos de l'ouvrage de M. Bergson, *Durée et simultanéité*," *Revue de philosophie*, XXXI (1924), 56–88.

———. "Replique à M. Bergson," *Revue de philosophie*, XXXI (1924), 437–39.

———. "Un dernier mot d'André Metz," *Revue de philosophie*, XXXI (1924), 440.

Meyerson, Emile. *La déduction relativiste.* Paris: Payot, 1925.

———. *Identité et réalité.* 2ᵉ ed.; Paris: F. Alcan, 1912.

Muller, Maurice. "Un aspect de la théorie bergsonienne de la physique," in Albert Béguin and Pierre Thévenaz, *Henri Bergson, essais et témoignages recueillis.* Neuchatel, 1943, pp. 227–32.

Nédoncelle, Maurice. "Quelques aspects de la causalité chez Bergson," *Actes du Xᵉ Congrès des Sociétés de Philosophie de Langue Française* (Congrès Bergson). Paris: Armand Colin, 1959, I, 255–60.

Nordmann, Charles. *Notre maître le temps, les astres et les heures, Einstein ou Bergson?* Paris: Hachette, 1924. (*The Tyranny of Time, Einstein or Bergson?* Translated by E. E. Fournier d'Albe. London: T. F. Unwin Ltd., 1925.)

Parodi, Dominique. "La durée et la matière chez Bergson," *Revue de métaphysique et de morale*, XLVIII (1941), 258–65.

Pflug, Günther. *Henri Bergson: Quellen und Konsequenzen einer induktiven Metaphysik.* Berlin: Walter de Gruyter & Co., 1959.

Rouges, Alberto. "La duración de Bergson, el tiempo físico y el acontecer físico," *Sustancia*, II (September, 1941), 317–26.

Rousseaux, André. "De Bergson à Louis de Broglie," in Albert

Béguin and Pierre Thévenaz, *Henri Bergson, essais et témoignages recueillis.* Neuchatel, 1943, pp. 271–80.

Sageret, Jules. *La révolution philosophique et la science, Bergson, Einstein, Le Dantec, J.-H. Rosny Aîné.* Paris: Félix Alcan, 1924 (esp. pp. 80–83, 104–108, 200–209, 230–35).

Serrus, Charles. "L'évolution de la physique et de la philosophie," 4th international weekly, *Synthèse,* I (1935), 79–95.

Stern, Alex. "Discussion of Bergson's Philosophy of Physics," *Actes du X*e *Congrès des Sociétés de Philosophie de Langue Française* (Congrès Bergson). Paris: Armand Colin, 1959, I, 13–16.

Truc, Gonzague. "Le bergsonisme et le mouvement," *Revue hebdomadaire,* March 3, 1923, pp. 61–68.

Voisine, G. "La durée des choses et la relativité. A propos d'un livre récent de Bergson," *Revue de philosophie,* XXII (1922), 498–522.

Watanabé, Satosi. "Le concept de temps en physique moderne et la durée de Bergson," *Revue de métaphysique et de morale,* LVI (1951), 128–42.

Whitehead, A. N. "The Problem of Simultaneity," *Aristotelian Society Supplementary Volume III,* Symposium: The Problem of Simultaneity, (1923), 34–41.

Virieux-Raymond, Antionette. "A propos du problème du discontinu dans la philosophie bergsonienne," *Actes du X*e *Congrès des Sociétés de Philosophie de Langue Française* (Congrès Bergson). Paris: Armand Colin, 1959, I, 327–31.

Zawirski, Zygmunt. *L'Évolution de la notion du temps.* Cracowie, 1934.

INDEX